INTEGRALISM AND THE COMMON GOOD

Selected Essays from *The Josias*

VOLUME 1
Family, City, and State

INTEGRALISM
AND THE
COMMON GOOD

Selected Essays from *The Josias*

⊕

VOLUME 1
Family, City, and State

Edited by
P. Edmund Waldstein, O.Cist.
and Peter A. Kwasniewski

 Angelico Press

First published in the USA
© Angelico Press 2021

All rights reserved

No part of this book may be reproduced or transmitted,
in any form or by any means, without permission.

For information, address:
Angelico Press
169 Monitor St.
Brooklyn, NY 11222
angelicopress.com

978-1-62138-788-6 pbk
978-1-62138-789-3 cloth

Cover design: Michael Schrauzer

CONTENTS

Preface 1

I. God and the Good

1. The Good, the Highest Good, and the Common Good
   Edmund Waldstein, O.Cist. 7
2. The Foundations of Christian Ethics and Social Order
   Peter A. Kwasniewski 31
3. Contrasting Concepts of Freedom
   Edmund Waldstein, O.Cist. 49
4. Freedom as Choosing the Good, Against the Nihilists
   Peter A. Kwasniewski 66
5. Notes on Moral Virtue
   Edmund Waldstein, O.Cist. 72
6. Natures as Words, Contraception as a Lie
   Edmund Waldstein, O.Cist. 83

II. The Family, the Village, and the City

7. Aristotle's Account of the Relationship of the Household to the State
   Beatrice Freccia 93
8. The End of the Family and the End of Civil Society
   Charles De Koninck 131
9. The Mirror of the Benedict Option
   Edmund Waldstein, O.Cist. 138
10. Nature and Art in the Village
    John Francis Nieto 151
11. Urbanism and the Common Good
    Nathaniel Gotcher 164

III. Economics

12. Thomism and Private Property
    W. Borman 171

13. Aquinas on Buying and Selling
    Thomas Storck 175

14. The Sin of Usury
    Thomas Storck 184

15. Robin Hood Economics
    Edmund Waldstein, O.Cist. 195

16. The Needy Immigrant and the Universal Destination of Goods
    Edmund Waldstein, O.Cist. 204

IV. Politics

17. A Note on the Legitimacy of Governments
    Daniel Lendman 213

18. The Duties and Rights of Subjects Toward the Civil Power
    Tommaso Maria Cardinal Zigliara, OP 217

19. The Illegitimate State as Chastisement
    Gregory de Rivière-Blanche 230

20. Catholics and the Ethics of Voting
    Joshua Kenz 237

21. Is Man an Individual?
    Ian Bothur 242

22. Logos and Leviathan: Leonine Perspectives on Democracy
    Zachary Thomas 250

23. The Politics of Nostalgia
    Edmund Waldstein, O.Cist. 267

24. Hard Liberalism, Soft Liberalism, and the American Founding
    Edmund Waldstein, O.Cist. 286

25. Liberalism's Fear
    Adrian Vermeule 306

26. "According to Truth"
    Adrian Vermeule 310

27. Integralism Versus the Marxist and Post-Marxist Left
    Vincent Clarke 316

28. Right, Left, Forward, or Back? Or Why I Am Neither Left nor Right
    John Francis Nieto 331

Preface

The two best things in life are friendship and wisdom. So, at least, the Socratic tradition of philosophy would lead us to believe. Those two best things are united when friends come together in the pursuit of wisdom. The essays contained in this volume came out of a group of such friends. Facebook is often mocked for its use of the term "friends"—as though "liking" each other's status updates on that platform were equivalent to the mutual love of benevolence in a shared life that the ancients called *philia*. And yet, it was indeed on Facebook that this group of friends originally began its common pursuit. Soon a website was founded—*The Josias*—where the results of our reflections could be posted. Most of the following essays were originally posted there, although some of them appeared on other websites. Spanning seven years of conversation, the essays share a basic perspective but have the sort of back-and-forth and development that one would expect in such a conversation.

The ambition of *The Josias*'s first editor, E.M., was for the website to become "a working manual" of Catholic political thought. Why political thought? Wisdom, in the full sense, is a matter of knowing something that is not subject to political deliberation: the First Principle and Last End of all things. Wisdom includes understanding the *order* of all things *from* that First Principle and *to* that Last End. That is an order that does not depend on human will and human political deliberation. And yet, the order that we, as human beings, establish in our own actions and in our common life in society ought to depend on the larger order that wisdom considers. Our lives and actions as human beings and human communities can and ought to be part of a greater order. Whenever we act as human beings we act for the sake of some good, and what is truly good for us (whether as individuals or societies) depends on our First Principle and Last End.

Integralism and the Common Good

The political implications of this truth have been obscured in the modern era by the errors of liberalism. Liberalism, as Pope Leo XIII defined it in the great encyclical *Libertas*, is the doctrine of a false supremacy of human reason, making man's own deliberation the only measure (or, indeed, in some sense the originator) of the good. From this follows that the order which human beings establish in their societies depends only on their own wishes and is not subject to God: "just as every man's individual reason is his only rule of life, so the collective reason of the community should be the supreme guide in the management of all public affairs."[1] Our shared conviction at *The Josias* has always been that there is urgent need to combat the errors of liberalism (both in the world and in the Church herself), in order to integrate human life into the greater order in which alone human beings can be truly happy.

The urgency of this task explains the political focus of *The Josias*. This focus is accompanied by a conviction: to truly overcome modern errors, a "broadening of reason" is necessary. We must draw on the deepest sources of philosophical and theological wisdom, on the deepest insights of human reason reflecting on the whole breadth of human experience, and on the supernatural light of Divine Revelation.

This first volume of essays from *The Josias* treats the main questions of practical philosophy: the principles of human action, and the common goods of natural human communities ranging from the smallest and most fundamental to the greatest and most encompassing: the household to the political community. The second volume will be devoted to the relations of those natural communities to the supernatural Kingdom established by Christ. The insight of the Socratic tradition into wisdom and friendship as the chief goods of human life seems to be confirmed by Divine Revelation. Eternal life is wisdom, the vision of God (cf. John 17:3). But it is also friendship, the union of mutual love with God and with our fellow creatures in God (cf. John 15:15). Grace does not destroy nature, but

---

1. Pope Leo XIII, Encyclical *Libertas Praestantissimum* (1888), 15; English translation from the Vatican website.

Preface

rather presupposes, heals, and perfects nature. It thus enriches and purifies our human friendships.

That is why the two volumes have as their main title "Integralism and the Common Good." As our three-sentence definition elucidates: "Catholic Integralism is a tradition of thought that, rejecting the liberal separation of politics from concern with the end of human life, holds that political rule must order man to his final goal. Since, however, man has both a temporal and an eternal end, integralism holds that there are two powers that rule him: a temporal power and a spiritual power. And since man's temporal end is subordinated to his eternal end, the temporal power must be subordinated to the spiritual power." This definition brings out the two essential conceptual steps—the first, concerning the end or *telos* of man, the second concerning the twofold power by which he achieves it—behind the two volumes of this set.

I want to thank the many friends who helped bring about this volume. In the first place, of course the contributors of the essays collected here. Next, and with a certain sorrow, those who were important at the beginning of our project but have since parted ways with us—particularly E.M., our founding editor, and K.J.G., who suggested that we name our project after the reforming King of Judah. I want also to thank the current editors of *The Josias*, Joel Augustine, Jonathan Culbreath, and Daniel Whitehead, for their help in the first publication of many of these essays; the editors of *Plough* and *Ethika Politika* for permission to include essays originally published by them; Ethan Mack for help in compiling the manuscript of this volume; our publisher John Riess of Angelico Press for his tireless work in getting this book to press; and last but not least my co-editor for this volume Peter Kwasniewski, who took the lion's share of the work of compiling the text for publication.

Gaaden, Austria
October 19, 2021
Feast of the North American Martyrs
EDMUND WALDSTEIN, O.Cist.

I

GOD AND THE GOOD

1

The Good, the Highest Good, and the Common Good

Edmund Waldstein, O.Cist.

The following thirty-seven theses give a basic overview of the Aristotelian-Thomist account of the good, as interpreted by Laval School Thomists such as Charles De Koninck, Duane Berquist, and Marcus Berquist.

I. The Good in General and the Human Good[1]

1. The good is what all want.

The word "good" seems to have at least two different meanings. If one were to ask a little boy, let us call him Tom, "What is good?," he might answer: "ice cream is good, pizza is good, TV is good, football is good, vacation is good." On the other hand, another little boy, let us call him Clarence, who is perhaps a bit of a goody-goody, might answer, "obeying your parents," or "not breaking the rules," or even "doing what God wants." There might seem to be a great distance between these senses of the good, but they are actually very closely related.

I begin with Tom, who seems to present a simpler meaning. What do ice cream, pizza, TV, vacation, sports, etc. have in common? They are all things that Tom wants. And this is the first definition of the good that Aristotle gives: the good is what all want, or desire.

---

1. Part I closely follows Duane Berquist's "Lectures on Ethics," available at https://archive.org/details/duaneberquistonethics.

2. The good is wanted because it is good.

One might think that because the good is defined from wanting or desire, it is desire that *makes* something good. This has great initial plausibility: it seems that if someone wants something, then it is good for him. If so-and-so wants to live in L.A., then it seems that it is good *for him* to live there. This is also suggested by the enigmatic character of desire as described by Freudian psychoanalysis; desire seems an illogical force that fastens on an object without prior cause. As an American agent puts it in David Foster Wallace's novel *Infinite Jest*, "What if you just love? without deciding? You just do."[2] If this were true, the definition of the good would be a definition of an effect from its cause. And if this were true, Clarence, the goody-goody, would be sadly mistaken—no one else, and no set of rules or laws, could tell him what is good for him. He should learn to listen to his desires and free himself from paternalistic oppression.

But there are also reasons to doubt the idea that it is wanting something that makes it good. For haven't we all had the experience of wanting something which we ourselves then admitted was not good? I wanted that last drink at the party, but afterwards I admit that it was not good for me. I wanted to drive 100 mph down the winding road, but later, on my hospital bed, I admit that it was not good. If wanting something made it good, then my wanting the last drink would have *made it* good for me.

Duane Berquist, in his lectures on Ethics, takes a great many examples of basic desires and their objects, and argues that in each case the object is not good because it is desired, but desired because it is good. Hunger is the desire for food, but food is not good because there is hunger. Rather, there is hunger because food is good and necessary for the preservation of one's substance. And it is the same with drink. Water is not good because animals are thirsty, rather animals become thirsty because water is good for them. Nature gives them thirst in order to ensure that they attain this good. It does not seem to be merely desire that makes sexual union good, but rather it seems to be desired because it is itself good and

---

2. New York: Back Bay Books, 2006, 108.

The Good, the Highest Good, and the Common Good

necessary for the preservation of a whole kind of being. And even in our experience of pleasure, it seems that it is the goodness of pleasure that causes our desire—we speak of being "attracted" by it. This list can be continued indefinitely: knowledge, friendship, art, etc. Even money is not good because people want it; they want it because it is so useful for buying things.

But then again, there are also difficulties with the idea that the good is desired because it is good. What is good, after all, is often *not* wanted. If good is the *cause* of desire, how can it be that people do not want what is good? If it is good for Tom to go to school, why does Tom not want to go to school? If it is good for him to eat his vegetables, why does he not want to eat them? How can the cause be good without the effect following?

Or, again, if good is the cause of desire, then it would seem that the contrary of good, bad, is the cause of aversion. But many people desire what is bad for them, as we saw in the examples of the last drink and the 100 mph drive.

But these objections can be answered. Before desiring a good, I have to know it in some way. If Tom had never tasted candy, he would never have desired it. If Romeo had never seen Juliette, he never would have desired her. If Socrates had not understood to some extent what wisdom was, he would not have desired it. The good is desirable *as known*, and therefore as long as it is unknown it is powerless to cause desire.

And the bad is not desired because it is bad, but rather because it appears, or seems to be in some way, good. I didn't take that last drink because of the bad things it would do to me, but because of the good pleasure I thought it would give me. Sometimes what is bad looks like what is good, and the former is mistaken for the latter. Thus, someone who eats poisonous mushrooms "by mistake" eats them because he thinks they are the good mushrooms they resemble.

3. *The good is the final cause.*

To define the good as "what all want" is therefore a definition not of an effect by its cause, but just the opposite: a definition of a cause by its effect. The good is a cause. It is the final cause, the end or purpose. Aristotle famously distinguishes four different causes: the material of which something is made, the form that that material has, the agent that gives the material its form, and the end for the sake of which the agent gives the material its form. A statue of Napoleon, for example, is made of bronze, in the form of a Corsican-French tyrant, by a sculptor, for the sake of honoring the tyrant. The final cause is realized last in time, but it must be present in intention first. It is the cause of the other causes because the form is given to the material by the agent, but the agent cannot act unless he has some purpose for acting. The final cause, the good, is thus the cause of causes.

4. The better is not better because it is more wanted.

If something is not good because it is wanted, then neither is it better because it is wanted more. If Socrates thinks the best goods are the goods of the soul, and the Athenians think the best goods are the goods of the body and of external possessions, the dispute cannot be resolved by saying, "For Socrates virtue and wisdom are better because they are what he wants; for the Athenians pleasure and wealth are better because those are the things they want." In reality, virtue and wisdom are better and the Athenians only prefer pleasure and wealth out of ignorance; they do not know wisdom and virtue well enough to see how good they are.

5. The whole is better than the part.

A whole chair is better than part of a chair. A whole car is better than part of a car. A whole garden is better than one flower. There might be a particular situation in which a part is more sought, e.g., someone fixing an antique chair may prize the right part, someone testing auto parts may focus on just the parts, and a painter may wish to depict one especially beautiful rose. But all things considered, it is obvious that a chair, as such, is what it is only when it's whole; a car serves its purpose only when it is whole; and those who love flowers seek to plant many, not just one.

6. The end is better than that which is for the sake of the end.

Health and medicine are both good, but medicine is for the sake of health, and health is better than medicine. Studying is good and knowing is good, but studying is for the sake of knowing (unless one is merely studying to "kill time") and knowing is better than studying.

7. A good is not better because it is more necessary.

What is better: to breathe or to play football? Clearly breathing is more necessary, but it is for the sake of being able to do other things. Tom breathes so that he can play football and not vice versa. Many economists claim that in any free exchange each party must think that they are getting something better out of the deal. But people are not such fools. A widow who sells her wedding ring in order to buy food is fully aware that her ring is better than the food, but she also realizes that food is more necessary. Far from being pleased at the "free" exchange giving her something better, she is sad that cruel necessity forces her to exchange the better for the worse.

8. Honorable goods are better than useful and pleasant goods.[3]

Our knowledge begins with sensation: with the things that we see, feel, taste, smell, and hear. And so the wants or desires of which we are first aware are sensible desires. And these desires are for goods that give sensual pleasures. Tom, the little boy in the first section, gives examples of this kind of good: ice cream and pizza, which please the senses of taste and smell; TV, which pleases the sense of sight as well as the internal sense of imagination; and so on. These goods are called "pleasant goods."

Our idea of the good begins with the pleasant good, but then we extend it to things that are useful for obtaining pleasant goods. These things are called useful goods. Because Tom wants ice cream, he wants the things useful for attaining ice cream such as money

---

3. For sections 8–9, see Sebastian Walshe, "The Primacy of the Common Good as the Root of Personal Dignity in the Doctrine of St. Thomas Aquinas" (https://www.scribd.com/document/450477856/234217445-the-Primacy-of-the-Common-Good-as-the-Root-of-Personal-Dignity-in-the-Doctrine-of-St-Thomas-Aquinas) and Michael Waldstein, "Dietrich von Hildebrand and St. Thomas Aquinas on Goodness and Happiness," *Nova et Vetera* 1.2 (2003): 403–64, https://stpaulcenter.com/09-nv-1-2-waldstein/.

and ice cream trucks. But it is clear that he wants the ice cream more than these things useful for obtaining ice cream. He also wants to buy ice cream, but for the sake of eating ice cream. So ice cream is better than the things and activities that are for the sake of ice cream (considered just insofar as they are useful for ice cream).

Our knowledge begins with sense knowledge, but then we develop rational, intellectual knowledge. And this knowledge leads us to understand more basic goods, such as the preservation of our life and health, and then higher goods, such as friendship, wisdom, justice, et alia. These goods are called the "honorable good" (*bonum honestum*), because they are worthy of honor. Honorable goods are better than pleasant goods. A man who sacrifices friendship or justice for pleasure is rightly called a "pig," because pleasure is a good of the senses, which we have in common with animals, whereas honorable goods are goods of rational nature. An honorable good is not wanted for the sake of getting something else, not even pleasure; it is wanted for its own sake.

Of course, one and the same thing can be good in several of these ways. Steak is a pleasant good, but it is also useful for preserving life. Indeed, all sense pleasures seem to be intended by nature to be connected to actions that lead toward the lower and more basic of the honorable goods, such as the preservation and reproduction of life. A friend can be useful in many ways, pleasant to be around, and also loved for his own sake. But the three kinds of goods are distinguished according to the primary reason for wanting them: useful goods are primarily wanted for their usefulness in getting other goods, pleasant goods for pleasure, and honorable goods simply because they are good and desirable in themselves.

9. An honorable good is better than the delight of reaching it.

The division of the good into the useful, the pleasant, and the honorable is used to distinguish between different things that are wanted for different reasons. But, as St. Thomas shows, similar distinctions are made in the getting and having of almost any good. Almost always there are steps taken to reach the good (corresponding to the useful), the good itself (corresponding to the honorable), and resting or delighting in the good (corresponding to the pleasurable). For example, in the case of Tom getting ice cream, we can distinguish his buying the ice cream, the ice cream itself, and his pleasure in eating the ice cream.

And we can see something similar in the case of honorable goods. There are the steps taken to reach an honorable good (useful), the honorable good itself (honorable), and a resting and delighting in the honorable good (pleasure). In the higher honorable goods, this delight is not sensible pleasure, but rather a rational or spiritual delight analogous to sense-based pleasure. For example, we can distinguish between learning a truth, the truth itself, and delighting in the truth. Or we can distinguish between taking steps to become friends with someone, the friend himself, and delighting in the friend. Delight in an honorable good can itself be an honorable good, but the good in which one delights is better than the delight. Delight in attaining a truth is an honorable good, but it is natural to love the truth itself more than one's delight in it. Delight in a friend is an honorable good, but one must love the friend himself more than the delight of being his friend. A sign of this is that a good friend wants what is good for the friend even if this means that he will be separated from him and will thus no longer be able to delight as much in his friendship.

10. An honorable good is better than the activity by which it is possessed or enjoyed.

Let's return to the example of Tom and his ice cream. We distinguished between buying the ice cream, the ice cream itself, and the pleasure of eating it. But we can also distinguish the *action* of eating from these, and this too is a good. So we have four goods: buying the ice cream, the ice cream itself, *Tom's eating the ice cream*, and Tom's pleasure in eating the ice cream.

Again, there is something analogous with honorable goods. We have the steps taken to achieve the good itself, *the activity of possessing or enjoying the good*, and the delight in that activity: learning a truth, the truth itself, *the act of knowing the truth*, the delight flowing from that action; getting to know a friend, the friend himself, *the activity of being friends with him*, the delight flowing from that activity.

Integralism and the Common Good

The activity of possessing the good is better than the delight that follows from it: knowledge of the truth is better than the delight that comes from knowledge, and the act of friendship is better than the delight that follows from it. But the good itself is better than the activity of possessing it: the truth itself is better than the knowledge of it, and the friend is better than my being his friend. The good itself is the primary thing—it is ultimately that which makes the activity of attaining it desirable. It is because the truth is good that the philosopher wants to know it. It is because a person is good that another person wants to befriend him.

11. All things desire participation in the eternal and the divine.

As we saw above (8), the first kind of desire that we experience is the desire that comes from sense knowledge, that is, the desire for sensible goods. But then we come to intellectual knowledge, and from this comes desire for goods known by reason. And the idea of desire can be extended. We can see in plants, which have no sense knowledge, and indeed even in inanimate things, a certain tendency to which we can extend the idea of desire. One can say that anything that acts at all must have something analogous to a desire for the good. This is because action is simply unintelligible without reference to some end or goal, since the final cause is the cause of causes. Aristotle shows in the *Physics* that natural things are things which have an internal principle of motion and that this motion is toward an end. Inanimate things seem to have at least a tendency to remain in existence and resist destruction. And this is still more evident in plants. Plants take in water and light in order to grow and continue existing. Moreover, plants reproduce, thus keeping their kind in existence. In Plato's *Symposium* (207d), Diotima explains the instinct to reproduce by saying that mortal nature seeks as far as it can to be always and immortal, and Aristotle echoes this in the *De Anima* (415a–b), arguing that everything that natural things do according to nature is for the sake of participating in the eternal and divine, and that therefore reproduction is the most natural of actions. Reproduction does not give an individual immortality, but it gives immortality to certain *kinds* of things.

The Good, the Highest Good, and the Common Good

12. All things desire their own perfection.

Natural things do not merely wish to continue existing, they wish to *complete* and *perfect* their natures. A seed strives to grow into a complete plant, and an animal into an adult animal. The nature of a thing is a principle impelling it to perfect itself. Tom wants to grow up, and he wants to develop his abilities, make his possibilities actual and real. As Tom grows older, he will want not only to complete his own individual nature, he will also want to help his friends and his children complete theirs. And he will want to help the communities of which he is a part—his football team, his business, his country—to complete theirs. Perhaps, he will even want to contribute something to the human race as a whole.

13. Human action is always for the sake of the last end of human life.

There are a great many goods that a little boy like Tom wants. Each of them is desirable to him because they contribute (or at least seem to contribute) in some way to his completion and perfection (or the perfection of some community of which he is a part). So his desire for them is caused by his desire for a complete perfection—it is only because he desires complete perfection that he desires them at all. And so, as St. Thomas shows, whenever he desires some good that is not complete perfection, he desires it *for the sake* of that complete perfection.[4] Complete perfection is *the final end* of Tom's life, and all other ends are means in comparison to it. This does not mean that Tom knows distinctly what the final end is, or what is necessary to attain it; it only means that to choose anything he has to see it as good, and this means seeing it as contributing to the purpose and end of his life.

14. Law aids in attaining the end.

Clarence, the goody-goody from section 1, identifies "good" with obeying authority, following rules, etc. We can now see how his concept of good is related to Tom's concept of the good as "things that he wants." A little boy does not know very distinctly what his

---

4. *ST* I-II, q. 1, a. 6.

final end is, and so he can be easily deceived about what contributes to it. His parents therefore command him to do certain things that help him begin to attain his good. The rules that his parents set up are therefore means useful for attaining what Clarence really wants. And therefore doing what his parents tell him is itself worthy of choice, good in a secondary sense. Something similar holds for the laws of human society, which are an aid to attaining its perfection, and the law of God which he gives all of creation in order to help it attain its end.

So Clarence's concept of the good is really reducible to Tom's. Neither of them, however, has a full account of the good. Tom identifies the good with those goods which are most known to him, even if they are not the most important ones for attaining the final end, whereas Clarence identifies the good with certain means for attaining the good, which are given him by his parents.

15. A thing's intrinsic final end is to do its own act well.

When a thing has fully developed its nature, it is able to do the act that either it alone can do, or at least that it can do better than other things. This act is called a thing's "own act," or its "proper act," or its "function." In discussing what a thing's own act is, Aristotle discusses the acts of particular human occupations, since these are most known to us.[5] A cook's own act is to cook, a roofer's is to make roofs, a teacher's is to teach. And in each of these cases, the purpose and end of the occupation is its own act. Why do we have a cook? To cook. Cooking is the purpose of a cook. And we have roofers for the sake of making roofs, and teachers for the sake of teaching. One can see the same thing in the case of human tools. A corkscrew's own act is to remove corks and so that is the end and purpose of corkscrews. A knife's own act is to cut, and cutting is the purpose of the knife. And the same thing holds for the parts of the body. The eye's own act is to see, and seeing is the purpose of the eye. The heart's own act is to pump blood, and this is the end of the heart.

So we can generalize and say that whenever a thing has some act that it alone does, or that it does better than other things, this act is

---

5. *Nicomachean Ethics* I.6, 1097b24–30.

its end or purpose. We must however qualify this, since one can distinguish between a thing's own act and the object of that act. The first is the intrinsic good of a thing, and the second is its extrinsic good. The intrinsic good of a cook is cooking, but a cook's extrinsic good is food.

A further qualification is that the end of a thing is to do its own act *well*. The purpose of the knife is not just to cut, but to cut well. To do its own act *well*, a thing needs a certain quality or qualities, traditionally called "virtues." (The word now has a very narrow, moralistic sense, but the sense used to be much broader—think of the "virtue" of herbs.) The virtue of a knife is sharpness because sharpness is the quality that enables a knife to cut well. So we can say that the *intrinsic* good of anything that has an act of its own is to do its own act with its own virtue.

16. The intrinsic final end of human life is the act with reason, done according to human virtue.

What is man's own act? It would be strange if cooks, roofers, teachers all had their own act but man as man had nothing to do. Aristotle argues that man's own act can't simply be growing and nourishing himself, which plants also do, nor can it be the life of the senses, which he shares with animals.[6] He concludes that it must be the life of reason. But the life of reason has two kinds of acts: the acts of reason itself—such as knowledge, understanding, and reasoning—and the acts of other parts of the soul as guided by reason—the acts of the will done reasonably, and the acts of the emotions guided and moderated by reason. All of these together can be called "the act with reason." The intrinsic final end of human life is thus to do the act with reason in accordance with those qualities that enable this act to be done well, namely, the intellectual and moral virtues.

17. Objective happiness is better than subjective happiness.

The intrinsic good of human life is the act with reason according to human virtue. And so the *extrinsic* good of human life would be

6. Ibid., I.6.

the object of that act. The object of this act must itself be something good. And it will be an honorable good, not a mere pleasant or useful good. But we saw above (*10*) that an honorable good is better than the activity by which one attains to it. So the extrinsic good of human life must be better than the intrinsic good.

At the beginning of the *Nicomachean Ethics*, Aristotle calls the end of human life by the name that most men give to their confused notion of complete perfection: happiness (εὐδαιμονία). This term can easily be misunderstood, since in English it is chiefly used to mean the delight of attaining a good. But we saw above (*9–10*) that the action by which one attains an honorable good is better than the delight of attaining it and that the good itself is better than either of those. All these things are so closely related that they can all be called happiness. In the Thomist tradition, man's intrinsic good (his own act done well) is called *subjective happiness*, while the object of that act, his extrinsic good, is called *objective happiness*. We can now see that most properly speaking the final end of man is objective happiness, rather than the subjective attainment of that end or the delight in attaining it. But what is the object of man's own act? What is objective happiness?

II. The Highest Good[7]

18. God is infinite perfection and goodness.

God is the one who Is. He possesses absolute fullness of being in the complete simplicity of His essence. "I am who am" (Ex. 3:14). There is nothing lacking in God. There is no division in Him, no distension of Him, no limit to Him. He is an infinite ocean of perfection, and He possesses it all at once in the eternal instant of His infinite life. There is no unrealized potential in God; He is pure act. And therefore He is infinitely and completely good. In the unspeakable happiness of the trinitarian life, God's infinite perfection is

---

7. For Part II, see my paper "On Peace as the Final Cause of the Universe" (https://www.scribd.com/document/31549176/On-Peace-as-the-Final-Cause-of-the-Universe) and my blogpost "Thomism, Happiness, and Selfishness," *Sancrucensis*, September 21, 2012, https://sancrucensis.wordpress.com/2012/09/21/thomism-happiness-and-selfishness/.

The Good, the Highest Good, and the Common Good

known, expressed, loved, and given between three persons who are each the one God.

19. God shares his goodness with the things he makes.

Looking on His goodness with infinite love, God wills to share it. Because, as St. Thomas says, "the things that we love for their own sake we want to ... be multiplied as much as possible."[8] But since the Divine essence is absolutely simple and one, it cannot be increased and multiplied in itself. The only way in which the Divine essence can be multiplied is by likeness, by a representation which always falls short of the original. The goodness of creatures is a *participation* in the goodness of God, a partial sharing by way of likeness to God's own goodness.

20. The goodness of creatures is found more in their creator than in themselves.

Since the perfections of creatures are merely likenesses of the divine perfection, sharing in His goodness in a partial way, their perfection is really more in Him than in themselves. The perfections that exist separately in the multitude of created things exist in a unified and more perfect manner in the God who made them.

21. The greatest created good is the order of the whole of creation.

Each creature reflects a different *aspect* of the Divine goodness as no one creature can represent the Divine goodness as a whole. But the unity of God belongs to the very account of this infinite goodness. As St. Thomas Aquinas teaches, "Unity belongs to the idea of goodness ... as all things desire good, so do they desire unity; without which they would cease to exist. For a thing so far exists as it is one."[9] Therefore, since creation is a likeness of a goodness that is essentially one, it follows that the multitude of creatures must be brought together, in some way, so as to imitate the divine unity. The unity that belongs to the multitude of creatures is the unity of order, the harmony that binds them all together. St. Thomas manifests this from the creation account in the book of Genesis: "The good of

---

8. *SCG* I.75.
9. *ST* I, q. 103, a. 3.

order among diverse things is better than any one of those things that are ordered taken by itself: for it is formal in respect of each, as the perfection of the whole in respect of the parts... Hence it is said (Gen. 1:31): 'God saw all the things that He had made, and they were very good,' after it had been said of each that they are good. For each one in its nature is good, but all together are very good, on account of the order of the universe, which is the ultimate and noblest perfection in things."[10]

22. Creatures do all that they do out of love for God.

Because the perfection of created things is more in God than in themselves, God is more desirable to them than they are to themselves. As St. Thomas says, "To be good belongs pre-eminently to God. For a thing is good according to its desirableness. Now everything seeks after its own perfection; and the perfection and form of an effect consist in a certain likeness to the agent, since every agent makes its like; and hence the agent itself is desirable and has the nature of good. For the very thing which is desirable in it is the participation of its likeness."[11] And again, "All things, by desiring their own perfection, desire God Himself, inasmuch as the perfections of all things are so many similitudes of the divine being."[12] Plants growing, birds singing, cheetahs running—all these creatures are trying to achieve their own perfection, but it is really more God that they seek than themselves. We can now see the reason for the thesis presented above (*11*) that all things desire participation in the eternal and divine; it is because they desire their eternal and divine creator.

23. Creatures naturally love God more than themselves.

St. Thomas compares the natural love of created things for God with that of a part for the whole.[13] Creatures are not parts of their creator (we are not pantheists), and yet they are ordered to their Creator in the way parts are ordered to a whole. The perfection that

10. *SCG* II.45.
11. *ST* I, q. 6, a. 1.
12. Ibid., ad 2.
13. *ST* I, q. 60, a. 5.

they have is a *participation*, a partial sharing, in His perfection. Therefore all creatures naturally love God more than themselves.

24. Only persons love God directly in Himself.

Plants, birds, and lions have no explicit knowledge of God. The plants are moved by a higher cause to develop their own perfection—their love is not elicited by their own knowledge. Although animals too are moved by nature, they are also moved by a knowledge of a sensible likeness of God. Only rational and intellectual creatures (persons) are able to know God as God and therefore have a love that attains to Him in Himself. But there are two kinds of knowledge of God: a natural knowledge that knows God indirectly as the cause of creatures and a supernatural knowledge that will behold God directly. And so there are two kinds of elicited love of God: a natural, and a supernatural love. The supernatural love of God is a gift of grace, which perfects natural love.

25. God is the objective happiness of all persons.

The desire of anyone who is capable of knowing the Creator cannot be satisfied with any creature. In every creature what is desirable is the likeness of the Creator, but every creature falls short of the infinite perfection of the creator. God alone can satisfy. He is objective happiness (cf. *17*).

26. Sin occurs when some lesser good is preferred to God.[14]

As we saw, there is a natural love of God in all things that is not elicited by an explicit knowledge of Him, but rather is the tendency toward divine perfection in the natures of things. This kind of love does not fail. In persons there is also a higher kind of love that follows on knowledge. But while God is naturally more lovable to creatures than they are to themselves, He is not more knowable to

---

14. See Charles De Koninck, *On the Primacy of the Common Good*, trans. Sean Collins, in *The Aquinas Review* 4.1 (1997): 42–45; the translation may be found at http://ldataworks.com/aqr/V4_BC_text.html, but without page numbers. An alternate translation was prepared by Ralph McInerny and published as *The Writings of Charles De Koninck*, vol. 2: *On the Primacy of the Common Good* (Notre Dame, IN: University of Notre Dame Press, 2009).

them. Creatures first know other things, and then God. This is true even of the angels. Apart from grace, they know their own nature directly, but God only indirectly as the cause of their natures. And so they can prefer the perfection of their own nature to God, and this is the sin of the fallen angels. Human persons can sin in this way too, but they can also sin in another way. Since human persons first know through the senses, and then abstract rational knowledge from sense knowledge, they can be led to prefer sensible goods (such as ice cream) to the higher goods of rational nature. There is nothing sinful about loving lower goods as long as they are not preferred to higher goods; sin comes about when they are loved more than the higher goods, or in a way that is not compatible with loving God above all things. A sin is *mortal* if a lower good is chosen in a way incompatible with loving God as the final end of one's life; it is *venial* if it is chosen in a way that "doesn't quite fit with the love of God, yet is compatible with it—one's final end remains God, but one is too much attached to something which is a means to God."[15]

III. Common Goods[16]

27. A common good is distinguished from a private good by not being diminished when it is shared.

The first goods that we know are sensible goods, such as ice cream. And these goods are diminished by being shared. If Clarence gives Tom part of his ice cream, then the part of the ice cream that Tom has Clarence no longer has. Clarence can no longer enjoy the part of the ice cream that he gave away. Following St. Thomas and Charles De Koninck, Marcus Berquist calls such goods *private goods* because they can only belong to one person *to the exclusion of others*. A private good is ordered to the one whose good it is. In loving a private good, one is actually loving the person for whom that good is intended. Aristotle says that one does not really wish wine well—

---

15. Fr. Joseph Bolin, "Commandments and Counsels," http://www.pathsoflove.com/blog/2009/01/commandments-and-counsels/.

16. Part III is largely based on Marcus Berquist's "Common Good and Private Good" (www.scribd.com/doc/61181449/Marcus-Berquist-Common-Good-and-Private-Good) and Charles De Koninck's *On the Primacy of the Common Good*.

The Good, the Highest Good, and the Common Good

one wishes rather that the wine will keep so that one might enjoy it, that is, one is really wishing oneself well.[17] And this is because wine is a private good.

A common good, on the other hand, is a good that is not diminished by being shared. If Tom tells Clarence a joke then he does not cease to enjoy the joke himself—in fact his enjoyment may be increased by sharing it.

28. Common goods are better than private goods.

A joke is only a pleasant good; true common goods are honorable goods. Goods such as truth, justice, peace are common goods in the full sense. They are not diminished by being shared. Moreover they are not ordered to us; we are ordered to them. One desires to promote justice and truth for their own sakes. And they are better than private goods. It is honorable to attain a good for one man, but it is better and more godlike to attain a good in which many can share.[18] The common good is not better merely as a sum of the private goods of many individuals. Nor is it the good of their community considered as a quasi-individual; rather a true common good is good for each of the persons who partake of it—a good to which they are ordered. This cannot be emphasized enough: the common good is a *personal good*. The subordination of persons to this good is thus not enslaving. They are not being ordered to someone else's good (the good of "the nation" or "humanity," considered abstractly); rather they are ordered to their own good, but this is a good that they can only have together in a community. The common good is a universal cause in the order of final causality. And the fact that it extends its causality to more effects than a private good shows how much better it is.

29. As persons develop, they order themselves to more and more universal common goods.

As a small boy, Tom has little knowledge of common goods. The first goods that he mentions are private goods, such as ice cream.

---

17. *Nicomachean Ethics* VIII.2, 1155b30.
18. Cf. ibid., 1094b.

But he comes to love goods in which his whole family can share without diminishing them: the peace and the joys of family life. And he begins to see that he has a responsibility toward these goods and can be punished if he harms them (this does not mean that he becomes a goody-goody like Clarence).

Tom begins to participate in practices, such as chess, football, and acting out Shakespeare plays, that enable him to share other common goods with his friends. Later Tom begins to see that his whole life is bound up with others in a political society in which great common goods, such as justice, can be realized, in which people hold each other accountable for what they do (see Roger Scruton on accountability,[19] and my response[20]), and in which a governing authority orders them.

30. The family is an incomplete society that can attain to some common goods.[21]

In one sense, the family (or household) is a complete society because it is concerned with every aspect of human life—with the "act with reason according to human virtue." There are certain common goods to which a family can attain: the common celebration of feasts, certain truths, the beauties of music, dance, and so on, and above all the tranquility of order of its own life. But if a family were isolated from all other families, as the Lykov family in Siberia was, its development would be stunted. It would consume almost all of its energy in the gathering of private goods, such as food and fuel, and there would be many common goods in which it could not participate. A family is thus in another sense *incomplete*, as it is naturally ordered to a greater society that enables it to achieve its own common goods better and to share in other, greater common goods.

---

19. "The Good of Government: Americans Need a Positive View of Government," *First Things*, June 2014, https://www.firstthings.com/article/2014/06/the-good-of-government.

20. See "Roger Scruton," *Sancrucensis*, September 20, 2014, https://sancrucensis.wordpress.com/2014/09/20/roger-scruton/.

21. See Beatrice Freccia's account in chapter 7.

The Good, the Highest Good, and the Common Good

31. Associations are incomplete societies that are able to achieve the common goods internal to a particular human practice.

Alasdair MacIntyre defines a "practice" as "any coherent and complex form of socially established cooperative human activity through which goods internal to that form of activity are realized in the course of trying to achieve those standards of excellence which are appropriate to, and partially definitive of, that form of activity, with the result that human powers to achieve excellence, and human conceptions of the ends and goods involved, are systematically extended."[22] Chess, architecture, history, painting, music, the inquiries of physics—these are all practices in MacIntyre's sense. (MacIntyre also considers politics a practice, but, as Thomas Osborne has argued, there are important differences between politics and other practices because politics is the practice of a complete community.) Such practices are aimed at achieving goods internal to them. Goods internal to a practice are goods that can only be had by participating in a practice. And when achieved, such goods are good for the whole community that participates in a practice. A community founded around such a practice is not a complete community because it is not concerned with the whole of human life, not with the whole "act with reason according to human virtue," but only with one particular area of it. (Again, I am omitting the practice of politics from consideration at this point.) Such communities are usually not given in the way one's family is; usually (though not always) one has to choose to enter them. I call such communities of persons engaged in a MacIntyrean practice "associations."

32. Philosophical contemplation is ordered to attaining the common good of all things.

On Plato's and Aristotle's accounts, the greatest natural human activity is the activity of philosophical contemplation, whereby persons can transcend the temporal world and attain to eternal truths, and finally to the ultimate cause of all things. This activity is similar to MacIntyrean practices, but it transcends them because it is not

---

22. Alasdair MacIntyre, *After Virtue*, 3rd ed. (Notre Dame: University of Notre Dame Press, 2007), 187.

concerned with the common goods of a particular part of human life, but (at least indirectly) with God Himself, the universal common good of all things, to Whom all other common goods are ordered.

33. A polity is a complete society, concerned with the whole of human life, that can attain to the greatest natural common goods.

Human life is naturally ordered. It is natural for many families to live close to each other and assist each other in the pursuit of common goods, and for their community to be ordered by rules. Aristotle calls the association of a few families a village (κώμη), but he argues that such a small community does not yet suffice to achieve all the common goods to which human nature is ordered.[23] And so it is natural for many villages to come together to form a city (πόλις), a complete or perfect society, which does not depend on any greater society to help it achieve its ends. Such complete societies (which we can call "polities" or "commonwealths") take many forms in different times and places, but they always include some kind of rule ordering them to the common good. As Coëmgenus puts it, "even where there is no 'government,' the people are governed (e.g., by tribal custom). In large complex societies, polity finds a formal expression (written laws, anointed kings, formal elections, etc.). In the liberal West, it takes the form of the constellation of institutions that we call a 'state.' Not all people live under a state, but every [complete] human community by definition is a polity." Polities enable families, local communities ("villages"), and associations to flourish by realizing many common goods, but polities also allow for the achievement of greater common goods.

The bewildering variety of forms that polities can take sometimes makes it difficult to distinguish between a polity and a village, between a complete and an incomplete society. How can one tell whether a community is able to achieve all the goals of human society? Following Thomas Osborne, I have argued that a sign that can be used to distinguish them is this: the complete society has the

---

23. *Politics* I.2, 1252b15–27.

authority to make coercive laws enforceable by the sword.[24] Even with this qualification, it can still be difficult to distinguish them. For example, before the emergence of the "sovereign" territorial state in early modernity, Western Christendom was an extremely complex system of overlapping authorities—counties, duchies, kingdoms, and the empire—all claiming authority to use the sword.

Contemporary nation states pose a different sort of problem. While they in many ways function as complete societies, they have difficulty justifying the authority to use the sword. They have all more or less adopted a liberal political ideology, which holds that polities should be ordered not to the common good, but to the private goods of individuals. A sign of this is the abolition of the death penalty in much of the contemporary West.[25] This is a logical development given their political principles, but it raises questions about the extent to which they are really complete societies, capable of achieving the primary common good of political life.

34. *The primary intrinsic common good of a polity is peace.*[26]

What is it that gives the complete community the right to enforce its laws with the sword? The authority to kill is a quasi-divine power, since God alone is the Lord of life and death. "If you do evil, then be afraid, since it is not for nothing that that minister wears a sword, since he is God's minister, vindictive in anger against the evildoer" (Rom. 13:4). The authority of the polity is derived from

---

24. See my essay "What is the Primary Intrinsic Common Good of Political (or Imperial) Community?," *Sancrucensis*, May 31, 2013, https://sancrucensis.wordpress.com/2013/05/31/what-is-the-primary-intrinsic-common-good-of-political-or-imperial-community/.

25. For a Thomist account of the death penalty, see Steven Long, "'Goods' without Normative Order to the Good Life, Happiness, or God: The New Natural Law Theory and the Nostrum of Incommensurability," *Thomistica.net*, September 18, 2011, https://thomistica.net/news/2011/9/18/goods-without-normative-order-to-the-good-life-happiness-or.html.

26. See, in addition to "What is the Primary Intrinsic Common Good," my essay "Accountability and Paternalism, Imbalance of Power and Civil Friendship," *Sancrucensis*, May 24, 2014, https://sancrucensis.wordpress.com/2014/05/24/accountability-and-paternalism-imbalance-of-power-and-civil-friendship/.

God because it is derived from the common good. The primary intrinsic common good of the polity is the unity of order, peace. This peace depends on the distinction of the different families, villages, and associations in the polity. In consists partly in the common enjoyment of the common goods of those communities. It consists partly in civic friendship and in the activity of governance. But this peace is itself a greater good than any of those partial goods (excepting the philosophical contemplation of God as first cause) because this peace is a participation in the order of all of creation, which, as we saw above (*21*), is the greatest created participation in the divine goodness. Thus, for any person, this good is better than any of their private goods. It is a good to which they can order themselves, for which they can give their lives in battle. And if they harm this good, they oppose the goodness of their own lives, and the authority that has care for this good can justly kill them.

Nevertheless, the common good of the state is not the greatest common good to which persons are ordered. As we saw above (*25*), persons are ordered to attain by knowledge and love God as the supreme common good of all things, a good infinitely surpassing the intrinsic good of an earthly polity.

35. The primary intrinsic common good of the City of God is the order of the whole of creation restored and elevated through grace.

Persons are destined to attain to God, not merely through natural philosophic contemplation, but through the supernatural vision of His essence given by grace. They are destined to enjoy this vision forever in the "Heavenly City," which is nothing other than the whole of creation restored. The extrinsic common good of that city will be God Himself seen by all the angels and saints together, but its intrinsic common good is the order of all creation, the greatest likeness of the divine goodness, made even greater by its being constituted by persons who have become like Him through seeing His essence: "We know that when he is revealed we shall be like him, because we shall see him as he is" (1 Jn. 3:2). But before the second coming, the City of God is present in a hidden and partial way here on earth in the Church militant. In this temporal life, we do not yet have the vision of the divine essence, but we know God through the

The Good, the Highest Good, and the Common Good

theological virtue of faith and love Him with the same love that we will have in Heaven.

36. The common good of temporal society is subordinate to that of the City of God.

Until the second coming, the Church, which is immediately ordered to the common good of the Heavenly City, exists alongside temporal polities, which are immediately ordered to the temporal common good. But the temporal common good is a participation in the order of creation itself, and so it can dispose those who share in it toward the eternal common good. The temporal common good is thus subordinate to the eternal common good, and the temporal rulers are subordinate to the hierarchy of the Church.[27]

37. The theological virtue of love brings us into the right relation toward the common good of the City of God.

The most necessary thing for attaining any common good is love of that good. And in order to love God as the common good of the City of God, the most necessary thing is to have the theological virtue of love. I conclude with a text from St. Thomas, explaining this thesis. It is rather long, but I quote it in full, as it contains virtually the whole account of the common good:

> The philosopher says in Book Eight of the *Politics* that in order to be a good political [person] one must love the good of the city. Now when someone is admitted to participation in the good of some city and becomes a citizen of that city, he must have certain virtues in order to do what a citizen must do and to love the good of the city.
>
> In the same way, when a man is admitted by divine grace to participating in heavenly beatitude, which consists in the vision and enjoyment of God, he becomes, as it were, a citizen and member of that blessed society which is called the heavenly Jerusalem, according to Ephesians 2:19: "You are citizens with the saints and members of the household of God." A person who is in this way counted as part of the heavenly city must have certain freely given

---

27. See "Religious Liberty and Tradition III," *The Josias*, January 2, 2015, https://thejosias.com/2015/01/02/religious-liberty-and-tradition-iii/.

virtues which are the infused virtues. The right exercise of these virtues requires a love of the common good that belongs to the whole society, which is the divine good as the object of beatitude.

Now one can love the good of a city in two ways: in one way to possess it, in another that it might be preserved. If someone loves the good of a city in order to have and own it, he is not a good political person, because in this way even a tyrant loves the good of a city, in order to dominate it, which is to love oneself more than the city. He wants this good for himself, not for the city.

But to love the good of the city that it might be kept and defended, this is truly to love the city and this makes a person a good political person, so much so that some expose themselves to the danger of death and neglect their private good in order to preserve or increase the good of the city.

In the same way, to love the good that is participated by the blessed, to love it so as to have or possess it, does not establish the right relation between a person and blessedness, because even evil people want this good.

But to love that good according to itself, that it may remain and be shared and that nothing be done against this good, this gives to a person the right relation to that society of the blessed. And this is love [*caritas*] which loves God for his sake and neighbors, who are capable of blessedness, as oneself.[28]

---

28. *De Virtutibus*, q. 2, a. 2, trans. Michael Waldstein.

2

The Foundations of Christian Ethics and Social Order[1]

Peter A. Kwasniewski

It is a well-known axiom of Thomistic ethics that whatever good a person loves he loves as his own good (*bonum suum*). How, then, can there be a true "ecstasy," that is, a true going out of oneself in love for the other?[2] How can there be authentic love of the other for the *other's* sake? Does not love collapse into egoism? And would not the only practical or theoretical alternative be altruism—a sort of spontaneous giving away to others that has no reference whatsoever to oneself or one's good?

The modern antinomy

The liberal democratic state and the collectivist or communist state are giant social embodiments of the seemingly inescapable antinomy of egoism and altruism. One system reduces human

---

1. The present article was developed out of a talk given at the XIth Colloquium of the International Group of Research in Moral Theology of the John Paul II Institute for the Study of Marriage and Family, on the theme "*Caritas Aedificat:* Love as a Principle of Social Life," held at the Pontifical Lateran University in Rome, 19–20 November 2010. An Italian version appeared as "L'amore come principio di communicazione nel bene," in *L'amore principio di vita sociale*, Juan José Pérez-Soba and Marija Magdič, eds., *Studi sulla Persona e la Famiglia* 12 (Siena: Edizioni Cantagalli, 2011): 73–87. The author thanks Jeremy Holmes and Stephan Kampowski for their critical remarks on an earlier draft.

2. The doctrine of the *extasis amoris* is developed by Saint Thomas in a number of works throughout his career. For texts and analysis, see Peter A. Kwasniewski, *The Ecstasy of Love in the Thought of Thomas Aquinas* (Steubenville, OH: Emmaus Academic, 2021).

Integralism and the Common Good

motivation to self-interest or selfishness, thereby hindering interpersonal communion, which requires the gift of self; the other system undermines human happiness by ignoring the dignity of the person as such, allowing the individual to be sacrificed for an alien "social good." The entire political climate of modernity almost forces us into envisioning reality as an insoluble conflict between egoism and altruism.

Because modern society has rejected traditional virtues in favor of materialistic consumerism and hedonism, the modern man habituated to think, feel, and act as a pleasure-seeking consumer is therefore habituated to the error of egoism, and trapped within it. Since there are so many needy people about whom he does not care, the egoist must be "forced" to help others. One thinks in this connection of rampant socialism, of government welfare programs and mandated health care that have taken the place of an organic subsidiarity guided by social justice and charity. Such a "welfare state" breeds cynicism, then resentment, and finally violence because it does not emerge from or appeal to genuinely possessed virtue; it represents an assault on the monstrous ego that modern society has produced. Put differently, modern society inculcates egoism instead of justice and charity, but, recognizing the result as a disaster, it tries to enforce altruism, which both reinforces and chafes against egoism. The result is social tension, antipathy, civil unrest. A further, more subtle result is that modernity, by relentlessly promoting a self distant from divine roots, detached from tradition-based rationality, and doomed to create meaning, empties the ego of the rich content that persons, in their native receptivity, stand to inherit from the society of persons preceding and surrounding them and destined to flow forth from them. The unexpected flip side of a disproportionate inflation of the ego is its evacuation and vacuity—a perverse imitation of Christological *kenosis*—which may develop into a powerful force of negation and annihilation.

In a seminal political philosopher like Thomas Hobbes (1588–1679) we find the presuppositions of this pervasive egoism. For Hobbes, everything is instrumental to my own good, which is understood as a merely sensible good; because self = body (indeed, reality = body), there can be no extension of love beyond the self, beyond the body.[3] Everything outside of oneself is, at worst, a threat to oneself; at best, a means to the end of self-preservation. The social contract is a mechanism which enables me to get more of what I want, while enabling you to get what you want. We cannot desire something common, because there is nothing truly common. All good is private good. Thus I cannot "will the good for another"; I cannot want another to be well for his own sake. Anything I want for another (potentially or actually) takes something away from me.

Hobbes exposes the roots of the modern antinomy of egoism and altruism, whose deep kinship can be formulated as follows. If I am an egoist, I subordinate everybody else's good to *my own* private good. If I am an altruist, I subordinate my good to what ends up being *somebody else's* private good. (Ironically, altruism, whether in theory or in practice, depends upon the basic assumption of egoism—namely, that my good and your good are simply alien to each other, and that I can help *you* only at the expense of *my* good.) Both alternatives are equally irrational, indeed anti-Christian: the indiscriminate ordering of others to self or of self to others.

This opposition between egoism and altruism is entirely foreign to Saint Thomas's doctrine of love. In his subtle realism, Thomas grasps well the relationship between my good, the good of other persons, and the transcendent source of all good, the tripersonal God. Human perfection consists *neither* in the fulfillment of a self sealed off from others, *nor* in a radical negation of the worth and selfhood of the person. Man's perfection consists in the giving of oneself to God and neighbor, going out of oneself to the other in a self-forgetful oblation that is also the height of self-perfection, because it involves communication in the common good. This doc-

---

3. Connected to this is the contemporary "cult of the body" which takes many and various forms ranging from relatively harmless to spiritually poisonous, e.g., preoccupation with television and magazine images, the health and fitness obsession, capitalist pampering products, increasingly costly and invasive medical technology, tattoos and piercing, pornography. What all these have in common is the error of taking the body or the sensible as if it were the *self*—the locus of attention, cultivation, and finality.

trine offers a genuine alternative to tedious debates about egoism and altruism, self-interest and spontaneous beneficence.[4]

Ecstatic generosity as the rule of creation

The human self is not sealed off from others in its fulfillment, but rather naturally inclines to what might be called "ecstatic generosity." Implanted in man's nature—or more precisely, in his *voluntas ut natura*—is the love of the good as such. As a being that is and is good by participation, man depends upon and is naturally ordered to the simple Good; he is inclined, already *before* choice, to live more truly in and for God than in and for himself. The many conscious manifestations of *extasis* follow upon this innate *extasis* of created being to uncreated being, finite good to infinite Good, likeness to exemplar, imperfect image to perfect Image. Ontological *extasis* precedes and sustains psychological *extasis* as nature precedes power and power precedes activity.

Man, like all creatures, has ecstatic power (Dionysius refers to it as *eros*), because he is made to the image of the all-powerful God whose generous love creates, conserves, and governs the world. The God who does *not* stand outside Himself because He is everywhere, held by nothing, is the Lover whose effects are the most ecstatic, for He creates by love the very beings from which He then entices the *extasis* of a responding love. In His superabundant goodness whereby He remains in Himself, He effects a world of beings which, to greater and lesser extent, stand outside themselves, imitating Him.[5]

God has made creatures to be not merely recipients of good, but also sources of it. *Ens creatum*, created being, has not only the negative side of poverty, which provokes appetite for the absent good, but the positive side of wealth, which promotes the diffusion of the good to others. As Norris Clarke explains:

---

4. See David Gallagher, "Gewirth, Sterba, and the Justification of Morality," in *Gewirh: Critical Essays on Action, Rationality, and Community*, ed. Michal Boylan (New York: Rowman & Littlefield, 1999): 183–89.

5. In God alone is the lack of *extasis* pure positivity, for there is no finitude that He must transcend in order to be Himself, as we must transcend our limits if we will enter fully into what we are to be.

The Foundations of Christian Ethics and Social Order

The real beings of our universe go out of themselves in action for two reasons: one, because they are poor, in that as limited and imperfect they are seeking completion of themselves from other beings; two, because they are rich, in that they actually exist and so possess some degree of actual perfection and have an intrinsic tendency to share this in some way with others.[6]

As the axiom has it: *bonum est diffusivum sui*, the good is diffusive of itself.[7] The nobler a good is, the more being it has, and the more it can be loved not only in itself but also as something sharable, diffusible, participable. The infinite divine good is infinitely sharable, and hence it is most fitting that the divine love which is identical with this good should freely share it by bringing into being recipients of the same good. Because the created recipient mirrors its uncreated source and imitates His activity—because, in short, created being is mimetic ecstasy towards God—it is *naturally* apt to communicate itself to others in the way this is possible, viz., by efficiently causing *in another* a likeness of its own actuality, thus sharing its good. On such an account it is natural for all things not only to obtain and preserve their own good, but also to share it with others. Anything with a capacity to be aware of something other than itself naturally loves something other than itself, and, according to its ability, works for its good.[8] The sparrow feeding its newly-hatched offspring is doing in its nest something analogous to what God is doing in the universe: giving something good to a dependent, not for the giver's benefit, but for the dependent's. Perhaps the best expression of this truth is found in the *Summa contra gentiles*:

---

6. W. Norris Clarke, *The One and the Many: A Contemporary Thomistic Metaphysics* (Notre Dame: University of Notre Dame Press, 2001), 33.

7. Texts in which Saint Thomas invokes this axiom: *Scriptum super libros Sententiarum* [*Sent.*] I, d. 34, q. 2, a. 1, ad 4; *Summa contra gentiles* [*SCG*] Bk. I, ch. 37 and Bk. III, ch. 24; *Summa theologiae* [*ST*] I, q. 5, a. 4 and q. 27, a. 5, ad 2; *ST* I-II, q. 1, a. 4, ad 1; *ST* II-II, q. 117, a. 6, obj. 2 et ad 2; *Quaestiones disputatae De veritate* q. 21, a. 1, ad 4. On the related principle *bonum se communicat*, see *Sent.* I, d. 2, q. 1, a. 4, sc; *Sent.* I, d. 10, q. 1, a. 5, obj. 3 et ad 3; *ST* I, q. 19, a. 2 and q. 106, a. 4; *ST* III, q. 1, a. 1; *Compendium theologiae* I, ch. 124.

8. The principle of likeness will be important, for "every animal loves its like, and every man his neighbor" (Sir. 13:15).

The more perfect a thing's power, and the higher its degree of goodness, the more universal is its desire for good, and the greater the range of goodness to which its appetite and operation extend. For imperfect things extend no further than their own individual good; but perfect things extend to the good of the species; more perfect things, to the good of the genus; and God who is most perfect in goodness, to the good of all being. Wherefore it is said by some, not without reason, that good, as such, is diffusive of itself, because the better a thing is, the further does the outpouring of its goodness extend. And since, in every genus, that which is most perfect is the exemplar and measure of all that belongs to that genus, it follows that God, who is most perfect in goodness, and pours forth His goodness most universally, is in His outpouring the exemplar of all things that pour forth goodness. Now one thing becomes a cause of another by pouring forth its own goodness into that other. And so it is again evident that whatever tends to be the cause of something else, tends to a divine likeness, and yet tends to its own good.[9]

The higher the creature, the more of itself it gives, for it has more of a self at the origin of the giving. "The word 'friendship,'" says Saint Thomas, "is properly applied to a love that spreads itself out to others."[10]

Nature is not inherently selfish

Here is the root of Saint Thomas's forceful disagreement with an axiom traceable to earlier scholastics and, further back, to Saint Bernard: *natura semper in se curva est*, or *natura est recurva in seipsa*.[11] A dramatic statement of it is found in Saint Albert: "The love of concupiscence belongs to nature, which is always curved into itself; and whatever it loves it twists back into itself, that is, to its proper, private good; and unless it is freely made to be elevated

---

9. Thomas Aquinas, *SCG* Bk. III, ch. 24 (Leon. 14:63, Ex quo).
10. Aquinas, *Sent.* III, d. 28, a. 6 (913, §57).
11. See Aquinas, *Quaestiones quodlibetales* 1, q. 4, a. 3; *ST* I, q. 60, a. 5; I-II, q. 109, a. 3; II-II, q. 26, a. 3; *Sent.* III, d. 29, q. 1, a. 3; cf. Réginald Garrigou-Lagrange, *The Love of God and the Cross of Jesus*, trans. Jeanne Marie (St. Louis: Herder, 1947), 1:89 et seq.

above itself by grace, everything that it loves it twists back to its proper good, and loves on account of itself."[12]

What disturbs Saint Thomas is not the idea that some love can be self-recursive, but that natural love *as such* deserves to be so defined. For if natural love is necessarily self-directed, then any kind of love for others, any *extasis*, is not only exclusively a result of grace but is also contrary to nature, destructive of the order of appetite. We have seen that for Thomas appetite is built along ecstatic lines, and even in the clearest cases of self-recursive appetite, such as an electron's leap for a more stable place, an animal's hunger for food, or a plant's leaning into sunlight, the creature is, without knowing or intending it, striving for assimilation to God, consolidating its divine likeness. This process, however, is not isolated and introspective; it is communal and extroverted. Spontaneously and naturally, a creature is no less inclined to share its good than to preserve it and enhance it. In Thomas's words: "Natural things have an inclination not only with respect to the proper good—to acquire it when it is not had, to rest in it when had—but also to pour forth good into others so far as it is possible."[13]

Love always involves ecstatic transcendence, whether it be the total oblation of creature to Creator, the hierarchically proportioned reverence of any inferior to its superior, the mutual affection and help of equals joined in friendship, or the gracious condescension of a superior to the inferior dependent upon the superior for being or well-being. Love and ecstasy are therefore not companions of chance, but the latter is the infallible mark of the species, quality, and intensity of the former. If a man may be known by the company he keeps, love may be known by the ecstasy it provokes. Love's participation in personal, spiritual reality is determined by the presence of ecstatic commitment and gift. *Love of things* as instruments or accidental perfections generates a quasi-ecstatic love that journeys outward only to return inward, bearing gifts for the master subject. *Love of persons* for their own sake generates a truly ecstatic

---

12. Albertus Magnus, *Summae theologiae* 2.4.14.4.2, corp., in *Opera omnia*, vol. 32 (Paris: Vivès, 1895).

13. Aquinas, *ST* I, q. 19, a. 2.

love, bearing the self as gift to another subject, in the form of sharing a common life that aspires most of all to common goods. In one love alone is the ecstasy towards the other all-encompassing, all-consuming: the unconditional love of man or angel for his divine Lord, in whom all good is found, to whom all worship is owed. As David Gallagher explains:

> In accord with this doctrine of participation, Thomas maintains that the perfections of all creatures, including rational beings, are found more perfectly in the unparticipated source than in the participating subjects. It is precisely this point that serves to explain the love of God for his own sake (*amor amicitiae*) even more than self. The very good that one loves in oneself is found more perfectly in the uncreated source of that good. . . . Thus we are more pleased by (i.e., have more *complacentia* in) our good as it exists in God than as it exists in ourselves, and accordingly we love God even more than ourselves. One might express it as follows: the complete good of the whole that is God is more my good than the particular and partial good that I as a particular subsisting being possess. God, as the pure source of all good, is more lovable than any particular good, even oneself.[14]

We began by saying that the human self is not sealed off from others in its fulfillment, and here we have the most direct way of stating why: the creature is inclined to love the common good, which is more like the God who is naturally loved, than its private good, which imitates Him less and is therefore less the *creature's* good and less beloved. If natural love were not already to some extent ecstatic, *amor amicitiae*, friendship-love, would be impossible, grace or no grace. One might put it this way: selfishness, the exaltation of the private over the common, is only a corruption and is never natural.[15]

---

14. David Gallagher, "Desire for Beatitude and Love of Friendship in Thomas Aquinas," *Medieval Studies* 58 (1996): 1–47, at 37.

15. Sin is not only rejection of grace; at the deepest level it is denial of nature. Sin is the privation or diminishment of mode, species, and order (see *ST* I-II, q. 85, a. 4). Love of God above self is natural for *integral* nature; it is no longer natural for *fallen* nature (*ST* I-II, q. 109, a. 3). In the fallen order, an ecstatic, generously self-diffusive love is possible only by the infusion of grace, actual or habitual, which empowers a person to love God above all and in all, and to love one's neighbor as oneself.

The Foundations of Christian Ethics and Social Order

The entire moral life—possibly the whole of created being—is suffused with a new light: except for the merely logical relation of oneself to oneself, all relationships are governed by the law of ecstatic communication, varying in potency as the relatives vary in weight of being, in dignity of subsistence.

The human self is fulfilled in the common good

Up to this point in our reflections we have seen that the way in which "the problem of love" is usually cast—that allegiance must be given to altruism or egoism—involves a false opposition from the start, built upon a superficial metaphysics. Because neither position recognizes ecstatic generosity as the rule of creation, neither position recognizes the fundamental distinction between private goods, which cannot be shared by many, and common goods, which *can* be shared by many. To this distinction we now turn.

As we saw in the case of Hobbes, the foundation of the modern egoism/altruism antinomy is the view that reality = body. But as it turns out, Hobbes was wrong: he missed the realm of rationality. Because men are rational animals, we are brought together by spiritual goods through their sensible manifestations. We cannot eat the same piece of meat, but we can share the same meal. We cannot use the same spoon, but we can dwell under one roof as brothers. We cannot speak the same word, but we can share a conversation that binds us in pursuit of truth or in its joyful attainment. We cannot see with the same eyes or hear with the same ears, but the intelligible beauty that underlies the visible or audible beauty can penetrate all of our souls in such a way that we are drawn towards it with a shared admiration and delight. We cannot think the very same thought, but our minds can be conformed to the very same object and so be united in the truth.

In all these ways, although we are many, we become one. To be rational means to be able to enter into goods that transcend the material order, the *hic et nunc*. It means that we can be a "one-many": not a simple unity, as is God, nor an ever-changing multiplicity, as are materials things, but a plurality unified in and through adherence to a higher good. Friendship is "two-as-one," "many-as-one." The beasts of the field can be together in a place, but they cannot be truly *one*. Only persons created in the image of the Trinitarian God have the godlike power to form an interpersonal reality, a *communio* or *koinonia*, that embraces and gives ultimate meaning to their distinctiveness, their separate selves. Such *communio* will be inherently spiritual, founded on and ordered to spiritual goods.

This last point deserves careful reflection. Saint Thomas observes that "spiritual goods are more communicable than bodily goods."[16] The converse of this position is formulated by Garrigou-Lagrange as "a truth often uttered by Saint Augustine and Saint Thomas," namely: "Contrary to spiritual goods, material goods divide men, because they cannot belong simultaneously and integrally to a number." Garrigou-Lagrange explains:

> A number of persons cannot possess integrally and simultaneously the same house, the same field, the same territory; whence dissensions, quarrels, lawsuits, wars. On the contrary, spiritual goods, like truth, virtue, God Himself, can belong simultaneously and integrally to a number; many may possess simultaneously the same virtue, the same truth, the same God who gives Himself wholly to each of us in [Holy] Communion. Therefore, whereas the unbridled search for material goods profoundly divides men, the quest for spiritual goods unites them. It unites us so much the more closely, the more we seek these superior goods. And we even possess God so much the more, the more we give Him to others. When we give away money, we no longer possess it; when, on the contrary, we give God to souls, we do not lose Him; rather we possess Him more. And should we refuse to give Him to a person who asks for Him, we would lose Him.[17]

Garrigou-Lagrange's mention of Saint Augustine brings to mind a famous passage in Book XII of the *Confessions* where Augustine is

---

16. Aquinas, *ST* Suppl., q. 56, a. 4; cf. *ST* III, q. 23, a. 1, ad 3; I-II, q. 28, a. 4, ad 2. For an extended application of this principle, see Peter A. Kwasniewski, "On the Ideal Basis and Fruition of Marriage," *Second Spring* 12 (2010): 43–53.

17. Réginald Garrigou-Lagrange, *The Three Ages of the Interior Life: Prelude of Eternal Life*, trans. M. Timothea Doyle (Rockford: TAN, 1989), 2:141; see also idem, "The Fecundity of Goodness," *The Thomist* 2 (1940): 226–36.

contrasting those who interpret Scripture out of pride and those who interpret it out of charity. The proud, he says,

> love their own opinion, and this not because it is true but because it is their own. Otherwise they would have as much love for the truth uttered by another: just as I love what they say when they say truth, not because it is theirs but because it is truth. Indeed, from the mere fact that it is true, it ceases to be theirs [alone]. But if they love it because it is true, then it is already both theirs and mine; it is the common property of all lovers of truth.... For Your truth is not mine or this man's or that man's; it belongs to all of us because You call us to share it in common, warning us most terribly not to possess it as our private property, lest we be deprived of it. Whoever claims for himself what You have given for the enjoyment of all, and wishes to have as his own what belongs to everyone, is driven from the wealth of all to his own poor wealth, that is, from truth to a lie. For "he who speaks a lie, speaks from his own" (Jn. 8:44).[18]

Truth is the kind of good one can *have* only if one does not have it *as one's own*, as owned by oneself. The moment it is seized as private, it ceases to be true; it becomes a falsified or distorted truth, a half-truth or no truth at all. This is why the truth of the Christian creed, or even the act of heroic sacrifice, amounts to nothing without charity, as Saint Paul teaches (1 Cor. 13). Even if such things are good and true *abstractly*, they are good and true concretely, *for the subject*, only when he embraces them with a good will, which is to say, with the *right* love of self, which necessitates love of God and neighbor.

It is in this context that the fundamental relationship of *bonum privatum* and *bonum commune* becomes evident: the common good, properly understood, is not something over and above what is "good for me" personally; it is precisely what is best for me and most perfective of me, simply speaking. That which is most com-

---

18. Augustine, *Confessions* 12.25, trans. F. J. Sheed (Indianapolis/Cambridge: Hackett, 1993), 251, slightly modified.

monly sharable is, in being shared, the most beneficial to all who partake of it.[19]

"One's own good" not only permits but necessitates that one's self be enlarged by loving others for their own sake, which involves loving goods truly common to many. There is more to *my* good as a person than the private goods or the perfections I possess. My identity grows, my goodness is amplified, when I unite myself affectively to another person or community in a love which seeks the good of this other for its own sake.

It sounds paradoxical, as do so many basic truths. My good is not simply *my* good, but includes *your* good; indeed, *our* good is more truly what is good for me than any good that is mine alone. The basis of a truly human friendship is the union of minds or spirits through goods that are common, communicable, and inexhaustible; such a relationship has the potential for continual growth and fruition. Material goods, which are inherently private (i.e., sharable only by predication), divisible, exhaustible, and potentially divisive, cannot be a stable basis for friendship.[20]

Genuine love not only builds up personal union, it destroys whatever is incompatible with it. Love not only sees to it that friends are rooted in the common good, it uproots them from

---

19. Any creature, insofar as it is a part of a larger whole, is naturally inclined (and should it be a free agent, morally obliged) to love the good of the whole—both the intrinsic common good which is the order of the universe, and the extrinsic common good which is God—more than its good as a part. Being by its very nature part of a whole, or more precisely, part of many concentric wholes, the creature is ordered to the whole not merely as to something superior to and constitutive of it, but as to that which, in its very universality, is most causative of and integral to its own proper perfection. The definitive treatment of this subject is that of Charles De Koninck, *The Primacy of the Common Good*. See also Michael Waldstein, "The Common Good in St. Thomas and John Paul II," *Nova et Vetera* 3.3 (2005): 569–78; Oliva Blanchette, *The Perfection of the Universe According to Aquinas* (University Park: The Pennsylvania State University Press, 1992).

20. True, material goods may and must be *used* virtuously as the basis of expressing the friendship of charity, and in this way they can become instruments even of loving God in loving one's neighbor for His sake. One might refer to the "sacramental principle" underlying the orders of creation and redemption: spiritual realities are communicated to us through material things that serve as instruments and symbols of those realities. In the absence of genuine virtues, however,

whatever private goods may stand in the way of communion. In order to unite, love also divides; it compels a man to cease clinging to himself, so that he may cling to another—so that he may pour out his time, his energy, his actions, his possessions, on behalf of others. Although friends are never merged into numerical identity, they enter into genuine communion with one another through the unifying, transformative power of love. When a person loves another as he loves himself, he comes to be outside himself by loving and promoting the other's good as he does his own. His identity is colored and eventually transfigured through ecstatic operation.

Good and bad self-love: the truth behind the modern antinomy

In outline, we have exposed and refuted the supposed antinomy of egoism and altruism, but now we must admit that its persuasiveness to modern man is rooted at least in part in its resemblance to the truth about our fallen condition. In our experience, there is—or can often be—a real conflict between self-love and love of the other. A full response to the opposition of egoism and altruism must be able to explain our experience. So, what real opposition is there between self-love and love of the other?

We begin by recalling something we have already said: the good that is *most* my good—the divine good, which is *per se* infinitely common—is ontologically *other than* me and can benefit me only when loved for its own sake and as sharable by all. That which is deepest in the causing of perfection, intimately present to all things by communicating being and goodness to them, is that which most transcends the self and most demands the homage of self-transcendence. The "self" of which Aquinas speaks is always and more fundamentally ordered to God in whom its own good more perfectly

---

material goods become a stumbling block for man in his progress towards happiness, a powerful incentive and mechanism for oppression either by their abuse or by their plotted absence. As Garrigou-Lagrange rightly maintains, in and of themselves, material goods serve rather to divide men than to unite them; indeed, because of fallen man's disordered concupiscence, they divide a man against *himself*, his lower passions and appetites against his rational good and intellectual destiny, and as we know, "a house divided against itself cannot stand."

exists. By nature and by grace, I am ecstatically ordered to God. Self-love is therefore understood to be good or well-ordered when (and only when) it actually orders a man to God, his true and final good outside of himself.

Herein lies the essential difference between how the good man loves himself and how the bad man loves himself. According to Saint Thomas, the good man loves what is most truly himself—his mind, in which is inscribed the *imago Dei*[21]—by ordering the lower powers to the higher and, if need be, sacrificing something of the lower for the sake of the fuller perfection of the higher.[22] In contrast, by ordering everything to his lower powers, the bad man makes a self-contradictory sacrifice of what is most truly himself to things which are less truly himself. As Saint Thomas remarks:

> The love of God is unitive (*congregativus*), inasmuch as it draws man's affections from the many to the one; and so the virtues that are caused by the love of God are connected together. But self-love disunites (*amor sui disgregat*) man's affections among different things, so far as man loves himself by desiring for himself temporal goods, which are various and of many kinds.[23]

At their extremes, the two types of self-love exhaust the total possibilities of human nature. The saint rises above himself into greater, more common, more permanent goods that his mind embraces by spiritual love; the sinner falls beneath himself into narrower, private, passing goods upon which he dissipates himself. He who lost what was least himself finds what is most himself, namely, the image of God, and through it union with God; he who found what is least himself loses his soul, and through this loss, loses God.[24]

Part of the difficulty in this discussion is the elusive and ambiguous notion of "self." Who or what is the "self"? If we take it to mean

---

21. See Aquinas, *ST* I, q. 93; cf. *Catechism of the Catholic Church*, nn. 356–68.
22. According to Aquinas, *ST* II-II, q. 25, a. 7, good men take to be primary in themselves the *mens rationalis*, the *rationalem naturam*, whereas the bad judge primary the *naturam sensitivam et corporalem*.
23. Aquinas, *ST* I-II, q. 73, a. 1, ad 3; see Garrigou-Lagrange, *Three Ages*, 2:399.
24. See Lk. 9:24–25; Jn. 12:25 and parallels; Mt. 13:12, 25:29, and parallels; and the parable of the prodigal son (Lk. 15:11–32), who "wasted his substance with riotous living," *dissipavit substantiam suam vivendo luxuriose* (15:13).

instantiated personhood, my human identity as distinctively mine, my unique interiority as expressed in and through my body, then it is obvious that the self is not *prior*, absolutely speaking, to everything else, especially other selves. There is, first, the mystery of my origin: I do not come into being "by myself" but from others, into a world that surrounds me, and with a nature given to me. Then there is the mystery of my sociality. From the beginning and throughout the whole of life, one's self is enmeshed in and shaped by relationships with other persons, relationships through which the self attains (or fails to attain) its maturity and most excellent condition. The virtuous agent submits himself to, and is prepared to sacrifice his life on behalf of, the common good, in which he superlatively finds his own good, his own *identity*. Perfection involves a dedication or consecration to what is good absolutely speaking; hence it makes absolute demands, and the good man is precisely the one who heeds these demands on account of goodness itself, not on account of private benefits. By so living he "assigns to himself the noblest and best goods" (as Aristotle says),[25] for one partakes of a common good by subordinating oneself to it. As we saw in the text from Saint Augustine, a common good can be possessed only *as common*, not "as mine" to another's exclusion. If the good man is to assign the noblest good *to himself*, then he must be referring and subordinating himself *to* that noblest good, which places him in the relationship of part to whole.

Existential distinction among rational creatures was willed by God with a view towards their association, formation of society, friendship, and mutual indwelling (*mutua inhaesio*).[26] The best thing about being an individual of a *rational* nature is that one can enter into communion—with God, first and foremost; with other rational creatures secondarily and in order more fully to adhere to and delight in God. The other becomes "another self"; put differently, my "self" is expanded or enlarged to include other selves. I take the friend as a part of who I am, so that his good becomes my good, and thus when I work for his good, I am not doing something

---

25. See Aristotle, *Nicomachean Ethics* IX.9.
26. See Aquinas, *ST* I-II, q. 28, a. 2.

unrelated to my good. The persons remain ontologically distinct, but as they participate more and more in what is truly common to rational beings, they develop a spiritual unity or *communio* that transcends their individual limitations, even as it draws out the image of God in their souls. *For creatures, to be a part is the only way to become whole.*

A society of charity

Saint Thomas's doctrine of love honors at every point the paradoxicality of love itself: the lover is made perfect only when and to the extent that he loves God more than himself—i.e., orders himself and all that is his to God *because* He is God—and seeks the good of other persons without subordinating their good to his own. Virtue is bound up with seeing the human good as primarily spiritual and common to many: the virtuous man sees himself as a "one-many," a part with roles to play, duties and rights to live out. Vice is bound up with reducing the good to material or bodily goods that cannot be shared: the vicious man behaves like a moral cyclops, a self-sufficient island with no needs or responsibilities towards others. If a man is virtuous, it is because he is capable of acting for the good as such, which can and should belong to many; if he is vicious, it is because he consistently chooses to act for goods that can be his either only or frequently at the expense of others. (One need only think of the abortion mentality of the culture of death.) As Catholic Social Teaching has always maintained, the *only* way to overcome the false opposition between "mine" and "thine" is to acquire those virtues that see the best goods as "ours."

The mutually exclusive alternatives of egoism and altruism, like their counterparts *eros* and *agape* in Anders Nygren's fantasy, are from the start hopelessly inadequate to the task of explanation, forcing one into conclusions that run against both reasonable reflection on experience and the revealed word of God.

In a magnificent text, Jacques Maritain identifies three theoretical possibilities for man, which might be paraphrased as (1) self-absorption, death by contraction, pure subjectivity—in a word, *egoism*; (2) self-dissolution, death by expansion, pure objectivity—in a word, *altruism*; (3) self-surrender, greater life by dying to the extremes, the enfolding of subjectivity within the divine Subject—in a word, *charity*.

> If I abandon myself to the perspective of subjectivity, I absorb everything into myself, and, sacrificing everything to my uniqueness, I am riveted to the absolute of selfishness and pride [think: ossified egoism]. If I abandon myself to the perspective of objectivity, I am absorbed into everything, and, dissolving into the world, I am false to my uniqueness and resign my destiny [think: drunken altruism]. It is only from above [think: infusion of divine charity] that the antinomy can be resolved. If God exists, then not I, but He is the centre; and this time not in relation to a certain particular perspective, like that in which each created subjectivity is the centre of the universe it knows, but speaking absolutely, and as transcendent subjectivity to which all subjectivities are referred. At such time I can know both that I am without importance and that my destiny is of the highest importance. I can know this without falling into pride, know it without being false to my uniqueness. Because, loving the divine Subject more than myself, it is *for Him* that I love myself, it is to do as He wishes that I wish above all else to accomplish my destiny; and because, unimportant as I am in the world, I am important to Him; not only I, but all the other subjectivities whose lovableness is revealed in Him and for Him and which are henceforward, together with me, a we, called to rejoice in His life.[27]

Ultimately, our perfection consists in being ordered to something, or rather Someone, who is *interior intimo meo et superior summo meo*,[28] more interior than what is innermost in me, and higher than what is highest in me—the source of my being, my goodness, my personhood, my destiny. What perfects me lies ever beyond me and yet is made mine by charity. This Good is not taken into me and assimilated like food, but I am taken by it and assimilated to it, along with all others who allow themselves to be drawn into its embrace. This is the basis for a society of charity—a society in which the members actualize their dignity as children of God

---

27. Jacques Maritain, *Existence and the Existent*, trans. Lewis Galantiere and Gerald B. Phelan (Garden City, NY: Doubleday, 1957), 82–83.

28. Augustine, *Confessions* 3.6.11.

through divine worship, contemplative leisure, friendship, and active service to the lowly; a society that pursues and rejoices in goods truly common: natural and supernatural truth, moral and intellectual virtues, the intelligible beauty of the fine arts, the joy of communities at peace; a society that even begins to conform, from afar, to the luminous exemplar of the Blessed Trinity, leading us *ex umbris et imaginibus in veritatem*, from shadows and images into the Truth.

3

Contrasting Concepts of Freedom[1]

Edmund Waldstein, O.Cist.

1. Two concepts of freedom, two forms of culture

The contemporary world is being dominated ever more by a secular, liberal, hedonistic anti-culture that is a threat to true human happiness and flourishing. This secular anti-culture originated in the West in a rejection of the traditional culture of Western Christendom, but it has now become a global force, and one therefore that Islam will have to contend with as well. One way of understanding the conflict between secular anti-culture and the traditional Christian culture against which it rebelled is to distinguish their very different concepts of freedom. In the following reflections I want to consider the concept of freedom found in the Bible and the Christian tradition (and to some extent in the philosophy of antiquity), and then contrast it with the secular concept, rooted in

---

1. A paper delivered at the Conference *Heute gerecht leben: Impulse zu Ordnungskonzeptionen aus katholischer, orthodoxer und schiitischer Tradition*, Vienna, September 19, 2016. A version of this essay was also published in Stefan Gugerel, Christian Machek, and Clemens Egger, eds., *Ordnungskonzeptionen für die Zukunft: Impulse aus schiitischer, orthodoxer und katholischer Tradition* (Vienna: Institut für Religion und Frieden), 125. I have revised my remarks in the light of the discussion at the conference. I would like to take this opportunity to thank all the organizers and participants in the conference especially Christian Machek, Taher Amini Golestani, the *Johannes-Messner-Gesellschaft*, the *Institut für Religion und Frieden* of the Austrian Military Diocese, the *International Institute for Peace and Religions*, and the *ViQo Circle for Catholic-Shi'a Dialogue on Religion, Philosophy, and Political Theory*. I would also like to thank Peter A. Kwasniewski, Alan Fimister, and Susan Waldstein for helpful comments.

the philosophy of the so-called Enlightenment. I shall try to show why the secular concept of freedom is so dangerous.

One can consider freedom on many different levels. For the sake of clarity I shall distinguish between three such levels: 1) exterior or political freedom, 2) interior or natural freedom, 3) moral freedom. The secular and Christian concepts of freedom differ on all three levels. I shall summarize the differences briefly before considering each view more closely.

1) For the Christian tradition *external freedom* means not being subordinated to another's good, not being a slave. Politically such freedom is realized by a political rule that orders people to their own true common good—a good that is truly good *for them*. For the secular tradition of the Enlightenment in contrast, external freedom means not being commanded by another to act in one way rather than another. Negatively this kind of freedom is realized by limiting the scope of government to the preservation of external peace, leaving each citizen free to seek whatever he thinks is the good. Positively it is realized by the participation of all citizens in political rule—so that everyone can claim to be "self-ruled."

2) *Interior or natural freedom* is taken in the mainstream of the Christian tradition to mean the ability of man to understand what is good, deliberate about how it is to be attained, and choose means suitable to attaining it. Unlike the animals, man is not determined by instinct, but is able to deliberate about his actions. On the secular view, however, internal or natural freedom is taken to mean a completely undetermined self-movement of will. On the secular view man is free not only to deliberate about how to attain the good, but *to decide for himself what the good is*.

3) *Moral freedom*, according to the Christian tradition, means knowing what the true good for man is, and what means are necessary to attain it, and being able to make use of those means. Moral freedom means being liberated from bad habits and disordered passions that lead us away from what we know is the good. To be morally free is to live in accordance with the nature that God has given us—it is to be virtuous and wise. For secular culture on the other hand, moral freedom means not being determined by cultural pressures, rejecting conformity for the sake of "authenticity" and "origi-

nality," and deciding on one's own peculiar way of living human life, based on one's own "freely chosen" (i.e., arbitrarily chosen) "values."

2. True freedom

The Book of Exodus is a story of liberation, of attaining freedom. The people of Israel is enslaved, they are forced to work hard for the Egyptians. Their slavery is in the first place an external slavery: they are forced to work for the good of their Egyptians masters rather than their own good, to realize their master's end, not their own end. Their liberation is therefore also in the first place an external, political liberation. They are to be liberated from the power of Egypt in order to attain to *their own* true good and end as the chosen people of God.

"Thus says the LORD, the God of Israel, 'Let my people go, that they may hold a feast to me in the wilderness'" (Ex. 5:1). God's message to Pharaoh demands an external, political freedom for his people in order that they might attain to their true good, which consists in worshiping God (holding a sacrificial feast in God's honor). But it becomes clear in the desert that the people need moral freedom as well as political freedom to be able to attain to their good. They are enslaved to the false gods of Egypt and to their own disordered passions—they fall back into idolatry, and long for the fleshpots of Egypt. They are unable to live as God's chosen people in peace and justice, worshiping Him alone.

The Ten Commandments can be seen as an aid that God gives to the people to teach them moral freedom. God introduces the commandments by reminding the people of their liberation from Egypt: "I am the LORD your God, who brought you out of the land of Egypt, out of the house of slavery" (Ex. 20:2). But the commandments are meant to bring them to a truer liberation: liberation from sin.

The giving of the commandments implies that the people have natural freedom, that is, "free will." They must be able to understand the good, and chose the means that lead to it. In Deuteronomy God emphasizes their need to make a *choice*:

> See, I have set before you this day life and good, death and evil. If you obey the commandments of the LORD your God which I

command you this day, by loving the LORD your God, by walking in his ways, and by keeping his commandments and his statutes and his ordinances, then you shall live and multiply, and the LORD your God will bless you in the land which you are entering to take possession of it. But if your heart turns away, and you will not hear, but are drawn away to worship other gods and serve them, I declare to you this day, that you shall perish; you shall not live long in the land which you are going over the Jordan to enter and possess. I call heaven and earth to witness against you this day, that I have set before you life and death, blessing and curse; therefore choose life, that you and your descendants may live, loving the LORD your God, obeying his voice, and cleaving to him; for that means life to you and length of days, that you may dwell in the land which the LORD swore to your fathers, to Abraham, to Isaac, and to Jacob, to give them. (Deut. 30:15–20)

The law shows the way to life, to the true good, and the people are able to understand this and to choose to obey the law.

In the New Testament, St. Paul tells us that the law was not enough. Human nature is wounded by original sin. And it is too difficult for persons with this wounded nature to follow the law, even though they know that it leads to life. But the grace of Christ heals human nature, and gives it the power to obey the law, and to attain to an even greater good than the life promised in the Old Testament. St. Paul teaches that Christ's grace frees us from the law, insofar as it enables us to do the good spontaneously without need for the law. I quote a famous passage from the Epistle to the Galatians at length:

> For you were called to freedom, brethren; only do not use your freedom as an opportunity for the flesh, but through love be servants of one another. For the whole law is fulfilled in one word, "You shall love your neighbor as yourself." […] But I say, walk by the Spirit, and do not gratify the desires of the flesh. For the desires of the flesh are against the Spirit, and the desires of the Spirit are against the flesh; for these are opposed to each other, to prevent you from doing what you would. But if you are led by the Spirit you are not under the law. Now the works of the flesh are plain: fornication, impurity, licentiousness, idolatry, sorcery, enmity, strife, jealousy, anger, selfishness, dissension, party spirit,

envy, drunkenness, carousing, and the like. I warn you, as I warned you before, that those who do such things shall not inherit the kingdom of God. But the fruit of the Spirit is love, joy, peace, patience, kindness, goodness, faithfulness, gentleness, self-control; against such there is no law. (Gal. 5:13–23)

The desires of the flesh prevent us from doing what we would, that is, what we truly desire, what leads to our true good. But the power of the Spirit enables us to be free from the law, not because it gives us permission to break the law, but because it enables us to fulfill the essence of the law, which consists in loving the good, easily and without coercion.

In the Gospel of John, Jesus teaches that He has come to liberate the people from slavery to sin:

Jesus then said to the Jews who had believed in him, "If you continue in my word, you are truly my disciples, and you will *know the truth*, and the truth will make you free." They answered him, "We are descendants of Abraham, and have never been in bondage to anyone. How is it that you say, 'You will be made free'?" Jesus answered them, "Truly, truly, I say to you, every one who commits sin is a slave to sin." (Jn. 8:31–34)

The Jewish leaders think that they are already free, but Jesus teaches them that true moral freedom will only come if they remain with Him, allowing themselves to be formed by Him, so that they know God as their true good and attain to unity with Him.

The vision of freedom given in the Bible was further unfolded throughout the Christian tradition. St. Augustine of Hippo (354–430) is the first great theorist of "free will," as a faculty of choosing.[2] This faculty chooses which of our inclinations to follow. But it is nat-

---

2. See Johannes Brachtendorf, Introduction to Augustinus's *De libero arbitrio–Der freie Wille*, vol. 9 of *Augustinus Opera–Werke* (Paderborn: Schöningh, 2006), 45; Eva Brann, *Un-Willing: An Inquiry into the Rise of the Will's Power and an Attempt to Undo It* (Philadelphia: Paul Dry, 2014), 22–37. Brachtendorf and Brann go slightly too far in saying that Augustine *invented* the will—the denial of the term "will" to ancient concepts such as the Aristotelian *boulesis* seems to me to be based on a too narrow, modern concept of will. As Brann herself admits, Thomas Aquinas's account of *voluntas* (will) corresponds to Aristotle's account of *boulesis*. If one can call the one "will," why not the other?

urally inclined to happiness; it chooses to follow inclinations, only because they seem to lead to happiness. All men want to be happy. *The will is not "free" to desire unhappiness.* Happiness is found in *wisdom,* which is the attainment of God as the highest good, and no one can be prevented from attaining God against his will. Therefore, no one can be made unhappy against his will. But everyone *wills* happiness. So why is it that so many persons are not happy? How is that possible? How can one both will to be happy and choose not to be happy? "How does anyone suffer an unhappy life by his will, since absolutely no one wills to live unhappily?"[3] Augustine's answer is that the will is able to err by choosing things that are incompatible with happiness, even while continuing to will happiness:

> All the people you mentioned, who follow different things, pursue good and avoid evil. Yet because different things seem good to one person and to another, they follow different things. Thus anyone pursuing what should not have been pursued—even though he pursues it only because it appears good to him—nevertheless is in error. [...] To the extent that all people pursue the happy life, then, they are not in error. But people are in error to the extent that they stray from the road of life that leads to happiness, even if they profess and protest that they only want to attain happiness; "error" means following something that does not lead where we want to reach.[4]

Here Augustine is arguing that those who err are deceived by a false appearance of good. But how does such deception arise? Augustine argues that there are three kinds of false appearance of good:

> The will sins when it is turned away from the unchangeable and common good, towards its private good, or towards something external, or towards something lower. The will is turned to its private good when it wants to be in its own power; it is turned to something external when it is eager to know the personal affairs of

---

3. *De libero arbitrio,* 1.14.30.100; *On the Free Choice of the Will, On Grace and Free Choice, and Other Writings,* trans. Peter King (Cambridge: Cambridge University Press, 2010), 25.

4. *De libero arbitrio,* 2.9.26.100–101; King, 50.

other people, or anything that is not its business; it is turned to something lower when it takes delight in bodily pleasures.[5]

The "great and fundamental good" of human beings is a common good, in the sense that "he who is unwilling to share this possession cannot have it,"[6] but for this very reason turning away towards one's own private good has an *appearance* of the self-sufficiency proper to God. In the *Confessions*, in wondering about why he had stolen pears as an adolescent, Augustine describes this false appearance in terms of apparent freedom:

> Of what excellence of my Lord was I making perverse and vicious imitation? Perhaps it was the thrill of acting against Your law—at least in appearance, since I had no power to do so in fact, the delight a prisoner might have in making some small gesture of liberty—getting a deceptive sense of omnipotence from doing something forbidden without immediate punishment.[7]

In struggling with the question of what led him to steal the pears, Augustine also explains turning toward the external and toward the lower in terms of deceptive appearances of likeness to God, and yet a mystery remains. For, Augustine teaches that it is natural for the will to be turned toward God, where true happiness is to be found.[8] The turning away is a defect, a weakness, a sort of nothingness, a failure to be what we are: "We admit that this movement is sin, since it is a defective movement, and every defect is from nothing."[9]

St. Thomas Aquinas further developed Augustine's account with the help of Aristotle. According to St. Thomas, will is a faculty that is dependent on the faculty of reason. It is *rational desire*. Just as there is a desire in the sensitive part of the soul when we sense something pleasurable to senses (e.g., when we smell good food), so

---

5. *De libero arbitrio*, 2.19.53.199; King, 70.
6. *De civitate Dei*, XV, 5; *The City of God*, trans. Marcus Dods (New York: The Modern Library, 1993), 483.
7. *Confessiones*, II,vi; *The Confessions*, trans. Frank Sheed, 2nd ed. (Indianapolis: Hackett, 2006), 32.
8. See William R. O'Connor, *The Natural Desire for God* (Milwaukee: Marquette University Press, 1948), 18–25.
9. *De libero arbitrio*, 2.19.53.200–2.20.54.204; King, 70–71.

there is desire in the rational part of the soul when we understand something good. And the faculty for this desire is the will. As soon as reason understands something as good, the will moves toward it. To understand something as good is to understand it as contributing to my perfection and completion—that is, as leading to the final end, which is happiness. Now since there are many individual good things that can lead to happiness, the will is free to choose among them.[10] The very highest good, the attainment of which is happiness, is God. In this life, however, the mind does not necessarily see the connection of God and happiness, and thus, while it necessarily desires happiness, it does not yet necessarily desire God. In Heaven, where we shall directly attain to God, it will not be possible for the will to turn away from Him.[11] In earthly life, however, the knowledge of God is indirect, and therefore weak.

Sharpening Augustine's account with Aristotelian notions, St. Thomas gives two ways in which we can be deceived by a false appearance of good. The first comes from the fact that in this life all our knowledge begins with sense-knowledge. Only with effort does the mind rise above sensible particulars to universal truths. Similarly the goods that we first know are sensible goods, and so the desires of man are first pulled down towards those goods, and only with effort does the will rise to desire more universal goods.[12] The second way in which we can be deceived comes from the fact that the God in Whom our happiness lies is the common good of all creation, but the good that is first known to us is the proper good of our nature. Thus to seek God as our good requires that we subordinate ourselves to Him. This requires a certain self-transcendence, which can fail.[13]

---

10. *ST* I, q. 83, a. 1.
11. "Until through the certitude of the Divine Vision the necessity of such connection be shown, the will does not adhere to God of necessity, nor to those things which are of God. But the will of the man who sees God in His essence of necessity adheres to God, just as now we desire of necessity to be happy" (*ST* I, q. 83, a. 1).
12. See De Koninck, *Primacy of the Common Good,* 10–71, at 45–46.
13. "Indeed, although natural inclination of the will is present in every volitional agent to will and to love its own perfection so that it cannot will the contrary of this, yet it is not so naturally implanted in the agent to so order its perfection to

Contrasting Concepts of Freedom

St. Thomas's account of freedom was officially endorsed by the popes of the nineteenth century in their struggle with modern liberalism. In his great encyclical *Libertas* (1888), Pope Leo XIII summarized St. Thomas's teaching on natural, moral, and political freedom. He explains that natural freedom is called *natural* because it is not acquired but is given to man by God as part of man's created nature.[14] Because man has universal, rational knowledge he knows not only particular, sensible goods, but also the good in general. He therefore understands that no particular good is necessary to man, and he can then choose those particular goods that he thinks are suitable means to his highest good and final end.[15] In order for a person to choose some particular good he must understand it as being *good*, that is, as desirable, as contributing toward the complete goodness of the final goal of life.[16] But because both reason and will are fallible, man can be deceived by a false appearance of good.[17]

Moral freedom is the freedom from such error: the ability to know which means really lead to happiness and the ability to make use of them. To attain such freedom man has a need for law, which is "a fixed rule of teaching" in which "reason prescribes to the will what it should seek after or shun, in order to the eventual attainment of man's last end."[18] Law is thus not contrary to freedom, but a great help in attaining it.

The most important kind of law is *natural law*, which is "our reason, commanding us to do right and forbidding sin." This voice of reason has the force of an obligatory law, because it is given to us by God, the author of our nature.[19]

---

another end, that it cannot fail in regard to it, for the higher end is not proper to its nature, but to a higher nature. It is left, then, to the agent's choice, to order his own proper perfection to a higher end" (*SCG* Bk. III, ch. 109).

14. Pope Leo XIII, Encyclical *Libertas Praestantissimum* (1888), 1; English translation from the Vatican website.
15. *Libertas* 3.
16. Ibid., 5.
17. Ibid., 6.
18. Ibid., 7.
19. Ibid., 8.

Integralism and the Common Good

Political freedom is attained when the laws of a society correspond to the natural law. In such a case the laws do not enslave the people by ordering them to someone else's good, but rather help them to attain what is really good for them—the common good in which their happiness lies; they help them to be morally free.[20] Thus Leo XIII teaches that political freedom is not dependent on any particular *form* of government, such as democracy. Any government that makes laws that are compatible with the natural law, whether it is monarchical, aristocratic, democratic, or some mixture of those three, gives its subjects or citizens political freedom.[21] Participation of the greater number of the members of a society in political life might be a good *means* to helping frame laws that are in fact ordered to the common good (rather than the private good of some faction), but such participation is only a means; the essence of political freedom consists in the ordering of the laws to the true common good.[22]

3. False freedom

The account of freedom that I have just sketched out sees human freedom at every level as being tied to an objective order of the good. But another account of freedom came to be dominant in modern times, an account that sees freedom as independent from any objective good. Such has, of course, ancient antecedents. Even

---

20. *Libertas* 10; cf. chapters 1 and 23 in this collection.
21. See Pope Leo XIII, Encyclical *Diuturnum Illud* (1881), English translation from the Vatican website.
22. "Unless it be otherwise determined, by reason of some exceptional condition of things, it is expedient to take part in the administration of public affairs. And the Church approves of every one devoting his services to the common good, and doing all that he can for the defense, preservation, and prosperity of his country. Neither does the Church condemn those who, if it can be done without violation of justice, wish to make their country independent of any foreign or despotic power. Nor does she blame those who wish to assign to the State the power of self-government, and to its citizens the greatest possible measure of prosperity. The Church has always most faithfully fostered civil liberty, and this was seen especially in Italy, in the municipal prosperity, and wealth, and glory which were obtained at a time when the salutary power of the Church had spread, without opposition, to all parts of the State" (*Libertas* 45–46).

in the book of Genesis the serpent tempts Eve to eat the fruit that God has forbidden by saying, "God knows that when you eat of it your eyes will be opened, and you will be like God, knowing good and evil" (Gen. 3:5). This can be understood to mean that you will be independent of the objective order of good established by God, and will yourself *decide* what is good and what is evil.[23] This is tempting because it flatters human pride, giving human beings an apparently more exalted status. St. Thomas Aquinas teaches that such pride is always the reason for rebellion against God.[24] The Roman poet Lucretius gave an account of freedom as "pleasure-driven randomness" that is similarly disengaged from any objective order of good.[25]

Yet it was only in modern times that such an account of freedom became dominant. Ironically, the modern view of freedom was developed out of the view that can be found in certain late-medieval theologians, who certainly did not want to rebel against God, but rather sought to emphasize the sovereignty of God's will. Peter of John Olivi (c.1248–1298),[26] John Duns Scotus (c.1266–1308),[27] and

---

23. That was famously the interpretation given by Heinrich Heine, who saw the parallels with modern philosophy in the shape of G.W.F. Hegel: "there are indeed many [...] beautiful and noteworthy narratives in the Bible [...] as, for example, just at the beginning, there is the story of the forbidden tree in Paradise and of the serpent, that little adjunct professor who lectured on Hegelian philosophy six thousand years before Hegel's birth. This blue-stocking without feet demonstrated very ingeniously how the absolute consists in the identity of being and knowing, how man becomes God through cognition, or, what is the same thing, how the God in man thereby attains self-consciousness. This formula is not so clear as the original words: When ye eat of the tree of knowledge ye shall be as God!" (Heinrich Heine, *Religion and Philosophy in Germany*, trans. John Snodgrass [London: Trübner and Co., 1882], 13, translation slightly modified).

24. "Aversion from God has the nature of an end, inasmuch as it is sought for under the appearance of freedom, according to Jer. 2:20: 'Of old you have broken my yoke, you have burst my bonds, and you have said, I will not serve'" (*ST* III, q. 8, a. 7).

25. Brann, *Un-Willing*, 14.

26. See Dominic Whitehouse, O.F.M., "Asserting the Absolute Freedom of the Will: Petrus Iohannis Olivi's Intertextual Dialectical Investigation of the Nature of *liberum arbitrium* in his *Quaestiones in secundum librum Sententiarum*," Doctoral Dissertation, University of Vienna, 2019.

27. See Brann, *Un-willing*, 60–64.

especially William of Ockham (c. 1287–1347)[28] developed a theory of free will that saw it as completely arbitrary determination, not constrained by natural desire for the good. They applied this account to God in the first place, but then also to man. According to Ockham, the choice of the will does not follow knowledge of the good, but rather precedes all other acts including knowledge: "For I can freely chose to know or not to know, to will or not to will."[29]

Partial anticipations notwithstanding, it was the French philosopher René Descartes (1596–1650) who must be seen as the true father of the modern idea of freedom. Descartes's philosophy of pure thought emptied the natural world of all inherent goodness and teleology.[30] The world was seen merely as material for human domination, the imposition of human will. Hence will was seen not as appetite for an objective good, but as pure self-determination. Descartes is very explicit that freedom of the will makes the human person independent of God: "freewill […] makes us in a certain manner equal to God and exempts us from being his subjects."[31]

Descartes's idea of freewill was highly influential on all of modern philosophy. Modern ideas of political freedom were especially indebted to him. If the freedom of the will means the will is not determined by the good, but only by itself, then political freedom can no longer consist in having laws ordered to the true good. Instead, modern so-called "liberal" political theory understands political freedom as self-legislation. Immanuel Kant (1724–1804), to

---

28. See Servais Pinckaers, O.P., *The Sources of Christian Ethics*, trans. Mary Thomas Noble, O.P. (Washington, DC: The Catholic University of America Press, 1995), chs. 10 and 14; also Peter Kwasniewski, "William of Ockham and the Metaphysical Roots of Natural Law," *The Aquinas Review* 11 (2004): 1–84.

29. Quoted in Pinckaers, *The Sources of Christian Ethics*, 331.

30. See the chapter on Descartes in my dissertation: www.academia.edu/13118432/Symbolic_Calculation_and_the_Scientific_Revolution.

31. René Descartes, Letter to Christina Queen of Sweden, November 10, 1647, in *The Philosophical Writings of Descartes*, trans. John Cottingham et al., 3 vols. (Cambridge: Cambridge University Press, 1985–1991), 3:326. Cf. Charles Taylor, *Sources of the Self: The Making of the Modern Identity* (Cambridge, MA: Harvard University Press, 1989), 147.

Contrasting Concepts of Freedom

take only one particularly clear example,[32] argued that a ruler who tries to order his subjects to their own true good would be acting against their freedom:

> A Government founded upon the principle of Benevolence towards the people—after the analogy of a *father* to his children, and therefore called a *paternal Government*—would be one in which the Subjects would be regarded as children or minors unable to distinguish what is beneficial or injurious to them. These subjects would be thus compelled to act in a merely passive way; and they would be trained to expect solely from the Judgment of the Sovereign and just as he might will it, merely out of his goodness, all that *ought* to make them happy. Such a Government would be the greatest conceivable *Despotism;* for it would present a Constitution that would abolish all Liberty in the Subjects and leave them no Rights.[33]

In order to preserve freedom, Kant argues, the government must be limited to balancing the freedom of different individuals:

> No one has a right to compel me to be happy in the peculiar way in which he may think of the well-being of other men; but everyone is entitled to seek his own happiness in the way that seems to him best, if it does not infringe the liberty [i.e., freedom] of others in striving after a similar end for themselves when their Liberty is capable of consisting with the Right of Liberty in all others according to possible universal laws.[34]

This is one side of modern political theory, and it has had tremendous consequences. One thing that it demands is the complete independence of the state from religion, since religion always proposes a definite idea of human happiness, and therefore is seen as a threat to freedom. In the West, this view of political freedom has

---

32. Similar accounts had already been given by "liberal" thinkers as diverse as John Locke (1632–1704) and Jean-Jacques Rousseau (1712–1778).

33. Immanuel Kant, "The Principles of Political Right Considered in Connection with the Relation of Theory to Practice in the Right of the State," in *Kant's Principles of Politics, Including his Essay on Perpetual Peace*, ed. and trans. William Hastie (Edinburgh: T. & T. Clark, 1891), 36.

34. Kant, "The Principles of Political Right," 36.

Integralism and the Common Good

been embedded in the laws. A particularly clear expression of it was given by the United States Supreme Court:

> At the heart of liberty is the right to define one's own concept of existence, of meaning, of the universe, and of the mystery of human life. Beliefs about these matters could not define the attributes of personhood were they formed under compulsion of the State.[35]

But there is also another side to the modern idea of political freedom, namely the demand that each citizen *participate* in the framing of the laws. Kant expresses the reason for this demand as follows:

> All right, in fact, depends on the laws. A public law, however, which determines for all what is to be legally allowed or not allowed in their regard, is the act of a public Will, from which all right proceeds and which therefore itself can do no wrong to anyone. For this, however, there is no other Will competent than that of the *whole* people, as it is only when all determine about all that each one in consequence determines about himself. For it is only to himself that one can do no wrong.[36]

This demand is fulfilled by representative democracies. Hence, in the modern view, the only legitimate form of government is democracy.[37]

It has often been noted that there is a certain tension between the two sides of the modern idea of political freedom, with some modern political movements giving more emphasis to the first, and others to the second. But almost all modern political movements accept both sides in some form or other.[38]

Another important element in the modern idea of freedom, what we might call the modern ideal of *moral freedom*, arose out of the Romantic reaction against the rationalism of philosophers such as

---

35. *Planned Parenthood v. Casey*, United States Supreme Court, 1992, http://caselaw.findlaw.com/us-supreme-court/505/833.html.
36. Kant, "The Principles of Political Right," 42–43.
37. See chapter 23.
38. Cf. Isaiah Berlin, "Two Concepts of Liberty," in *Four Essays on Liberty* (Oxford: Oxford University Press, 1969), 118–72.

Contrasting Concepts of Freedom

Descartes and Kant. The eighteenth- and nineteenth-century Romantics rejected the Cartesian idea of cool, disengaged will and reason, confronted with a neutral meaningless world of extension. But Romanticism did not return to a pre-Cartesian, teleological worldview. It wanted to preserve the sovereignty of the human subject, but in a new way. Therefore it imagined an inchoate "current of life" underlying all things that expresses itself through living things, striving for ever higher expression. Man's spirit is stirred by the sublime in nature, and this allows him to "create" new expressions of spirit that articulate and bring into being what was only potential before.[39] This Romantic vision underwent many developments and changes over time, but what remained was the idea that for human beings to be really free they had to express themselves in their own unique way. Human desire, on this view, is not *elicited* by good things, but is rather a potential force that expresses itself, and brings "value" (as the good now comes to be called) into existence. Freedom means being "true to oneself" by finding an "authentic" way of expressing one's desires, and thus creating one's own "values."[40]

The Romantic, expressivist idea of freedom was an important element in bringing about the so-called "sexual revolution" of the 1960s, which continues to our own day. Sexual desire being particularly strong and ecstatic, contemporary culture sees sexual expression as a key to "authenticity" and freedom. Hence the proliferation of various forms of sexual perversion, all seen as "authentic self-expressions," giving value and meaning to human life. And hence the violent opposition to the natural law, which forbids such perversions, when it is proclaimed by traditional Christians and Muslims.

4. Conclusion: the slave of sin

The modern idea of freedom, and the "liberal" culture built on it, have many attractions. Their individualistic, self-determining approach to the good does do away with some of the limits and self-

---

39. See Taylor, *Sources of the Self*, ch. 21.
40. Cf. Charles Taylor, *The Ethics of Authenticity* (Cambridge, MA: Harvard University Press, 1991).

sacrifices demanded by an approach based on a common pursuit of objective ends. It gives room for movement and an independence from others. Moreover, such an individualistic approach can avoid some of the conflicts that arise from different views of what the objective good for man is. In such a liberal order individuals are free to accept religious teaching on God as the final end of human life, the good in whom alone we can find happiness.

But the advantages of the modern view of freedom come at a great price. The attempt to determine one's own "values" for oneself often means that one becomes dominated by one's own passions, the desires and loathings that arise from the sense-knowledge in which all our knowledge begins. This is not freedom, but slavery. The American novelist David Foster Wallace spoke of the "default settings" of human beings as being the "worship" of things like money, sexual allure, and power, but that the "worship" of such things will "eat you alive."[41] To become free of such things requires great effort, and usually a *communal* effort.

The claim that the modern culture of liberal freedom leaves room for those who hold to an older notion of freedom as related to objective good to follow their beliefs has to be qualified. The very fact that the whole culture is based on the competing, modern, "liberal" view of freedom exerts tremendous pressure to conform on those who would hold an older view . As David Schindler put it:

> Liberalism invites us to adopt only its freedom and its institutions while (putatively) permitting us to supply our own theories which will give meaning to freedom and free institutions; but liberalism does so—paradoxically—all the while hiding the very theory (of liberalism) which alone justifies this (purported) extrinsic relation between freedom, institution, and theory. In fact, this very extrinsic relation, which is taken to guarantee a supposedly "empty freedom," already embodies a definite, though hidden, conception of human nature and destiny.[42]

---

41. David Foster Wallace, "Kenyon Commencement Speech," in Dave Eggers, ed., *The Best American Nonrequired Reading* 2006 (Boston: Houghton Mifflin, 2006), 355–64, at 362.

42. David L. Schindler, *Heart of the World, Center of the Church: Communio Ecclesiology, Liberalism, and Liberation* (Grand Rapids: Eerdmans, 1996), 33–34.

Contrasting Concepts of Freedom

Thus, the crisis of religious faith that we are witnessing in the West today is a logical outcome of the prevalence of this liberal idea of freedom, which inevitably leads to viewing religion as a limit on freedom. The supposedly neutral view of the good, in which each person decides his values for himself, really turns persons away from their true good, in which alone true happiness can be found. In its place it sets an ethics of arbitrary self-expression that is becoming more and more perverse and irrational by the day. This is not freedom, but slavery: "every one who commits sin is a slave to sin" (Jn. 8:34). I am therefore convinced that we should oppose the modern view of freedom by every possible means. The most important means of opposition is the revival of the traditional and true account of freedom.

4

Freedom as Choosing the Good, Against the Nihilists

Peter A. Kwasniewski

All the same, one might enquire how what happens under the impulse of desire can be self-determined [i.e., voluntary] when desire leads one to what is outside oneself and has deficiency in it; for that which desires is *led,* even if it is led to the good. And a difficulty must be raised about intellect itself, whether, when its activity is what it is by nature and as it is by nature, it could be said to have freedom and anything in its power, when it does *not* have it in its power not to act [for the sake of the good].... But then how can there be freedom when even these higher beings [intellects] are slaves to their own nature? Now, to speak the truth, where there is no *compulsion* to follow another, how can one speak of slavery? How could something borne towards the good be under compulsion, since its desire for the good will be voluntary if it *knows* that it is good and goes to it *as* good?

Plotinus, *Ennead* VI.8

The connection between choosing the good and attaining greater freedom is not easy to set forth deductively. Let us begin with the end. Willing and final causality are utterly wed to each other. Where there is a natural power, there is a natural purpose. There is no willing that is not for some end; there is no voluntary end which is lacking a moral content. This moral content, the object of the act of willing itself, is what gives the species or type to the action. The moral content, the intentional target of the deed, is what enables us to classify an act of killing as murder or as self-defense—the former punishable, the latter praiseworthy.

The will is a power that inclines towards the good apprehended

Freedom as Choosing the Good, Against the Nihilists

by reason. That the will can choose false goods or lesser goods over genuine or higher goods is due to the fact that reason is capable of viewing things from many different angles, and can therefore see some limited good in what is nonetheless evil for the whole man. If a good is cognizable, reason can apprehend it and the will can choose it. Hence, we may glimpse the answer to the question, Does choosing the good necessarily lead to more freedom? Freedom is the perfection of the natural faculty of will; the ultimate perfection of a faculty results from its proper use, its being put to the right use again and again. If a state of freedom (self-command) is the result of choosing what is objectively *best*, namely the genuine good, then freedom should be *defined* as a perfection of the will when it has chosen consistently well. In light of this, we see the extent to which the will's perfection depends upon the condition of man's reason, how reason views various desirable things. If reason is in good estate, the will is the first beneficiary.

Is the truth of things the object of the intellect? Is the goodness of things the object of the will? If one answers "no" to either question, one is compelled to maintain either that there is no natural end to the intellect and the will, i.e., the power is wholly indeterminate and has no orientation whatsoever, or that the end is arbitrarily chosen and set up, in the manner of an idol. Either position destroys objectivity and morality, leaving us with no way of arguing against *any* intellectual or moral position, however absurd, cruel, or disgusting. Any human being who takes seriously his own life and the lives of other people implicitly accepts an objective order (however difficult it may be to articulate it) by which the wiser and better person can judge the actions of others who offend against the principles of this order. Try to think or live as though there were not a built-in predetermined purpose to your faculties; it will not work. The orientation to goodness is not a gloss on the dark purposelessness of nature, nor is it a condition that compromises freedom. In order to be truly free, does one have to be free to *create* oneself? Modern existentialists look upon *all* determination or form as irrational impositions over which the individual has no control; the individual, they say, ought to be absolutely free to determine what and who he will be. This is none other than a doctrine of uninhibited metaphysical license that has as its counterparts political anarchy, ethical relativism, and intellectual nihilism.

Is it problematic, on the other hand, to say that one is free to determine the *way* in which one will *realize* his own good—that one can choose what is to count as happiness for himself in this life, even though happiness is the end all men desire by nature? Such an individual does not lose his freedom, if, with an eye towards happiness, he can choose the manner of life he wants to lead. What sort of freedom is the existentialist looking for—freedom to create new worlds, to pursue *un*happiness as an end, to annihilate himself, to experiment with the space-time continuum? Judging from the remarks of some philosophers, one would think the very notion of an end is arbitrary and stifling. Yet *nothing* can exist without ordering to an end; it is against the nature of being itself. One cannot think "being" without co-thinking "end"—another way of saying, with Aristotle, that the formal cause cannot be divorced from the final cause. In short, only nothing has no purpose.

Moderns assert that to have freedom is to be able to determine oneself absolutely. To be free, they hold, one must be able to give oneself an end. But what else could this mean, except to give oneself a *nature*—which amounts to *creating oneself*? The very thing which distinguishes creation from making is that the maker (or poet) only makes some part or aspect of the thing made, whereas the creator brings the whole thing, including its act of being, into being. Now to bring a thing into being means to bring a "this something" into being; there is no *creatio* without some boundaries as to the appetites and abilities characterizing the *creatum*. To create is to give being to something—and this something, even to *be* a something, must have a certain form and thus a certain end, since form and end are unintelligible apart from each other.

It seems to me, therefore, that to speak of a rational creature, a creature having as its highest reality a power by which to apprehend the true and the good, that nonetheless does not have as its necessary end the resting in that very truth and goodness, is to speak without meaning. It is to say that a creature is made capable of partaking in the perfections of its origin, yet is left wholly on its own as to the end towards which it will be inclined to go, or without determination as to whether or not it will even *have* an end. I do not see how any sense can be made out of that.

All men desire happiness, or, if the word reminds you too much of Hollywood, substitute another term: completion, fulfillment, enduring bliss. There is nobody who does not will this end, because to be rational is to be the sort of creature that (a) is capable of knowing or being aware of itself; (b) in knowing itself recognizes that there is such a thing as the full possession of and rejoicing in what is good, viz., happiness; (c) upon glimpsing the possibility of happiness, desires it ardently as a way of reaching the zenith of what it, the creature, is; and (d) strives always to reach this maximum actuality. The question of what exactly is *taken* as the end should not be mixed up in this discussion. We are only concerned with the universal question: what does it mean to live a human life? It means to work for one's completion. We should not ask why man desires this end; for how could he not? A creature endowed with the power to partake of truth and goodness is inclined towards that which he takes to be true and good. This is not compulsion or slavery, this is simply a precondition of all action and passion. If a man did not *naturally* want something, he could never move himself to want anything *voluntarily*. We never deliberate about means until some end is fixed; we would never deliberate at all were there no distant target which was seen as the ultimate justification of our actions. If *we* designated our final end, if we created our own natures, action could not be other than totally arbitrary, neither right nor wrong, and neither describable in itself nor communicable to others. We could not act in concert with other human beings; we could not even act as a single subject of a life of action. Each man would be his own species, or non-species; each act would be an isolated fact with no prelude, no postlude, no context. And then we would have to ask: could love or hatred, the most basic of our responses to the world and its inhabitants, survive in this metaphysical wilderness?

A large impediment to accepting the Thomistic account is the routine failure to distinguish between the end as given generically, and the end as "colored" by a particular person's life, choices, habits, opinions. Our *perceptions* of what makes for happiness can differ dramatically, as is obvious from living in a world where some people would identify fulfillment with (say) endless and unfatiguing electronic entertainment. Because reason can have different apprehensions of the *good*, the will can tend towards different goods in the right or the wrong order, putting lower goods above higher ones, or, albeit more rarely, higher goods above lower ones when it is not appropriate to do so. The will is not automatically harnessed to the natural and supernatural means of human perfection, nor is the intellect prepackaged with instructions as to what will ultimately fulfill it. This is why Aristotle says that education counts for just about everything, together with habituation to virtuous or vicious actions (and, as Christians, we can add the presence or absence of grace). If men can mentally locate their fulfillment in wealth or pleasure, the two most common follies of our fallen race, then they can go about living as though wealth or pleasure really *were* the final end for which they exist. There has been a conscious decision, a choice or free act to orient oneself to some "x" as constitutive of happiness, where "x" can be anything that is perceived to have some degree of goodness in it.

Perhaps, after all, the modern replies: to have freedom to choose what I will construe to be my happiness is no freedom at all, if I am still naturally made for a certain final end and will be miserable if I do not choose it.

Yet is this argument sound? Consider some examples. Is the murderer not free because he commits an action that will make him miserable? Is any man less free for doing something stupid? In one sense, of course, he is not as free as he might be if he were acting in a way that would *perfect* him rather than *damage* him, but he is free as long as the origin of action remains in him and is not the result of instinct, chance, or coercion. If this freedom were not real, would there be any basis for distinguishing between manslaughter and murder, as criminal investigators and courts of law do on a daily basis? It seems as though moderns need to go back to school with Socrates in the *Gorgias*. The entire point of having morals, of striving to be virtuous, is to live in such a way that one will *not* be miserable. To be tending towards happiness or misery is, at least on the natural level, within our power.

The modern may still object that if the rational creature has been

Freedom as Choosing the Good, Against the Nihilists

given a will, it should be free to choose what it is going to be for. That is perfectly true if by "choosing what it is going to be for," one means the choices all men make about what goods to pursue here and now, what to construe as happiness, for what (or whom) am I living my life. It is obvious that not only are we free to do this, we are *always* doing it. Our experience of freedom is undeniable and all-pervasive: we are in charge of ourselves whenever we say "I could do this or that or neither, but I choose to do this." All of a man's life is taken up with decisions about this step or that, this object or that. Reading the plays of Sartre, one might almost begin to think that such decisions are irrelevant and somehow too ignoble to be taken seriously as free acts! Comparatively speaking, speculation about the final and absolute good is a luxury for the few who are capable of bearing the strain of concentration. Most people carry on from day to day trying to be happy in some fashion, without rising to the level of secondary reflection where we pose the question "what's it all for."

On the other hand, if the statement "the rational creature should be free to choose what it is going to be for" is taken to mean that a rational creature should be free to endow itself with an end or have authority over its orientation to the good, then I say: impossible. Doing so would involve defining what is actually good, producing goodness as an artist produces an artifact. The creature would cease to be a creature; it would become God, and a strange God at that, since there would no longer be any such thing as "the good." All would be chaos, relativity, meaninglessness. But the Good Itself cannot be defined by the creature; not even *God* defines the Good. He *is* the Good, He cannot be otherwise, and there is no need for Him to be able to be *Not*-Good in order for Him to be *free*.

The existentialist is worried about preserving the creature's freedom. If he were thinking rationally, he might rather turn his mind to the problem of God's freedom. For on his view, God not only could not be free, He would be the most unfree being of all—He would be a total and complete slave. Yet what thinker at this point would not blush from embarrassment and retire to his room, eager to find a less ridiculous position?

5

Notes on Moral Virtue

Edmund Waldstein, O.Cist.

1. Virtue in general

1.1. Etymologies

Like so many words in English, "virtue" is derived from the Latin. This Latin derivation has the disadvantage of obscuring the original experience from which the concept signified is abstracted. Moreover, the cultural history of nineteenth-century Britain has given "virtue" a sort of missish ring, whereas it and similar words in other languages originally had martial connotations. Unfortunately, there is no good Anglo-Saxon equivalent still in use. The closest would be "dought" or, in the more common adjective form, "doughty," derived from Old English *dohtig*, which now has an almost comically archaic ring to it: "Yet many doughty warriors often tride / In greater perils to be stout and bold."[1] Doughty now means "brave," and that was probably its oldest meaning as well, but in the eleventh century it was used in an extended sense to mean "competent" and "good" as well. Thus Bosworth-Toller cites the following line from a charter of Earl Godwin from sometime around the year 1016:

Ðyssa þinga is gecnǽwe ǽlc dohtig man on Kǽnt and on Súþ-Sexan

("Of these things is cognizant every good [doughty] man in Kent and Sussex").[2] *Dohtig* is related to *dyhtig* (strong) and *dugan* (to be

---

1. Edmund Spenser, *The Faerie Queene,* Book IV, Canto 10, Stanza 18.
2. T. Northcote Toller, ed., *An Anglo-Saxon Dictionary: Based on the Manuscript Collections of the Late Joseph Bosworth*, vol. 1 (Oxford: The Clarendon Press, 1882),

fit, able, strong). It is thus etymologically equivalent to the Modern German word for virtue, *Tugend*, from *taugen* (power, ability, efficiency).

In any case, the Latin *virtus*, from which the Modern English "virtue" is derived, has a similar history to *dohtig*. *Virtus* is derived from *vir*, man, and originally meant manliness, bravery, or valor. It was thus the equivalent to the Greek ἀνδρεία (*andreia*, courage). It was, however, used as a translation of the Greek ἀρετή (*arete*), which is probably related to the name of *Ares*, the God of war. *Arete* too originally meant bravery, valor, etc. *Arete* is the word used for virtue in Greek philosophy and in the Septuagint and the New Testament. It is therefore worth examining more closely.

1.2. The general meaning of arete *from Homer to Aristotle*

In Homer *arete* means in the first place the qualities that make a good warrior, namely, those qualities that allow a warrior to be effective in battle. But it is also extended to mean the qualities that allow men, women, and children to do well the actions their respective station in life requires, whatever that station might be: "In the Homeric poems a virtue is a quality the manifestation of which enables someone to do exactly what their well-defined social role requires."[3] This is then extended beyond human beings to animals and even inanimate objects: "the *arete* of a horse consists in its swiftness of foot, the *arete* of soil in its fertility, the *arete* of a woman in her being a good housewife, the *arete* of a slave in his or her loyalty to a master."[4]

It is basically the Homeric idea of virtue that Meno gives in his first attempt at defining virtue in the *Meno*:

> First of all, if you take the virtue of a man, it is easily stated that a man's virtue is this—that he be competent to manage the affairs of his city, and to manage them so as to benefit his friends and harm

---

s.v. "dohtig;" cf. Benjamin Thorpe, ed., *Diplomatarium Anglicum Ævi Saxonici* (London: MacMillan & Co., 1865), 313.

3. MacIntyre, *After Virtue*, 183–84.
4. Margalit Finkelberg, ed., *The Homer Encyclopedia* (Oxford: Wiley-Blackwell, 2011), s.v. "aretê."

his enemies, and to take care to avoid suffering harm himself. Or take a woman's virtue: there is no difficulty in describing it as the duty of ordering the house well, looking after the property indoors, and obeying her husband. And the child has another virtue—one for the female, and one for the male; and there is another for elderly men—one, if you like, for freemen, and yet another for slaves. And there are very many other virtues besides, so that one cannot be at a loss to explain what virtue is; for it is according to each activity and age that every one of us, in whatever we do, has his virtue; and the same, I take it, Socrates, will hold also of vice.[5]

Meno merely lists the various kinds of virtue, without making the implicit account explicit. Aristotle, in the *Ethics*, will however follow this line of reasoning to come to a general definition:

We must explain, therefore, that virtue perfects everything of which it is the virtue, rendering both the possessor good and his work (ἔργον αὐτοῦ) good. Thus the virtue or power of the eye makes good both the eye and its operation, for it is by the power of the eye that we see well. Likewise the virtue or excellence of a horse makes the horse good and also makes him good for running, riding, and awaiting the enemy. If this be true in all other things, then human virtue will be a habit making man good and rendering his work good.[6]

The key term here is "his work," *ergon autou*. This is what is often translated as a thing's "own act" or "proper act." As Duane Berquist puts it, "A thing's own act is the act which that thing alone can do or, at least, do better than other things."[7] From this he derives Aristotle's entirely general definition of virtue: "Virtue is the disposition of a thing which makes it good and its own act good."[8]

---

5. *Meno*, 71e–72a.
6. *Nicomachean Ethics* VI.2, 1106a, trans. C.I. Litzinger, O.P.
7. Duane Berquist, "Note on End or Purpose of Man," 1, https://archive.org/details/10NoteOnTheEndOfMan.
8. Berquist, "End or Purpose," 3.

Notes on Moral Virtue

2. Human virtue

If virtue is what enables a thing to do its own act or work well, then human virtue is what enables a human being to do the proper act of a human being well. But what is the proper act of a human being? Aristotle raises this question in determining the end of human life in *Ethics* I:

> For just as for the flute-player and the sculptor and every artist and generally everyone for whom there is something to do (πρᾶξις) and some act (ἔργον), the good and well-being seems to be in doing this, so also it would seem for man if there is something he does (ἔργον). Are there then some doings and acts of the carpenter and the shoemaker, but of man there is none, and he is by nature without anything to do? Or just as there seems to be something done by the eye and the hand and the foot and generally by each of the parts, should one also lay down something that man does besides all these? What then will this be? To live seems to be common even to the plants, but what is man's own is sought. The nourishing and growing life therefore should be set aside. Following this, there would be something sensing. But this also seems to be common to the horse and the ox and every animal. There remains the doing of what has reason. But of this, the one as obeying or persuaded by reason and the other as having reason and thinking.[9]

What is proper to human beings, what distinguishes them from other bodily, living things, is reason. The absolutely final end of human beings is an act of reason that completely transcends human nature: Beatific Vision. In the natural order, the highest act is the contemplation of God through His effects in philosophical wisdom. Wisdom is the highest intellectual virtue—the others are understanding (knowing the first principles of reasoning), science (knowing the conclusions of reasoning), and (in a qualified way) art and prudence.

But Aristotle points out that there are parts of the human soul beside reason itself that have acts proper to human nature: namely

---

9. *Ethics* I.7, 1097b–1098a, trans. Duane Berquist.

the parts that obey or are persuaded by reason. These are the parts of the soul that have to do with desire in all its forms. "For the vegetative element in no way shares in reason, but the *appetitive and in general the desiring element* in a sense shares in it, in so far as it listens to and obeys it" (1102b). Taken together, we might call these desiring parts "the heart." The virtues of these parts of the soul are called "moral virtues," because, as Aristotle points out, when we speak of someone's morals (ἤθους), we mention temperance and good-temper rather than wisdom (1103a). There seems to be a puzzle here. The highest activity of a human being is found in the acts of the intellect, and yet when we say that persons are "good," without qualification, we mean that they have the virtues of the heart, rather than those of the intellect.

St. Thomas explains the reason for this. Virtue is what makes both a thing and its proper act good without qualification. Now, what moves a person toward an end as good is the heart (any one of the desiring faculties). Thus, in order to do one's own act well, and thus be oneself good, one's heart must be rightly directed toward the good. If I do not desire the good, I will not do the actions which lead to it or in which it consists, and therefore I will not myself be good. Thus St. Thomas writes:

> When we speak simply of virtue, we are understood to be speaking of human virtue. But as was explained above (q. 56, a. 3), a human virtue, in the most perfect sense of virtue, is a virtue that requires rectitude of appetite [i.e., the heart], since a virtue not only bestows a facility for acting well but is also a cause of the very use of a good work (*usum boni operis causat*). Still, in a less perfect sense of virtue, a virtue does not require rectitude of appetite, since it only bestows a facility for acting well but is not a cause of the use of a good work.[10]

Moral virtue causes the right *use* of the intellectual virtues. It will be desire for the good that moves me to use the intellectual virtues to actually contemplate some truth. And therefore, the virtues

---

10. St. Thomas Aquinas, *ST* I-II, q. 61, a. 1. In the translation I follow Alfred Freddoso, except that I have translated *usum* as "use" rather than "execution." This sounds clumsy in English, but is essential to the meaning.

which rectify the desires are necessary for the proper use of intellectual virtues. As Henri Grenier puts it:

> The intellectual virtues give man the power of performing good acts, but do not give him the right use of this power, i.e., do not make him use this power in a right manner. Hence they render good the operation of a particular faculty, but do not make man good in an absolute sense; e.g., as a result of intellectual virtue, a person can be a good philosopher, but yet not a man who is good in every respect, for he can knowingly, and without sinning against intellectual virtue, be the author of sophistries. The moral virtues not only give man the power of performing good act[s], but make him use this power rightly, for the moral virtues perfect the appetite, whose function consists in moving the other powers to act. Hence the moral virtues make man good in an absolute sense.[11]

The moral virtues not only immediately enable persons to do the acts of the faculties of the heart well, they are also necessary to use the other faculties—even the higher faculties of the intellect—well. A person who has the virtue of science can use that virtue to lead his students astray, and the habit of science does not prevent this. Indeed, it is *because* he has science that he will be good at inventing sophistries. But if such a person also has the virtue of justice, this will mean not only that he will do acts of the will well, but also that he will do the acts of reason perfected by science well—leading his students to the truth.

Human virtues in the strict sense are therefore the moral virtues, which perfect the heart, the desiring and appetitive parts of the soul. But, as we shall see, the greatest of the moral virtues is prudence, which in terms of its subject is an intellectual virtue.

3. The powers and passions of the soul

3.1. The powers of the soul

Human beings are rational animals. They are distinguished from

---

11. Henri Grenier, *Thomistic Philosophy*, vol. 4, *Moral Philosophy*, trans. J. P. E. O'Hanley (Charlottetown: St. Dunstan's University, 1950), §929.

the other animals by having the spiritual power of reason. They are distinguished from the angels by having senses, dependent on material organs. Human knowledge begins with sensation. The world is sensed through the five external senses, and the sense-impressions are received into the interior senses (the common sense, memory, imagination…). And then these sense experiences are illuminated by the intellect, and the intellect abstracts universal truths from them.

The intellect can be considered in two ways: as theoretical, and as practical. The theoretical (or "speculative," i.e., "looking") intellect simply looks at and contemplates the truth. The practical intellect looks at the truth of reality insofar as it contains attainable goods and orders this knowledge to action.

The knowledge of the good causes a desire for the good, or a striving after the good. This takes place already at the level of the sensible soul. The sensible good (the pleasant) is "known" by the external and internal senses, and this causes the sensible appetites to desire that good or the overcoming of what threatens the good. There are two desiring powers at the sensible level: the concupiscible appetite, and the irascible appetite. The first and more fundamental is the concupiscible appetite, or concupiscence. This is what is usually meant when we say the "desiring part of the soul." It answers to *epithymia* (ἐπιθυμία) in Plato's tripartite division of the soul. This power strives after the pleasurable and flees the painful. The second is the irascible appetite. This appetite depends on concupiscence, and it is concerned with overcoming difficulties and repelling threats to the goods desired by concupiscence. It answers to *thymos* (θυμός) in the Platonic division.

Desire for the good as *good*, and not merely as pleasant, belongs to the practical intellect, which can understand the good and the end. Intellectual knowledge of the good leads to a spiritual desire of the good in the "rational appetite" known as the will. The two levels, the sensible and the rational, mutually influence one another. Sensible appetite has an influence on our knowledge of the good, and therefore our will. But on the other hand, sensible appetite can also be directed by reason and will.

3.2. The passions

Passions are movements of the sensitive desiring faculties, resulting from the sense-knowledge of good or evil, accompanied by bodily changes. The fundamental passion is sensual love which arises in the concupiscible appetite. Love is a conformity of the concupiscence to some desirable object. From love arise desire (when the loved object is not yet possessed) and joy (when it is possessed). From love also arises the opposite sensible passion, hatred, which is the lack of conformity that the appetite has with some sensible evil. To love something implies hating its opposite (to love pleasure is to hate pain). From hatred arise flight (when the evil has not yet come to pass) and sorrow (when it has come to pass).

In the irascible appetite, the passions of hope and despair arise with respect to goods apprehended as difficult to attain, whether possible (hope) or impossible (despair). With respect to evils, the irascible appetite brings forth fear (aversion from an evil considered unconquerable), daring (turning toward an evil considered conquerable), and anger (the inclination to inflict evil for evil). The following diagram gives a rough sketch of the passions. (A deeper consideration would show that more distinctions are necessary.)

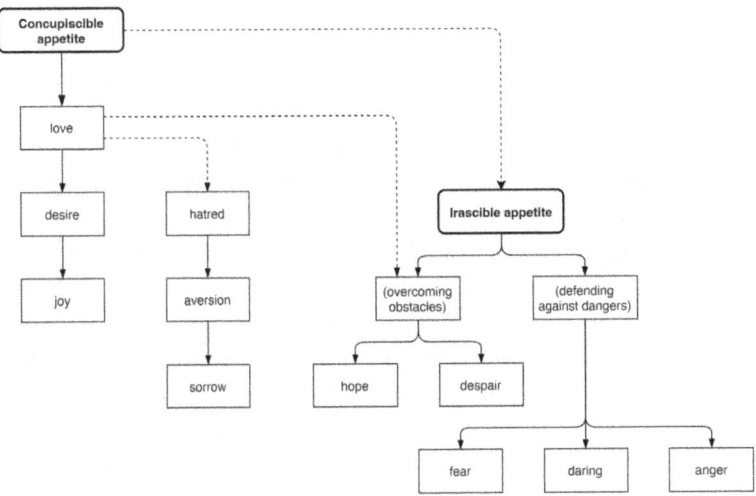

4. The cardinal virtues

Thus, there are four powers of the soul that are immediately concerned with the good to be attained through human action: practical intellect, will, concupiscence, and the irascible appetite. There are therefore four principal virtues, dispositions of the soul that allow human beings to do the actions arising from these four powers well:

> i. A virtue of the practical *intellect* that allows persons to know their good easily and direct their actions to the good: PRUDENCE, or practical wisdom.
>
> ii. A virtue of the *will* that enables persons to easily will not only the goods closest and most known to them, but also the good of other persons and the more universal and common goods to which they are ordered: JUSTICE.
>
> iii. A virtue of the *irascible appetite* that renders it, and the passions arising from it, subject to reason: COURAGE.
>
> iv. A virtue that perfects the *concupiscible appetite* and renders it, and the passions arising from it, subject to reason: TEMPERANCE.

These four virtues are called *cardinal virtues,* from the Latin *cardo,* meaning hinge, because all the other virtues hinge on them.

5. The mean

The goods and evils with which sensible appetites are concerned are destroyed by excess and defect. For example, it is good to eat food because this is necessary to conserve our substance, but it is bad to eat too much or too little food. It is good to face dangers in pursuing the good, and it is bad to face danger too little (cowardice) or too much (foolhardiness). Thus it is evident that the virtues of temperance and courage are concerned with a mean relative to the subject. The mean is not in this case mediocrity, but perfection, just as in Greek music, the tonic note was called the "mean note" because the scale moved both toward and away from it.

Justice is also concerned with a mean because it is concerned with giving to each his due. But this is an objective, rather than a subjective mean. It is the mean between giving someone more than he is objectively due (e.g., punishing a criminal more than he deserves) or less than he is objectively due (e.g., giving a store keeper less than the price of his wares).

In each case, the mean is determined by prudence: prudence rules the other moral virtues by laying down what the mean is for them. By analogy *ad unum*, therefore, we can say that prudence is also concerned with the mean.

6. Habit

The powers of the soul are not limited to one fixed activity but are capable of acting in various ways. It is therefore necessary that they be determined to good activity by stable dispositions or habits. Such dispositions are acquired by repeatedly acting in the right way, until it becomes easy. This ease of action allows the pleasure of good activity. Aristotle compares the acquisition of moral habits to the acquisition of skill in making things (art):

> Again, it is from the same causes and by the same means that every virtue is both produced and destroyed, and similarly every art; for it is from playing the lyre that both good and bad lyre-players are produced. And the corresponding statement is true of builders and of all the rest; men will be good or bad builders as a result of building well or badly. For if this were not so, there would have been no need of a teacher, but all men would have been born good or bad at their craft. This, then, is the case with the virtues also; by doing the acts that we do in our transactions with other men we become just or unjust, and by doing the acts that we do in the presence of danger, and being habituated to feel fear or confidence, we become brave or cowardly. The same is true of appetites and feelings of anger; some men become temperate and good-tempered, others self-indulgent and irascible, by behaving in one way or the other in the appropriate circumstances. Thus, in one word, states of character arise out of like activities. This is why the activities we exhibit must be of a certain kind; it is because the states of character correspond to the differences between these. It makes no small difference, then, whether we form habits of one kind or of another from our very youth; it makes a very great difference, or rather all the difference.[12]

12. *Nicomachean Ethics* II.1, 1103b.

In the case of the virtues of the sensitive part of the soul, habituation rectifies the appetites by training them to delight in the mean determined by reason. Since our knowledge begins with the senses, our desires begin with the senses as well, and the desires most obvious to us are the desires for sensual pleasure. It therefore requires training for the appetites to participate in reason. The habits resulting from such training are temperance, courage, and the other virtues that flow from them.

In the case of the will, training is necessary so that the will can not only choose the closest and most immediate good (the proper good of the one willing), but also love a more transcendent good (the good of the other). This is justice: willing the due good of the other.

In the case of the practical intellect, habituation is necessary simply because of the variety of circumstances in human affairs, and the quasi-infinite number of the means that can lead towards the end. The result of such habituation is prudence.

If virtue in general is the disposition of a thing which makes it good and its own act good, then we can now see that moral virtues are habits that make the powers of the human soul concerned with practical action good, and the actions proceeding from those powers good.

These notes have only considered natural or "acquired" virtue. There is a higher kind of virtue that is not acquired by training, but is "poured" directly into the soul by God. Such "infused" virtues are in reality a participation in a higher life, the Divine Life. Through the infused virtues, human beings have a foreshadowing and beginning of supernatural happiness.

6

Natures as Words, Contraception as a Lie

Edmund Waldstein, O.Cist.

One of the main obstacles to understanding the Catholic teaching on contraception is an ignorance of the relevant meaning of the concept of *nature*. What sense of nature is being used when one says that contraception is "contrary to nature"? An exactly parallel sense of "contrary to nature" is used in the Church's teaching on lying. And although the teaching on lying is as obscure to many as is the teaching on contraception, I think that a comparison of the two is illuminating. The teaching on lying is particularly illuminating, because the natures of created things can in a real sense be said to be "words" of the Creator.

Natures as words

St. Thomas Aquinas follows Aristotle in using "nature" to mean a principle of change and rest that is in a thing, making that thing be what it is. So the "nature" of a tree is the principle in the tree according to which the tree grows and stops growing, stretches out toward the sun, bears fruit, and so on. Aristotle shows in the *Physics* that nature is directed toward a goal, toward a good, that the thing is supposed to realize. So one could define nature as a kind of direction within a thing toward a particular good that it is supposed to realize.

St. Thomas Aquinas takes this Aristotelian account and develops it further by arguing that to act for an end presupposes some kind of knowledge. So he defines nature as an impression of the Divine Reason on creatures; the nature of each thing is a kind of participation in the divine wisdom by which that thing is directed towards its end.[1] This is the sense of nature from which natural law is derived: human beings are directed by this innate impression of divine wisdom to seek self-preservation, reproduction, friendship, knowledge of God, and so on, and to shun what is destructive of those goods. Charles De Koninck in commenting on this passage says that every nature can be called a "Divine *logos* ... a Divine word."[2] *Logos* can of course mean *reason* as well as word and De Koninck notes that the nature of irrational things is "a substitute for intellect," but a nature is also a word in a much more literal sense.

God's principal intention in creating is to manifest his own glory,[3] and so each nature is a sign by which God leads rational creatures to a knowledge of Himself. As St. Thomas puts it:

> The creatures made by God's wisdom are related to God's wisdom, whose signposts they are, as a man's words are related to his wisdom, which they signify. And just as a disciple reaches an understanding of the teacher's wisdom by the words he hears from him, so man can reach an understanding of God's wisdom by examining the creatures He made.[4]

Maurice Dionne thus argues that the "natural works" of God, that is the natures of natural things, are given us as "principles which permit us to discover certain divine names."[5]

That creatures are words of their Creator is in principle knowable by natural reason, but revelation deepens our understanding of this truth. All things are created through the Eternal Word, the *Logos* Who is the perfect expression of the Father's knowledge of Himself. And creation reflects that Word. But rational nature is in a special sense a reflection and even an image of the *Logos*. Human contemplation of God is an image of the eternal generation of the Word,

---

1. See *Commentary on Aristotle's Physics,* lecture 14, n. 268.
2. *On the Primacy of the Common Good,* Appendix.
3. See my paper "On Peace as the Final Cause of the Universe."
4. *Commentary on 1 Corinthians,* lecture 3, n. 55.
5. "The Grace of Mary is of the Hypostatic Order," 1, https://www.scribd.com/document/238167087/The-Grace-of-Mary-is-of-the-Hypostatic-Order.

and human speech is a sign of the Incarnation, in which the eternal Word was manifest in the sensible world.[6]

Two ways in which an action can be contrary to nature

So natures are words of the Creator, and they make a thing to be what it is. A tree is a tree because of the sort of participation in the divine wisdom that it has, a participation that orders it to the sort of good that can be realized by a tree, and that signifies something about its creator. Similarly a human being is human because of human nature. But not only the substantial natures of things are Divine *logoi*—everything was made through the Word, and without the Word nothing was made. Thus human *actions*, which flow from human nature and are ordered to an end, can also be said to be Divine words, and to have "natures" in this sense. One can look at a kind of human action and ask, "what is the nature of this sort of act"—i.e., what is the innate ordering to a goal that this kind of act has. Thus one can look at human speech and ask: What is human speech? What makes it to be what it is and not something else? This is crucial for understanding the teaching of *Humanae Vitae*. In the case of sexual intercourse too one has to ask: What is the nature of this act? What is the innate order toward a good goal in it that makes it to be sexual intercourse and not something else?

It follows, then, that there can be two ways in which an action is "contrary to nature." In one way it can be contrary to the end of human nature as a whole—this is true of any evil action, since all evil actions are against "right reason" and contrary to the final goal of the human person. But in a more particular sense something can be "contrary to nature" if it is against the particular nature of the kind of act that it is.

We can see this in the case of speech. One can sin by saying something mean or indiscreet, and this is contrary to right reason, and thus contrary to one's nature, but it is not against the particular nature of speech. But there is one kind of sin in speech that is

---

6. See John Francis Nieto's exposition of this point in his lecture "*Nil Hoc Verbo Veritatis Verius*: A Christian Reflection on Lying," audio at https://www.thomas aquinas.edu/news/photos-audio-st-thomas-day-2012.

indeed against the nature of speech itself. As the *Catechism of the Catholic Church* teaches: "By its very *nature*, lying is to be condemned" (CCC 2485). St. Thomas argues for this position in the *Summa theologiae* through an analysis of the nature of speech.[7] Speech is by its nature, that is its particular nature as a certain *kind* of act, ordered to communicate the thoughts that a person has in his mind. So, if one says something that is directly contrary to what he thinks, then he violates the nature of speech: the action is "unnatural."

Of course, communicating the truth is not the only good that speech realizes—speech also strengthens relationships, sounds nice, and so on. But it is communicating truth that gives speech its nature—it is the primary natural end of speech from which all the others flow. Hence St. Thomas teaches that even the so-called "friendly lie" (lying out of politeness: "you look great"), or the jocose lie (April fool's jokes), is sinful. The whole class of actions called lies is intrinsically bad and can never be good.[8] And St. Thomas teaches something precisely similar about sexual sins. He argues that there are two ways in which a sexual act can be sinful: first, through being contrary to right reason, and this is common to all lustful vices; secondly, because, in addition, it is contrary to the natural order of the venereal act as becoming to the human race.[9] In the first class are sins such as adultery and fornication—they are contrary to right reason, contrary to the final end of the human person, but they are not contrary to the nature of the sexual act. An act of adultery still has the *nature* of a sexual act, and this because it preserves the natural order toward the end of that kind of act. The primary end of sexual intercourse is reproduction. Of course sex also realizes other goods: the union of the spouses, pleasure, etc. But the one that *defines* it, that makes it to be what it is, that gives it its nature, is reproduction. Thus adultery and fornication are not contrary to the nature of sex. But sins such as sodomy and masturbation *are* contrary to the nature of sex. It is not merely that in doing

---

7. *ST* II-II, q. 110, a. 3.
8. Again, see Nieto, "*Nil Hoc Verbo Veritatis Verius.*"
9. *ST* II-II, q. 154, a. 11.

such acts one is not *intending* to reproduce; it is that the *kind of act* one is choosing is not a reproductive kind of act at all. It doesn't have the nature of proper sex, and hence it is unnatural. It is like a lie.

Pope Paul VI teaches (and Pope John Paul II expands on his teaching at great length) that contraception belongs to this category of acts. Contraception is wrong not because people contracepting are not *intending* to reproduce (however true that might be); it is wrong because it contradicts the nature, the Divine *logos* of the act. It uses the faculty of generation in a way that directly frustrates the defining end of that faculty, the end that gives that faculty its nature. It is perverse because it is contrary to the nature of the faculty in the same way that lying is contrary to speech: It changes the kind of act that you are doing into a kind of act in which a faculty is used to contradict itself. As Elizabeth Anscombe puts it, "The action is not left by you as the kind of act by which life is transmitted, but is purposely rendered infertile, and so changed to *another sort of act* altogether."[10]

Thus, contraception is *always* sinful. It always contradicts the impression of the Divine wisdom that is imprinted in sexual nature. This is why Paul VI speaks of contraception as contrary to the "meaning" of the conjugal act,[11] and why John Paul II speaks of the *language* of the body: "the *truth* of the *language of the body* can be expressed only by safeguarding the procreative potential."[12]

Lying is to equivocation as contraception is to natural family planning

While lying is *always* sinful, it can in certain emergencies be morally good to deceive someone by equivocation, that is, by saying something true that one's interlocutor is liable to misunderstand. A classic example: St. Athanasius, fleeing his persecutors by boat, orders his men to turn the boat around and sail straight toward the

---

10. "Contraception and Chastity" (1975), https://issuu.com/catholictruthsociety/docs/contraception___chastity.
11. *Humanae Vitae* 13.
12. General Audience of November 21, 1984.

persecutors. The persecutors ask his men, "Have you seen Athanasius?" And his men answer (on his orders), "Yes, he is nearby." The persecutors hurry on up stream.

What is the difference between lying and equivocating in such a situation? In both cases one is intending to deceive. But in the case of a lie you are directly acting against the nature of the act of speech—it's the wrong *kind* of act that you are doing. When you equivocate you are certainly not *intending* to communicate truth, but the act nevertheless is the right *kind* of act—it has the *nature* of true speech—even though in this case you hope it won't succeed in communicating truth.

Something similar can be seen when comparing "Natural Family Planning" (NFP) and contraception. Contraception is *always* sinful because it doesn't have the *nature* of sex; it is like a lie. But NFP is more like equivocation. In an emergency situation (for example, inability to support more children due to unjust economic structures), one does not want the sexual act to result in pregnancy. So one chooses to engage in a true sexual act, but in such a way that it will not (likely) result in pregnancy, just as Athanasius's sailors say something *true* but in a way that will not communicate the truth. Thus in certain circumstances, using NFP can be morally good. As Pope Paul VI teaches:

> Neither the Church nor her doctrine is inconsistent when she considers it lawful for married people to take advantage of the infertile period but condemns as always unlawful the use of means which directly prevent conception, even when the reasons given for the latter practice may appear to be upright and serious. In reality, these two cases are completely different. In the former the married couple rightly use a faculty provided them by nature. In the later they obstruct the natural development of the generative process.[13]

The difficulty that many Catholics have in understanding this teaching is caused (at least in part) by the modern concept of nature, which is very different from the true one. The natural world

---

13. *Humanae Vitae* 16.

is seen by much of post-Cartesian modernity as a kind of machine with parts acted on by blind force, rather than an order of things directed from within by impressions of the divine wisdom. In his Introduction to John Paul II's series of Wednesday audiences, *Male and Female He Created Them* (otherwise known as *The Theology of the Body*), Michael Waldstein has argued that one of the Pope's main points was to try to recover the traditional view of nature on which this teaching is based. In the final audience of the series, John Paul says that the whole series was ordered to understanding the teaching of *Humanae Vitae*. What he tries to show finally is that this teaching is about our very structure as creatures of God; about the impression in us of the divine wisdom.

II

THE FAMILY, THE VILLAGE, & THE CITY

7

Aristotle's Account of the Relationship of the Household to the State

Beatrice Freccia

1. Introduction

At the outset of his *Ethics*, Aristotle points out that one cannot expect an equal degree of precision in the treatment of all subjects, particularly of those subjects that ethics and politics address:

> Problems of what is noble and just, which politics examines, present so much variety and irregularity that some people believe that they exist only by convention and not by nature. The problem of the good, too, presents a similar kind of irregularity, because in many cases good things bring harmful results. There are instances of men ruined by wealth, and others by courage. Therefore, in a discussion of such subjects, which has to start from a basis of this kind, we must be satisfied to indicate the truth with a rough and general sketch: when the subject and the basis of a discussion consist of matters that hold good only as a general rule, but not always, the conclusions reached must be of the same order. The various points that are made must be received in the same spirit. For a well-schooled man is one who searches for that degree of precision in each kind of study which the nature of that subject at hand admits: it is obviously just as foolish to accept arguments of probability from a mathematician as to demand strict demonstrations from an orator.[1]

---

1. Aristotle, *Nicomachean Ethics* I.3, 1094b14, trans. Martin Ostwald (Upper Saddle River, NJ: Prentice Hall, 1999); hereafter, *Ethics*.

Integralism and the Common Good

Because the matters that Aristotle treats of in the *Ethics* and the *Politics* are inextricably tied up with particulars, there can be no scientific demonstrations about such matters, and it would be ridiculous to expect such a thing. This is a highly satisfactory explanation of the obvious differences between Aristotle's treatment of, say, justice, and his treatment of logic in the *Categories*. But it sometimes seems as if Aristotle's *Ethics* and *Politics* are "rough and general sketch[es]" not only in terms of the degree of precision which they admit of; for often the reader is left to his own devices when it comes to synthesizing the concepts discussed—"bridging the gaps," as it were.

A particularly good example of an issue that is only outlined (but about which there is no dearth of material to synthesize) is the relationship between the family and the state.[2] Aristotle's explicit treatment of the matter in the *Politics*[3] is exceedingly spare, but what he says explicitly is remarkably consistent with not only his implicit references to the matter elsewhere (both in the *Ethics* and the *Politics*), but also with his general theories about human nature (e.g., moral and intellectual virtue, friendship, happiness, and rule). It is perhaps the case, given this degree of consistency, that Aristotle felt that the "general sketch" that he provides gives the student everything he needs to formulate an answer to the question "What is the relationship of the household to the state, according to Aristotle's account?"

This essay will attempt to make a beginning in answering that question. It will argue that, though the primary end of the family is rightly said to be "the supply of men's everyday wants,"[4] the family is, in a secondary sense, also ordered towards the true state's end of

---

2. Aristotle uses the Greek word *polis*, which more literally means "city-state." Although we will use the word "state" (since English has no direct equivalent to *polis*), it is understood that the "state" we are discussing here, since we are examining Aristotle's thought, is a community closer to the modern idea of the city than to the modern idea of the state or nation (see Aristotle's *Politics* VII.4).

3. *Politics* I.2, 1253a19, trans. Benjamin Jowett, in *The Basic Works of Aristotle*, ed. Richard McKeon (New York: Random House, 1941). Unless otherwise noted, this translation will be cited.

4. Ibid., I.2, 1252b12.

ensuring that its citizens "live well."[5] The household prepares its members for their life within the state by developing the virtues appropriate to each of them, a task which is integral to the health of the state. Further, the role which the household plays in the proper functioning of the state is a role for which the household is peculiarly suited, and which only it can play.

We will first briefly address Aristotle's general definitions of the family and the state, as well as his explicit treatment of the relationship between the two. A more thorough investigation of the nature of the household will follow. For, as Aristotle says at the beginning of the *Politics*:

> The complete household is made up of slaves and free persons. Since everything is to be sought first in its smallest elements, and the first and smallest parts of the household are master, slave, husband, wife, father, and children, three things must be investigated to determine what each is and what sort of thing it ought to be. These are expertise in mastery, in marital [rule] (there is no term for the union of man and woman), and thirdly in parental [rule] (this too has not been assigned a term of its own).[6]

Each of these three relationships, then, will be examined in detail. Having acquired a clearer picture of the relationships within the household, the peculiar degree of "other-self-ness" and the having-of-things-in-common within the household will be addressed, as well the particular ways in which the household develops the virtue of its various members. Finally, the necessity of the household will be addressed. This last consideration is dependent on the peculiar other-self relationships and the having-of-things-in-common within the household, as well as on the household's development of the virtue of its members.

2. Defining the family, the state, and the relationship between them

A brief treatment of Aristotle's definitions of the family, the state,

---

5. *Politics* II.9, 1280a31, trans. Carnes Lord (Chicago: The University of Chicago Press, 1984).
6. *Politics* I.3 (Lord), 1253b4.

and their relationship will of course be a necessary preliminary to a closer examination of these three. These are defined in Aristotle's *Politics*, which presupposes his *Ethics*. In the *Ethics*, Aristotle defines virtue as an activity, discusses the individual's need for other men if he is to develop moral virtue,[7] presupposes moral virtue to intellectual virtue (because it orders the parts of the soul),[8] defines happiness as activity in conformity with the virtue of the highest part (the rational element),[9] and, since happiness will lack nothing, notes that happiness will be marked by self-sufficiency.[10] It is theoretical knowledge which is self-sufficient[11] and loved for its own sake, and the perfection of the pursuit of theoretical knowledge will require other men, insofar as it requires intellectual discourse.[12] Finally, in a transition to the *Politics*, Aristotle discusses the need for laws, if men are to continue in virtue their whole lives.[13] And since laws are the "product of politics,"[14] it would seem that there is a need for the state.

It is to "complete... our philosophy of human affairs,"[15] then, that the project of the *Politics* is embarked upon. It is in chapter 2 of his *Politics* that Aristotle treats of the origins of the family and the state:

> In the first place there must be a union of those who cannot exist without each other; namely, *of male and female*, that the race may continue (and this is a union which is formed, not of deliberate purpose, but because, in common with other animals and with plants, mankind have a natural desire to leave behind them an image of themselves), and of natural ruler and subject, that both may be preserved.
>
> Out of these two relationships between man and woman, mas-

---

7. *Ethics* IX.9, 1169b12, 1170a2, 1170a7; X.8, 1178b4.
8. Among others, *Ethics* VI.13, 1145a6 suggests that intellectual virtue presupposes moral virtue.
9. *Ethics* X.7, 1177a12, 1177b27.
10. *Ethics* X.6, 1176b5.
11. *Ethics* X.7, 1177a27, 1177b.
12. Ibid., 1177a35.
13. *Ethics* X.9, 1180a14.
14. Ibid., 1181a25.
15. Ibid., 1181b15.

Aristotle on the Relationship of Household to State

ter and slave, the first thing to arise is the family.... The family is the association established by nature for the supply of men's everyday wants.... But when several families are united, and the association aims at something more than the supply of daily needs, the first society to be formed is the village....

When several villages are united in a single community, large enough to be nearly or quite self-sufficing, the state comes into existence, originating in the bare needs of life, and continuing in existence for the sake of a good life.[16] And therefore, if the earlier forms of society are natural, so is the state, for it is the end of them, and the nature of a thing is its end. For what each thing is when fully developed, we call its nature, whether we are speaking of a man, a horse, or a family. Besides, the final cause and end of a thing is the best, and to be self-sufficing is the end and best.[17]

Finally, as to the relationship of the family to the state, Aristotle has the following to say:

Further, the state is by nature clearly prior to the family and to the individual, since the whole is of necessity prior to the part; for example, if the whole body be destroyed, there will be no foot or hand, except in an equivocal sense, as we might speak of a stone hand; for when destroyed the hand will be no better than that. But things are defined by their working and power; and we ought not to say that they are the same when they no longer have their proper quality, but only that they have the same name. The proof that the state is a creation of nature and prior to the individual is that the individual, when isolated, is not self-sufficing; and therefore he is like a part in relation to the whole.[18]

This brief exposition of the relationship between the family and the state leaves the reader, as we have said, with a great many questions. The issue of the priority of the state to the family is a particularly perplexing one—is the family really ordered to the state, as an organ is to the body? How can this be the case, when they have been said to have different ends? While an exhaustive treatment of the various ways in which the "priority of the state" could be inter-

---

16. On this, see also *Politics* III.9, 1280a31.
17. *Politics* I.2, 1252a26.
18. Ibid., 1253a19.

preted is outside of the scope of this essay, we will nevertheless keep in mind, while examining the relationship of the household to the state (and in particular, the ways in which the family might be said to be ordered to the state), how this relationship might bear on the question of priority.

3. Relationships within the household: husband and wife

Before entering into a discussion of the relationship between husband and wife, it will be helpful to review Aristotle's discussion of friendship in his *Ethics* (which precedes his discussion of the various relationships within the household), since the ideal marriage would seem to be a sort of friendship.

At the beginning of Book VIII of the *Ethics*, having already considered diverse opinions about friendship, Aristotle concludes that "the object of affection" is the lovable. The lovable, he writes, is divided into three types: the good, the pleasant and the useful. Through a dialectical consideration of friendship, he arrives at some basic requirements for a relationship to be called a friendship: "To be friends men must have good will for one another, must each wish for the good of the other on the basis of one of the three motives mentioned [the good, the pleasant, and the useful], and must each be aware of one another's good will."[19] Thus, there are three kinds of friendship, corresponding to the different sorts of lovable things.[20] But, Aristotle says of friendships of use and pleasure, "these two kinds are friendship only incidentally, since the object of affection is not loved for being the kind of person he is, but for providing some good or pleasure."[21] Having eliminated these two kinds of friendship from the consideration of true friendship, he states:

> The perfect form of friendship is that between good men who are alike in excellence or virtue. For these friends wish alike for one another's good because they are good men, and they are good per se. Those who wish for their friends' good for their friends' sake

19. *Ethics* VIII.2, 1156a3.
20. *Ethics* VIII.3, 1156a8.
21. Ibid., 1156a17.

are friends in the truest sense, since their attitude is determined by what their friends are and not by incidental considerations. Hence their friendship lasts as long as they are good, and goodness or virtue is a thing that lasts. In addition, each partner is both good in the unqualified sense and good for his friend.[22]

And then, just afterwards:

Now this kind of friendship [the friendship between virtuous equals] has all the requisite qualities we have mentioned and has them per se, that is, as an essential part of the characters of the friends. For in this kind of friendship the characters are like one another, and the other objects worthy of affection—the unqualified good and the unqualified pleasant—are also found in it, and these are the highest objects worthy of affection. It is, therefore, in the friendship of good men that feelings of affection and friendship exist in their highest and best form.[23]

It is important to note that, as Aristotle sees the matter, the relationship of the husband and wife does not meet the qualifications for the highest, most ideal friendship. This is because the husband and wife are not equals in Aristotle's schema. According to his account, the husband and the wife do not give each other the same things. We will see shortly why it might be that Aristotle believes this to be the case.

Suppose that the husband and wife are unable to give each other the same things: this is problematic because of the role that justice plays in Aristotle's conception of true friendship. He says that "It is natural that the element of justice increases with [the closeness of] the friendship, since friendship and what is just exist in the same relationship and are coextensive in range."[24] Now, the pure form of reciprocal justice (which is the sort of justice concerned with exchange) involves an equal exchange, and an unequal exchange constitutes an injustice.[25] So it would seem that friendship is impos-

---

22. Ibid., 1156b7.
23. Ibid., 1156b22.
24. *Ethics* VIII.9, 1160a7.
25. "Now, the just in transactions is also something equal (and the unjust something unequal)..." (*Ethics* V.4, 1131b32).

sible between two people who cannot make an "equal exchange." Nevertheless, Aristotle believes that the relationship between the husband and the wife *is* a friendship—but that it is a special case of friendship in which one of the partners is superior to the other. (Father-son and ruler-subject pairs are other kinds of friendships of inequality.) About these various kinds of relationships between unequals, Aristotle says:

> These kinds of friendship are different [not only from those which involve equality, but] also from one another.... For in each of these cases, the virtue or excellence and the function of each partner is different, and the cause of their affection, too, is different. Therefore, the affection and friendship they feel are correspondingly different. It is clear that the partners do not receive the same thing from one another and should not seek to receive it....[26]

The question still remains, how can we consider these relationships to be friendships, when this inequality is believed to exist between the partners? It would seem to be a sort of injustice, or, at the very least, grossly unfitting, considering what we have already seen of Aristotle's notions about the role of equality in true friendship. There is, however, a way in which this difficulty can be seen to be resolved:

> In all friendships which involve the superiority of one of the partners, the affection, too, must be proportionate: the better and more useful partner should receive more affection than he gives, and similarly for the superior partner in each case. For when the affection is proportionate to the merit of each partner, there is in some sense equality between them. And equality, as we have seen, seems to be a part of friendship.[27]

Now, because the relationship is one of a superior to an inferior, it will of necessity involve rule, as well as friendship—as will all other relationships between unequals. According to Aristotle's account, the husband, as the superior partner, rules over his wife. But it is important to note that there are different kinds of rule. The

---

26. *Ethics* VIII.7, 1158b12.
27. Ibid., 1158b23.

husband does not rule over his wife in the same way that he rules over, say, his slaves.

> For that which can foresee by the exercise of the mind is by nature intended to be lord and master, and that which can with its body give effect to such foresight is a subject, and by nature a slave; hence master and slave have the same interest. Now nature has distinguished between the female and the slave. For she is not niggardly, like the smith who fashions the Delphian knife for many uses; she makes each thing for a single use, and every instrument is best made when intended for one and not for many uses. But among barbarians no distinction is made between women and slaves, because there is no natural ruler among them: they are a community of slaves, male and female....[28]

So the wife does not blindly carry out her husband's wishes, as the slave carries out the will of the master (because the slave's rational principle is, in fact, external and present in the master). If, then, the wife has the capacity for reason (which would seem to be what distinguishes her from the slave), why does she need someone to rule over her? What is it that renders her inferior? A bit later in the *Politics*, Aristotle addresses this very question:

> Almost all things rule and are ruled according to nature. But the kind of rule differs;—the freeman rules over the slave after another manner from that in which the male rules over the female, or the man over the child; although the parts of the soul are present in all of them, they are present in different degrees. For the slave has no deliberative faculty at all; the woman has, but it is without authority, and the child has, but it is immature. So it must necessarily be supposed to be with the moral virtues also; all should partake of them, but only in such manner and degree as is required by each for the fulfillment of his duty. Hence the ruler ought to have moral virtue in perfection, for his function, taken absolutely, demands a master artificer, and rational principle is such an artificer; the subjects, on the other hand, require only that measure of virtue which is proper to each of them. Clearly, then, moral virtue belongs to all of them; but the temperance of a man

---

28. *Politics* I.2, 1252a32.

and of a woman, are not, as Socrates maintained, the same....
And this holds of all other virtues....[29]

Thus, the inequality between the husband and the wife, as Aristotle sees it, is not a matter of convention or "cultural conditioning." The male and the female are simply not capable of giving each other the same things—their virtues and abilities are not the same. Of course, they can pervert their activities so as to not follow from the character of their respective sexes, but this does not change the fact of what they are naturally capable of giving each other as man and as woman. At any rate, the fact that they do not give each other the same things turns out (as we shall see) to be for the good of the household.

But how to understand the subtleties of the husband-wife relationship? Surely there is more to say about Aristotle's position on the matter than merely that he feels the husband is superior to his wife on the basis of the fact that he possesses the authority necessary for rule, and she does not. Indeed, Aristotle does take pains to develop a clearer picture of the way the relationship between the husband and the wife works. In both the *Ethics* and the *Politics*, he compares the relationship between husband and wife to forms of political rule. (He also compares the other relationships in the household to types of political rule, but we will wait until we discuss those relationships to discuss those analogies.)

The first comparison of the husband-wife relationship to a form of political rule is in Book VIII of the *Ethics*:

> Resemblances to these forms of government—models, as it were—can be found in the household.... The association of husband and wife is evidently aristocratic. For the husband's rule depends on his worth or merit, and the sphere of his rule is that which is proper to a man. Whatever is more suited to a woman he turns over to his wife. But whenever the husband takes authority over all [household] matters into his hand, he transforms the association into an oligarchy, since in doing so he violates the principle of merit and does not rule by virtue of his superiority. Sometimes the wife rules because she is an heiress. But of course

29. *Politics* I.13, 1260a7.

this kind of rule is not in terms of excellence or virtue, but is based on wealth and power, just as in oligarchies.[30]

Here, Aristotle has likened marriage to an aristocracy because both in marriage and in aristocracy, superiority on the basis of worth or merit determines who is to rule. One can also see here that Aristotle believes men and women to have "sphere[s]" of activity which are proper to them. Failure to recognize the distinction between these two spheres of activity (as when a husband insists on managing *everything*, even those things in which he should delegate his authority to his wife, or when the wife rules over her husband) constitutes a perversion of the natural order. Just as the three good forms of the state are true states,[31] and their corresponding perversions are not, so too are male-female relationships which pervert the natural order not true marriages.

Soon after the passage cited above, Aristotle again compares the relationship between spouses to an aristocracy: "The friendship between husband and wife is the same as that in an aristocracy. It is based on excellence or virtue: the superior partner gets a larger share of good, and each gets what is suited to him, and the same relationship holds for what is just."[32] In an aristocracy, what the state has to offer is distributed according to the merit of the citizens.[33] Thus, as a true aristocracy (one based on genuine merit) is a just form of government, so is a true marriage a just exchange of the particular gifts and abilities men and women are given, respectively.

But, like all analogies, the comparison of marriage to an aristocracy falls short of fully illuminating its subject. It is perhaps to flesh out our understanding of the husband-wife relationship that Aristotle compares marriage to a second form of political rule in Book I of his *Politics*:

> A husband and father, we saw, rules over wife and children, both free, but the rule differs, the rule over his children being a royal,

30. *Ethics* VIII.10, 1160b24.
31. Ibid., 1160a31.
32. *Ethics* VIII.11, 1161a22.
33. *Ethics* VIII.10, 1160b12.

over his wife a constitutional rule. For although there may be exceptions to the order of nature, the male is by nature fitter for command than the female, just as the elder and full-grown is superior to the younger and more immature. But in most constitutional states the citizens rule and are ruled by turns, for the idea of a constitutional state implies that the natures of the citizens are equal, and do not differ at all. Nevertheless, when one rules and the other is ruled we endeavor to create a difference of outward forms and names and titles of respect, which may be illustrated by the saying of Amasis about his foot-pan. The relation of the male to the female is of this kind, but there the inequality is permanent.[34]

Here, Aristotle points out the fact that the wife and children are "both free," and that the conception of a constitutional state implies that "the natures of the citizens are equal." Later in the *Politics*, Aristotle defines constitutional rule as that "which is exercised over freemen and equals by birth...."[35] This comparison of the husband-wife relationship to a second type of rule illustrates the fact that, although the husband merits a certain position in the household (and is in that sense superior to his wife), both parties are nevertheless equal, under another consideration: they are both rational human beings, and as such are freemen. The wife is no less a human being than her husband is.[36]

The story about Amasis and the foot-pan (which Aristotle mentions in the last paragraph cited above) may help to illustrate the fact that the husband and wife are equal in this respect. This story (found in Herodotus)[37] tells of an Egyptian king who, when his common birth was spoken of disparagingly, secretly had a golden foot-pan melted down and made into an idol. When his subjects began to worship the idol, he revealed its humble origins, saying that he himself was like that footbath. The husband and the wife are both human—just as the foot-pan and the idol were both gold—

---

34. *Politics* I.12, 1259a39.
35. *Politics* III.4, 1277b9.
36. "Others suppose that if they are equal in a certain thing, such as freedom, they are equal generally" (*Politics* III.9 [Lord], 1280a23).
37. Herodotus, *Histories* II.172.

but the form which each takes (their respective sexes) determines the role each is to have. (Most literally, in generation, but also, as a result, in their common endeavors within the household.)

We have seen, then, that Aristotle believes that the husband merits rule over his wife by virtue of his having an authority that is uniquely male, and that this authority is permanent, but that they are nonetheless both equal in their dignity as freemen, on account of their rational nature. It was stated above that the wife does not blindly follow her husband's orders as the slave does. It can now be said that since the wife has the "deliberative faculty," she is free to deliberate as to the best means to achieving the ends her husband has chosen with authority. Because she has this deliberative element, she is a suitable partner and counsel for her husband, and can contribute to the decisions he makes concerning his family and property. It is their ability to reason that distinguishes the husband and the wife (and, in potency, their children) from the slave, and characterizes them as freemen. Their rational capacities allow them to have an understanding of the end of the state in which they live, and this understanding enables them to knowingly direct their actions to that end, and so have a role in the life of their state.

Now that we have discussed the ways in which the husband and the wife are said to be both unequal and equal, we can examine more closely the ways in which these considerations bear upon their actions. It was pointed out above that virtue is not the same for the male and the female, and that they each have their own virtues and abilities. These differences between the husband and the wife would seem to flow from the respective roles they play in generation—not merely in the act of generation, but also the different roles they play with respect to the rearing of their children. (Remember that it is this common endeavor that is the reason for their union in the first place, and thus constitutes the essence of their lives together.) The characteristics of their respective sexes render them suited to distinct but complementary sets of activities.

But what are these complementary activities, and how do they follow from the respective sexes of the husband and the wife? The roles that both the man and the woman play in generation are fixed and determined by nature and so, to a certain extent, are the roles they play in the raising of their child once he is born. Before he is born, the child grows within and is nourished by the body of his mother. In his infancy, his mother continues to nourish him with her body. Both the child's growth within his mother's body before birth and his being nourished by that same body after birth contribute to their relationship having a specific character. The character of the mother-child relationship is distinct from the character of the father-child relationship—it is not insignificant that the father's relationship with the child in a sense can be said to begin only after birth, and that, even then, the relationship is significantly more removed than that of the mother to her child. The differences between these two relationships could be said to contribute to the fact that the mother takes a different sort of interest in the child as an individual than his father does (and has a different and necessary sort of affection for him), and the relative distance between the father and the child contributes to his ability to fairly discipline the child—he is able to be more objective in his judgments. The roles of the parents in generation and child-rearing are certainly different, but they are undoubtedly complementary. The child needs both sorts of relationships to become a whole, well-ordered individual, and each parent's distinct experiences of a child informs the other's.

The matter of the husband's capacity for authority is a difficult one (and thus, we will not be able to fully address it within the confines of this essay), but it is fair to say that the husband's unique possession of authority may ultimately be said to be for the good of the relationship. On the subject of rule, Aristotle says in Book I of the *Politics*: "For whatever is constituted out of a number of things—whether continuous or discrete—and becomes a single common thing always displays a ruling and a ruled element; this is something that animate things derive from all of nature, for even in things that do not share in life there is a sort of rule, for example in a harmony."[38] Certainly, the husband and wife have, as a result of their common endeavor, joined together to form "a single common thing," and as such, there is a necessity for one element to rule over

---

38. *Politics* I.5 (Lord), 1254a27.

the others. The fact that the wife has the deliberative element means that their endeavor is truly a common one, but ultimately, order is secured (and conflict is prevented) by the fact that, within a properly ordered household, only one party rules. So the fact that there is one—and only one—element that is capable of ruling over the others within the household would seem to be both advantageous and ideal.

It is particularly difficult to see why it must be the husband who rules, and what he derives his authority from. Within the *Ethics* and the *Politics*, Aristotle seems to assume the husband's authority as a principle (and thus does not argue to it), but there is still some basis for conjecture about the subject. First, there is the consideration we made above about the husband's relative distance from the children—this allows him not only a sort of objectivity in the rearing of his children, but also the ability to have a life apart from them: not only with regard to the other elements of the household, but outside of the household and within the state. This life outside of the household gives him a better picture of what is best not only for his children, but for his household as a whole. Further, he is better able to see the relationship between his household and the state, and make decisions concerning his family that correspond to the way in which the state endeavors to order its citizens.

A second consideration that might contribute to Aristotle's claim about the superiority of the husband to the wife may be found in Book VII of the *Politics*, when Aristotle states that "spiritedness is a thing expert at ruling and indomitable."[39] Unfortunately, he does not expand upon what he means by spiritedness, but it would seem that he means some sort of dominance peculiar to male animals. After all, he says in the first book of the *Politics* that "the relation of male to female is by nature a relation of superior to inferior and ruler to ruled. The same must of necessity hold in the case of human beings generally."[40]

True and natural marriage comes about when both partners realize their true and proper sphere of activity and the purpose of their

---

39. *Politics* VII.7, 1328a5.
40. *Politics* I.5, 1254b12.

union, and act as nature intended them to act. This alone makes harmonious partnership possible.

> The friendship between man and wife seems to be inherent in us by nature. For man is by nature more inclined to live in couples than to live as a social and political being, inasmuch as the household is earlier and more indispensable than the state, and to the extent that procreation is a bond more universal to all living things [than living in a state]. In the case of other animals, the association goes no further than this. But human beings live together not merely for procreation, but also to secure the needs of life. There is division of labor from the very beginning and different functions for man and wife. Thus they satisfy one another's needs by contributing each his own to the common store.[41]

It seems clear, then, that in every marriage there will be a division of labor, that each will contribute "his own to the common store," and that their actions will follow from the different characters of their respective sexes. But it would also seem that, since there is an inequality, their actions would also have to do with "rectifying" that inequality. In what way do the actions of the husband and wife serve to rectify the inequality between them, so that friendship may occur?

> In those friendships, too, in which one partner is superior to the other, disagreements occur. Each partner thinks that he is entitled to more than the other, and when this happens the friendship is dissolved. If one partner is better than the other, he thinks he has more than the other coming to him, since the larger share ought to be assigned to the good. The same thing happens when one of the partners is more useful than the other; people say that a useless man should not have as large a share [as a useful person]. A friendship becomes a public service if what the man gets out of his friendship is not what he deserves on the basis of his contribution. The usual view is that a friendship should be like a business partnership: those who contribute more should also take more of the proceeds. The inferior partner who stands in need takes the reverse position. It is the mark of a good friend, he argues, to come

---

41. *Ethics* VIII.12, 1162a17.

to the aid of the needy. What is the use of being a friend of a man of high moral standards or power, they ask, if you are to get nothing out of it?

Now it seems that both partners are right in their claims: each is entitled to get a larger share from the friendship, but not a larger share of the same thing. The superior partner ought to be given a larger share of honor and the needy partner a larger share of profit. For the reward of excellence and beneficence is honor, whereas profit is the [form taken by] assistance to one in need.[42]

How does the wife profit by the relationship? First of all, there is the obvious fact that she profits materially. Since she does not have an income, she is supported entirely by the work of her husband. But let us not forget about the issue of the husband's having the authority his wife lacks. This authority allows the husband to take the initiative that creates the marriage in the first place. Thus, though both parties need each other to realize their own ends, only the husband can create the union that makes possible the realization of those ends.[43]

And what does it mean for the wife to "honor" her husband? The wife is entrusted with management of the household matters that her husband delegates to her, as well as with the upbringing of the children. Aristotle says in Book III of the *Politics* that "household management differs for a man and a woman as well, for it is the work of the man to acquire and the woman to guard."[44] The wife is entrusted not only with her husband's material possessions, but also with the protection of his reputation. One of the ways in which she does this is by always acting in the way her husband would with regards to the duties that are delegated to her. Not only is she never to act in such a way that might cause his integrity to be doubted, but she is to strive to act in such a way that she (and by extension, her husband) is praised for her virtue.

It is important to note that though Aristotle thinks the inequality

---

42. *Ethics* VIII.14, 1163a23, trans. modified.
43. Remember that, on Aristotle's account, any authority that the wife holds in the management of the household is received through her husband.
44. *Politics* III.4 (Lord), 1277b23.

between the husband and wife results in their possessing distinct virtues, this does not preclude their having a friendship based upon those virtues. Indeed, because they satisfy each other's needs by contributing to the common store, "this kind of friendship brings both usefulness and pleasantness with it, and if the partners are good, it may even be based on virtue or excellence. For each partner has his own peculiar existence and they find joy in that fact."[45] Within a properly ordered marriage, the husband and wife realize that their actions are complementary, and they love each other on account of the good each possesses. This is the source of the affection that is a part of what they exchange,[46] and that affection strengthens the relationship between the two. And this is no small thing, for the husband-wife relationship is one of the two relationships from which the household arises, and its strength is the strength of the household as a whole.

4. Relationships within the household: parents and children

Now that we have addressed the first ruler-ruled pair within the household, we move on to that which naturally flows from it: the parent-child relationship. Now, it was mentioned above that the relationship between parents and children is also a relationship between unequals, but that it differs in kind from the other relationships between unequals.[47]

As with the relationship between husband and wife, Aristotle chooses to first illuminate the relationship between fathers and children by analogy to a form of political rule (in this case, kingship):

> The friendship of a king for those who live under his rule depends on his superior ability to do good. He confers benefits upon his subjects, since he is good and cares for them in order to promote their welfare, just as a shepherd cares for his sheep. Hence, Homer spoke of Agamemnon as "shepherd of the people." The friendship

---

45. *Ethics* VIII.12, 1162a24.
46. *Ethics* VIII.7, 1158b12.
47. "The friendship which parents have for their children is not the same as that which a ruler has for his subjects, and even the friendship of a father for his son is different from that of the son for his father…" (*Ethics* VIII.7, 1158b14).

of a father [for his children] is of the same kind, but it differs in the magnitude of benefits bestowed. For he is the author of their being, which is regarded as the greatest good, and he is responsible for maintaining and educating them.... Furthermore, it is by nature that a father rules over his children, ancestors over their descendants, and a king over his subjects. These kinds of friendship depend on superiority, and that is why we [do not only love but] also honor our parents. Accordingly, in those relationships the same thing is not just for both partners, but what is just depends on worth or merit, and the same is true for friendship.[48]

So once again we are presented with a conundrum: we know that the relationship between parent and child is a relationship between unequals, and thus they cannot give each other the same things. But in order for there to be a friendship at all, there must be some exchange of what each is able to give, and what each owes to the other, in order to make right the inequality between them, to the extent that this is possible. So now we must investigate what it is that is given and exchanged, if we are to know anything further about the relationship between the two.

We have already seen that the father, as the author of the child's being, gives him a good that is regarded by some as the greatest good, and one which is certainly impossible to repay. Further, he is responsible for the education and maintenance of his children. So what is it that the child can possibly give his parents in return? About this Aristotle says the following:

> Friendship demands the possible; it does not demand what the giver deserves. In some cases, in fact, it is impossible to make the kind of return which the giver deserves, for instance, in the honors we pay to the gods and to our parents. Here no one could ever make a worthy return, and we regard a man as good if he serves them to the best of his ability.[49]

Thus, what is expected of the child is that he honor his parents as much as is possible (because honor is what he is capable of giving), never forgetting that they have given him his very being, without

---

48. *Ethics* VIII.11, 1161a11.
49. *Ethics* VIII.14, 1163b15.

which none of the other things which he enjoys would even be possible.[50]

The parents' responsibility for their child's education refers not just to his formal education, but also to his moral education. The moral education of the child could even be said to be the parents' primary duty towards their children. For indeed, the formal education of the child begins comparatively late in his development—say, at age seven or so. But the parents' role in the moral education of their child could be said to begin almost as soon as the child is born. Children begin to absorb information quite early, even before they are really capable of communicating. The family environment—the character of which is determined entirely by the parents—has a tremendous influence on the child's later outlook on life.

The parents are responsible for the discipline of their children, and this lays the foundation for the child's moral life. During the child's journey towards full rationality, he relies on his parents to direct his passions where he lacks the rationality to do so. The parents' punishment of the child (corporal or otherwise) helps the child to develop the proper attitudes towards pleasure and pain, which are integral to the development of the habit of virtue. And the example of the child's virtuous parents provides him with models for his own development. A child who grows up within a strong, properly ordered marriage and household, in which all of the adult members aim at the good, has a significant advantage when it comes time for him to devote himself to the art of household management.

It seems that for the parent who is himself virtuous, and thus correctly understands the end of man, the desire to "create something in his own image"[51] extends further than merely producing offspring. Rather, he desires for his child to reach maturity and realize his own end as a rational animal. A parent is grief-stricken when his

---

50. The gift of one's being is so great that the debt which the child owes to his parents is even owed to the parent who neglects the child in other respects—say, formal education. The parent who neglects his responsibility to his child has still given the child his being, and thus deserves the respect of the child.

51. See *Politics* I.2, 1252a30.

child dies before reaching maturity not merely because he has lost his child, but also because that child died before he was able to have children of his own and enjoy the rational perfection that is attainable only in adulthood.

At any rate, while the virtuous parent cannot attain moral perfection *for* his child, he will understand the importance of laying the proper foundation for the child's later moral development. In short, he does as much to ensure his child's mature happiness as he possibly can.

5. Relationships within the household: master and slave

At the very beginning of the *Politics*, Aristotle says that household arises out of two relationships: the relationship between man and woman and the relationship between master and slave.[52] We have already examined the relationship between man and woman, and the parent-child relationship which stems from the marriage of man and woman. Now we turn to the master-slave relationship.

Just as man and woman cannot exist without each other, but must unite so that the human race may continue, so must there be a union of master and slave, "that both may be preserved."[53] "For that which can foresee by the exercise of the mind is by nature intended to be lord and master, and that which can with its body give effect to such foresight is a subject, and by nature a slave; hence master and slave have the same interest."[54] Hence, the slave is a "living instrument," by which the will of the master is effected. This is not to the master's advantage in a way that is detrimental to the slave. It is according to nature, and thus, it is to the advantage of both. For "ruling and being ruled belong not only among things necessary but also among things advantageous."[55]

In this particular case, it is clear that the advantage of the ruler lies in receiving the services of his slave. If the household exists to secure the necessary advantages of life, it would seem that the

---

52. *Politics* I.2, 1252b9.
53. Ibid., 1252a31.
54. Ibid., 1252a32.
55. *Politics* I.5 (Lord), 1254a21.

nuclear family will require more than slight assistance in doing so, and the employment of slave labor makes this possible. The advantage to the slave is more difficult to see. Aristotle puts it thus:

> Accordingly, those who are as different [from other men] as the soul from the body or man from beast—and they are in this state if their work is the use of the body, and if this is the best that can come from them—are slaves by nature. For them it is better to be ruled in accordance with this sort of rule, if such is the case for the other things mentioned. For he is a slave by nature who is capable of belonging to another—which is also why he belongs to another—and who participates in reason only to the extent of perceiving it, but does not have it. (The other animals, not perceiving reason, obey their passions.)[56]

Without his master, the slave would be left in the thrall of his passions. He would neither see the proper ends nor the means for reaching those ends.

Now it is obvious that it will be better for a man to be enslaved only if his relationship to his master is according to nature, and the master desires to direct the slave towards his proper end. Further, the fact that Aristotle conceives of natural slavery as being of mutual advantage to both master and slave does not mean that he believes all slavery to be just. If one were to enslave someone perfectly capable of determining the proper ends and the means for reaching them, one would do a grave injustice.

We should not neglect to note here that, as with the other ruler-ruled relationships within the household, Aristotle compares the master-slave to a form of political rule: "The association of master and slave, too, is tyrannical, since it is the master's advantage which is accomplished in it."[57] Despite the fact that Aristotle elsewhere condemns tyranny as an unjust form of rule, he says immediately after this last quote that the tyranny of masters over slaves is a "correct" form of tyranny—undoubtedly because, as we can see from what has been cited above, he believes that the slave does in fact exist

---

56. Ibid., I.5, 1254b16.
57. *Ethics* VIII.10, 1160b29.

for the sake of the master, almost as a part of his own body. This is different from political tyranny, in which a free man perfectly capable of deliberation and choice is forced to live for the sake of another—a grave injustice, and contrary to nature, as was discussed above.

This is, perhaps, one of Aristotle's most controversial doctrines, but it is not within the scope of this thesis to discuss whether or not natural slaves actually exist. Rather, for our purposes it has been sufficient merely to outline what Aristotle says about natural slaves, so that we can develop a comprehensive idea of what Aristotle believes the household to consist of, and so that we may see that he believes the household to be able to incorporate and order all the members of society.

6. Other selves and commonness within the household

Now that we have discussed the basic aspects of all of the ruler-ruled relationships within the household, we will turn our attention to how the household relates to the state. One of the primary ways in which the household prepares those within it for their life in the state is through friendship within the family. The household is peculiarly able to develop its members' idea of friendship: not merely because it provides one's first experience of companionship, but because the experience of "another self" within the household is had in a unique way and the experience of a common life is thorough-going. And it would seem that these two things are fundamental to friendship, and that a good understanding of them (which a well-ordered household can provide) will be essential to a full conception of the meaning of friendship outside the household.

Though the idea of the "other self" and the having of things in common are present to a greater or lesser extent in all of the relationships within the household, this essay will closely examine their role in only two relationships: the parent-child and fraternal friendships.[58] Not only are the idea of the "other self" and commonness

---

58. Of course, the strength of the relationship between the husband and the wife—which is also based on the idea of the "other self" and on commonness—is presupposed to the strength of the parent-child and fraternal relationships.

perhaps more apparent in these two relationships than in the others, but it would seem that it is in these two relationships that these elements play the most significant role in developing those involved. Because the parent sees his child as another self, he has a bond with the child that strengthens his ability to contribute to the child's formation. Likewise, the child is more easily formed by his parent because he will eventually in turn see his parent as another self. Finally, the high degree of commonness within the household (especially between siblings) contributes to the proper development of the child's understanding of what is essential to friendship—an understanding that will influence the formation of his mature friendships within the state.

First, we will address Aristotle's idea that in the ideal friendship, each party will look upon the other as an "other self." He says in the *Ethics*: "The perfect form of friendship is that between good men who are alike in excellence or virtue."[59] So he establishes the idea of likeness, which is important because, as he reminds us: "[Friendship between virtuous equals], then, is perfect and complete friendship, both in terms of time and in all other respects, and each partner receives in all matters what he gives the other, in the same or in a similar form; that is what friends should be able to count on."[60] The idea of the other self is explicitly established in Book IX of the *Ethics*:

> We count as a friend a person who wishes for and does what is good or what appears to him to be good for his friend's sake; or a person who wishes for the existence and life of his friend for his friend's sake.... We regard as a friend also a person who spends his time in our company and whose desires are the same as ours, or a person who shares sorrow and joy with his friend.... A good man has every one of these sentiments towards himself.... He has the same attitude toward his friend as he does toward himself, for his friend really is another self....[61]

---

59. *Ethics* VIII.3, 1156b7.
60. *Ethics* VIII.4, 1156b33.
61. *Ethics* IX.4, 1166a3.

Aristotle on the Relationship of Household to State

In Aristotle's account of the matter, the other self in the friendship of the good man is not a clone, but an extension of one's self.[62] As such, the good of the other self is in some sense the good of the individual himself. And while the other selves found within the family are of necessity somewhat different from those found in the perfect friendship of virtuous equals, the other selves within the family make particularly manifest this idea of the extension of self, since the idea could be said to be less analogous within the family than elsewhere.

It would seem that since the child is from his parents, the parent would see the child as another self. It would also seem that, given the child's imperfect understanding of the world around him, it would take longer for the child to see the parent as another self, and even then, that it would be to a lesser degree. Aristotle discusses the parent-child relationship while discussing how all of the friendships between kinsmen seem to depend on parental friendship:

> For parents love their children as something which belongs to them, while children love their parents because they owe their being to them. But parents know better that the offspring is theirs than children know that they are their parents' offspring, and the bond which ties the begetter to the begotten is closer than that which ties the generated to its author. For that which has sprung from a thing belongs to its source, for example, a tooth, a hair, and so forth belongs to its source, but the source does not belong at all—or only to a lesser degree—to that which has sprung from it.[63]

The parents' role in the creation of the child, their awareness of themselves and their action as cause of the child's being, and of his being as the *particular* individual that he is, with a specific material form, contributes to their seeing the child as an "other self." He has his father's eyes, his mother's nose, sets his jaw like his father when angry, and has his mother's love of animals. It is the parents who provide the matter which individuates the child and makes him the

---

62. "For, as we have stated, all friendly feelings toward others are an extension of the friendly feelings a person has for himself" (*Ethics* IX.8, 1168b5).
63. *Ethics* VIII.12, 1161b18.

particular human being that he is. As such, he resembles them in innumerable ways, but particularly in his appearance and temperament. Further, since they are the first people he knows, and it is within their home that he grows toward adulthood, he will resemble them in his speech (i.e., vocabulary and idiom) and mannerisms and opinions—the things that are learned.

The child springs from the union of his parents, but as soon as he is born he begins to make continuous progress towards the point at which he will be completely independent of them. It is always clear to the parent that the child is of their union, and belongs to them even in his very form, but the parents do not belong to the child in the same way.

> Moreover, [there is also a difference between the love of parents and the love of children] in point of time: parents love their children as soon as they are born, but children love their parents only as, with the passage of time, they acquire understanding or perception. This also explains why affection felt by mothers is greater [than that of fathers].[64]

As we discussed earlier, the child comes into existence within his mother's body, during which time the child is continuous with her, and then, after she is delivered of the child, she nourishes him with her own body. There is never any question that the child is of *herself*. The father, not having the same physical connection with the child, will probably only begin to feel a strong attachment for the child as his own when the child is born, when he can begin to *see* that the child is like him and when he begins to form him after himself by teaching him what he knows. The child, on the other hand, needs to acquire an *understanding* of his parents as a cause of himself, needs time to realize his particular connection to them, and to discover the various ways in which he resembles his parents. As this knowledge unfolds, he will begin to ask his parents questions about what they were like at the corresponding stages of their development, and see that they can give him better advice because of their similar experiences—not just as human beings, but as human

---

64. Ibid., 1161b30.

beings with similar personalities. That is to say, he begins to recognize the fact that his parents have selves like his own.

Brothers, too, see each other as "other selves."

> Brothers love one another because they were born of the same parents: the identical relation they have with their parents makes them identical with one another. This is the origin of expressions like "of the same blood," "of the same stock," and so forth. Brothers are, therefore, in a sense identical, though the identity resides in separate persons. Of great importance to friendship is common upbringing and closeness in age....[65]

The sharing of parents means more than a common experience, more than merely being raised in the same household: everything that is meant by the child having a formal resemblance to the parent is also implied here. Brothers are similar in appearance and in tendencies—they share in a lineage and upbringing that shapes their identity and their experience of the world.

This emphasis on the role of the "other self" is not to imply, however, that the "having of things in common" (both materially and in terms of having a common experience) is of lesser importance to the relationships within the family. Aristotle addresses this specifically in the *Ethics*:

> Friendship is present to the extent that men share something in common, for that is also the extent to which they share a view of what is just. And the proverb "friends hold in common what they have" is correct, for friendship consists in community. Brothers and bosom companions hold everything in common, while all others only hold certain definite things in common—some more and others less, since some friends are more intense than others.[66]

The having of things in common takes place to the greatest extent within the family. Not only do the members of the family share in the "necessaries of life," as well as in a common experience and a common end, but they have these things in common with people who are "other selves." Further, because every family springs from

---

65. Ibid., 1162a8.
66. *Ethics* VIII.9, 1159b29.

the union of unique individuals, the character of every family is different, even amongst families that alike understand the proper aim of the family and are properly ordered. These differences between families create a unique environment and experience for those within the family.

Aristotle believes that, in fact, the relationships within the family are more pleasant and more useful because of the high degree of commonness.

> But [the friendship between children and parents] has also a higher degree of what is pleasant and useful than does friendship with persons outside the family, inasmuch as the partners have more of their life in common. Friendship between brothers has elements which are also found in friendship between bosom companions. It has them in a higher degree when the brothers are good men and, in general, when they are like one another, inasmuch as they are more closely linked together and have been loving one another since birth, and inasmuch as children of the same parents, who have been brought up together and have received a similar education, are more alike in character. Also, there is the test of time to which brothers are subjected more thoroughly and reliably than anyone else.[67]

It is only difference in age which causes inequality between brothers within the same family, and this inequality is only temporary—it will cease to exist when they reach maturity. Thus, the high degree of commonness between brothers likens their friendship to the friendship between equal bosom companions. Further, commonness develops a trust and familiarity between brothers which contributes to the strength of their unique bond. The "test of time" that Aristotle refers to at the end of the last quote brings to mind something he says earlier in the *Ethics*, about the ideal friendship between virtuous men:

> Such friendships [between men alike in excellence or virtue] are of course rare, since such men are few. Moreover, time and familiarity are required. For, as the proverb has it, people cannot know each other until they have eaten the specified salt together. One

---

67. *Ethics* VIII.12, 1162a8.

cannot extend friendship to or be a friend of another person until each partner has impressed the other that he is worthy of affection, and until each has won the other's confidence.[68]

The closeness between family members, which has to do with both the idea of the "other self" and commonness, is especially important to the formation of the children. Firstly, it makes possible the bond between parents and children that both moves the parents to care for their child's formation, and which disposes the child towards being formed by his parents. Secondly, it provides the child's first experience of love and companionship, and as such is the standard by which all of his subsequent friendships outside of the family will be measured. It is important that the children have this standard because, as we have seen, it is the best and most ideal friendships, the friendships between virtuous equals, which (outside the household) place the greatest emphasis on "other-self-ness" and commonness, and which most resemble brotherhood. The more an individual desires these things in a friendship, and the more inclined he is to require them, the more likely he is to form pure, lasting friendships in which both parties aim at the good, both for each other and universally. Just as the moral virtues properly order and dispose the soul to aim at the good (and so cultivate and perfect the intellectual virtues), so do healthy friendships within the family dispose one to seek the right things in extrafamilial relationships.

It is these friendships between virtuous equals which are necessary both to the development of the moral virtues (for a man is said to be just in relation to his fellow men) and to the development of the intellectual virtues (by making discourse possible)—and which are, as a result, ultimately necessary to man's complete happiness. Of course, these friendships are both impossible without the state and are integral to its aim, to its end of securing the happiness of its citizens. Now that we have seen what a key role properly ordered friendships within the family play in the health of mature, adult friendships within the state, we have a better idea of the importance

---

68. *Ethics* VIII.4, 1156b26.

Integralism and the Common Good

of the health of the family to the effectiveness of the state in achieving its end.

7. The development of moral virtue within the household

We now turn to a consideration of the ways in which the household can be said to form its members with regard to moral virtue.[69] We have already touched on the fact that the parents' approach towards the raising of the children must be one which results in the children having the proper attitude towards pleasure and pain. (Remember that the moral virtues, for Aristotle, are of necessity concerned with pleasure and pain.[70]) The parents' discipline of the children, whether corporal or otherwise, should be such that the child is brought to take pleasure in his right actions, and find his wrong actions causative of pain. Since these attitudes towards pleasure and pain would seem to be more malleable during childhood than they are later in life, the parent must take especial care with the child's moral education.

But it is not only the children who have their moral formation within the household. Recall that Aristotle divides household mastery into three parts: expertise in mastery [over slaves], expertise in marital [rule], and expertise in parental rule. Having addressed each of these three kinds of rule in the *Politics*, he observes that "it is clear that household management attends more to men than to the acquisition of inanimate things, and to human excellence more than the excellence of property which we call wealth...."[71]

Concluding that the excellence of all of the household's members is of primary importance to its head, Aristotle asks whether slaves,

---

69. Though it is true to say that the household can give the child a foundation for intellectual virtue—say, through the development of the child's sense of wonder—the child's formal education is, on Aristotle's account, properly the province of the state. Further, intellectual perfection will be attained through the friendships one forms within the state. It is important to remember that since moral virtue is presupposed to intellectual virtue, and since the household is ordered towards the perfection of all of its members, the household's development of the moral virtue of its members is done with an eye towards the formation of intellectual virtue.
70. See, *inter alia*, Aristotle's *Ethics*, 1104b2–1105a17, 1153b12, and 1153b25.
71. *Politics* I.11, 1259b17.

women, and children can be said to be virtuous. Ultimately, he concludes that they can in fact be said to be virtuous, but that each group has a peculiar virtue suited to its peculiar character. So, then, the head of the household is responsible for a moral formation of those over whom he rules. (We have already seen, of course, that in each of the relationships within the household it is the head of the household—the husband, father, and master—who is the ruler, though the ruled and the character of the rule are different in each relationship.)

In ensuring that there is a proper relationship between ruler and ruled in each of these relationships, the ruler orders things correctly, according to the order of nature. It is a reflection of the social nature of human existence (to say nothing of Aristotle's idea of virtue) that the members of the household do not achieve excellence independently of each other. Rather, the idea of each one's excellence is inextricably linked to his relationship with the other members of the household.

But why is this excellence important to the health of the state? Why should it concern us in our inquiry into the relationship of the household to the city-state? Aristotle concludes the section of the *Politics* in which he discusses the particular virtues of women, children, and slaves with this statement:

> For, inasmuch as every family is part of the state, and these relationships are parts of a family, and the virtue of the part must have regard to the virtue of the whole, women and children must be trained by education with an eye to the constitution, if the virtues of either of them are supposed to make any difference in the virtue of the state. And they must make a difference: for the children grow up to be citizens, and half the free persons in the state are women.[72]

Simply put, then, the virtuousness of the state (which exists for the sake of its citizens living well) is dependent on the virtuousness of its individual members. And this is not merely the concern of the ruler and lawgiver, but also of those who are charged with house-

---

72. *Politics* I.13, 1260b12.

hold management, because it is clear that the ordering nature of rule has the ability to make the ruled excellent. (We remember that moral virtue is itself a correct ordering of the parts of the soul.) Further, ruling well is itself an excellence. So the work of perfect virtue, though not necessarily *completed* within the home, can *at least* be said to be begun there.

The degree to which the perfection of an individual is effected within the household differs, depending on the individual's role within the household. For the head of the household, who is a mature male, the fulfillment of his duties within the household forms only a part of his perfection. His excellence as husband, father, and master is certainly necessary to his possessing the full complement of the moral virtues—to his being a just man. But he has obligations outside of the household, and friendships outside of the household, and so one could not say that all that is required of him lies within the confines of his estate. If he is truly to be just, he must also be excellent with regard to his relationships outside of the household.

The wife and mother can be said to be perfected *within* the household, as can the slave. This is because on Aristotle's view, neither of these can properly be said to have duties outside of the household. The mother is concerned with her husband, her children, and her husband's property (which includes management of the slaves, through the authority delegated to her by her husband). Though the fact that she is rational (and therefore free) allows her to knowingly act for the good of the state (as in, say, the raising of her children), her work with regard to the state remains within the context of the household. And the slaves, as we have said, exist solely to carry out the will of their master with regard to the management of his household and property. As his instruments, they cannot have any legitimate concern with anything that is not their master's.

Finally, the children can in no way become *perfect* within the household, since, as children, they are imperfect, and so must their virtue be imperfect. The male children will ultimately be perfected in adulthood, both through becoming heads of their own households and having a life within the state, outside of their own households. The female children will reach maturity and become wives and mothers, and thus be perfected inside of a household distinct from the one they were born into. Nevertheless, there is still much work to be done with the children, as we have addressed above. Besides their moral formation, their parents are to be concerned with cultivating their sense of wonder (so that they might have a foundation for the intellectual virtues), as well as with communicating to them a sense of the importance of civic virtue, with an eye towards their future as citizens of the state. In all of these things, the example of the parents is of equal importance to direct instruction and discipline.

8. Development of civic virtue within the family

The household can also be seen to contribute to the development of its members' perfection in civic virtue—a particular sort of virtue with regard to one's participation in the political life. One way in which the household can be seen to develop this particular virtue is with regard to the parents. If the end of the particular state that they live within is truly the good for man, they will of course desire to contribute to the perpetuation of that state, so that it may continue to accomplish its end. As such, they will bring forth offspring with an eye towards those children participating in the life of the state, and they will educate their children such that the children have a correct understanding of the regime and its aim.

The children are prepared for the life within the state not only by their parents' instruction, but also by participating (both directly and through observation) in the types of political rule modeled in the relationships within the household. These help them not only to better understand the particular regime under which they live, but also political rule generally.

Finally, all of the freemen within the household (even those who are only properly freemen in potency, as are the children) are brought to a better understanding of the common life and end of the state by their experience of the common endeavor of the household. The household, as that which is better known to all of its members, provides a foundation for understanding the life of the freeman within the state, and as such, plays an irreplaceable role in the strength of the state as a whole.

9. Necessity of the household

Now that we have made a beginning in the investigation into Aristotle's conception of the household and the ways in which it prepares and perfects its members for their life within the state, it is important to consider the fact that the family is a natural institution and, as such, a necessary one. Not only is the work of the family, when properly realized, complementary to the work of the state, but the role that the household plays in the perfection of its members is a role that only the household can play. To destroy the household is to destroy the state.

The first way in which this can be seen to be the case has to do with our earlier discussion of the peculiar nature of both the other-self relationship and commonness within the family. Man has a natural desire to perpetuate his species, a desire which corresponds to the animal aspect of his nature. Parents know their child as a thing which has sprung from them, and they see that child as another self, forming a bond between the parent and the child that could never exist between that child and the state. The fact that the child is "another self" to his parents gives his parents a unique interest in his moral and personal formation—they desire that he realize his end. Further, the parent has a knowledge of his child that enables him to better form that child.[73]

Further, the commonness that occurs within the family contributes to the particular bond that family members have, a bond which, as we have seen, is integral to the moral formation of the members of the household. This particular bond cannot be reproduced outside the household, for the state can give children material things in common, and even a common upbringing and a common end, but it cannot give them the sort of commonness that arises from the knowledge of having sprung from one's parents as from a common source, and from having had alike a personal, formative relationship with those same parents, and with others from the same source.

---

73. The fact that nature imposes limits on the number of children a woman can give birth to contributes to the personal nature of the upbringing one receives within a family.

Aristotle on the Relationship of Household to State

The second way in which the household plays a particular and irreplaceable role in the state has to do with the ordering nature of the ruler-ruled relationships within the household.[74] Here, it will be helpful to look at Aristotle's general treatment of rule, at the beginning of chapter 5 of the *Politics*:

> Ruling and being ruled belong not only among things necessary but also among things advantageous. And immediately from birth certain things diverge, some toward being ruled, others towards ruling. There are many kinds both of ruling and ruled, and the better rule is always that over ruled that are better, for example over a human being rather than a beast; for the work performed by the better is better, and wherever something rules and something is ruled there is a certain work belonging to these together.[75]

For Aristotle, then, the members of the household will properly be either ruling or ruled beings, by nature and from birth. Not only will they have this character, but if they neglect it, there will be disorder and unhappiness. For if ruling and being ruled are not only necessary, but advantageous, and there is a certain work that belongs to ruler and ruled together, then both will be at a disadvantage if that work is not taken up.

Of course, the members of the household may be rulers in some respects and ruled in others, as the head of the household may rule all within, but may himself be subject to a monarch, when considered as citizen. Further, they may be suited to be ruled for a time—as children are—but at some point (say, as children do, upon reaching maturity) become themselves capable of rule. What is important to see here is that a given individual must be properly ordered *in every area of his life in which there can be said to be a ruler-ruled relationship.*

In order to better understand this, it will be helpful to see examples of the various ruler-ruled relationships which a given individual might be expected to order himself in relation to. Just after the

---

74. Recall that Aristotle says that expertise in household mastery has to do with the three kinds of rule: mastery, marital rule and parental rule (*Politics* I.5 [Lord], 1253b8).

75. *Politics* I.5, 1254a21.

general discussion of rule quoted above, Aristotle goes on to give specific examples of various ruler-ruled relationships.

> For whatever is constituted out of a number of things—whether continuous or discrete—and becomes a single common thing always displays a ruling and a ruled element; this is something that animate things derive from all of nature.... But an animal is the first thing constituted of soul and body, of which the one thing is the ruling element by nature, the other the ruled....
>
> It is then in an animal, as we were saying, that one can first discern both the sort of rule characteristic of a master and political rule. For the soul rules the body with the rule characteristic of a master, while intellect rules appetite with political and kingly rule; and this makes it evident that it is according to nature and advantageous for the body to be ruled by the soul, and the passionate part by intellect and the part having reason, while it is harmful to both if the relation is equal or reversed.... Further, the relation of male to female is by nature a relation of superior to inferior and ruler to ruled. The same must of necessity hold in the case of human beings generally.[76]

Here, Aristotle begins with what is most fundamental: the fact that the body is properly ruled by the soul. And the soul itself is divided into the rational and irrational parts, and according to nature, the rational is to rule the irrational. Finally, he gives an example of human beings ruling each other, saying that nature also dictates that the male rule the female.

So we can see that an individual man will have many ruler-ruled relationships that he must account for, both within himself and between himself and others. Since all of these exist according to nature, it is clear that the proper ordering of each of them is to his advantage. Further, if any one of them were to be neglected or perverted, the ordering of his entire being (necessary for moral and intellectual virtue, and thus, for the attainment of his highest end) would be adversely affected. Thus, the household is necessary to the complete ordering and perfection of the individual.

Finally, Aristotle can be seen to argue for the necessity of the fam-

---

76. Ibid., 1254a28.

ily in Book II of the *Politics*, but from a different perspective: not from the nature of the family, but from the nature of the state. He does so in addressing the errors of Socrates' view of the state:

> Further, with respect to the end which he asserts the city should have, it is, as has just been said, impossible; but how one should distinguish [a sense in which it is possible] is not discussed. I mean, that it is best for the city to be as far as possible entirely one; for this is the presupposition Socrates adopts. And yet it is evident that as it becomes increasingly one it will no longer be a city. For the city is in its nature a sort of multitude, and as it becomes more a unity it will be a household instead of a city, and a human being instead of a household; for we would surely say that the household is more of a unity than the city, and the individual than the household. So even if one were able to do this, one ought not to do it, as it would destroy the city. Now the city is made up not only of a number of human beings, but also of human beings differing in kind: a city does not arise from persons who are similar.[77]

Now, we have already established the benefits of the citizens of the state being alike in ideal virtue, and how this makes possible the sort of friendship necessary to their ultimate perfection. So it is clear that when Aristotle says that the city is not constituted of people who are similar, he wants to emphasize the fact that they must have complementary skills and intellectual abilities to offer each other. Indeed, he says soon afterward:

> It is evident in another way as well that to seek to unify the city excessively is not good. For a household is more self-sufficient than one person, and a city than a household; and a city tends to come into being at a point when the partnership formed by a multitude is self-sufficient. If, therefore, the more self-sufficient is more choiceworthy, what is less a unity is more choiceworthy than what is more a unity.[78]

It is, then, the diversity of the contributions of its citizens that makes a polity self-sufficient. These diverse contributions are made possible primarily by the fact that the state consists of different

77. *Politics* II.2, 1261a13.
78. Ibid., 1261b10.

classes of people,[79] but also by the fact that the state is composed of a multitude of households, each of which will have a unique character (derived partly from the fact that it stems from the partnerships of unique individuals) even within a given class, and which will produce citizens with complementary perspectives and abilities. To eliminate the household is to destroy an aspect of the plurality of the state, and so also to destroy its self-sufficiency.

10. Conclusion

It is true to say that the end of the household is properly "the supply of men's everyday wants," because this is what the family is able to bring about *completely*. But we have also seen that, in various ways, the household makes a beginning in the state's project of perfecting its citizens, and that it is the only institution which can play this most necessary role. The fact that the household cannot complete the process of perfection which it begins returns us to our earlier inquiry into the nature of the state's priority to the household. Only the state, because it is self-sufficient and lacking in nothing, can secure man's perfection. Thus, though we are not able to make a comprehensive inquiry into the state's priority, we may ascribe priority to the state at least on the basis of its self-sufficiency, for "to be self-sufficing is the end and best."[80] And this understanding of the priority of the state to the household would seem to inform our primary discussion of the ordering of the household to the state. For if the members of the household are to find the perfection and happiness that they seek, they must realize that only the state can perfect them.

---

79. See *Politics* III.4, 1277a4, and IV.3, 1289b27.
80. *Politics* I.2, 1252b34.

8

The End of the Family and the End of Civil Society

Charles De Koninck

Editorial Note

In 1943 the Belgian-born dean of the department of philosophy at the University of Laval in Quebec, Charles De Koninck (1906–1965), published his controversial book *On the Primacy of the Common Good: Against the Personalists*, in which he argued that the private good of persons is subordinate to their common good. While De Koninck took pains to show that his position is not totalitarian, nevertheless, many of his critics remained unconvinced. One of the objections that he anticipates, but which was nevertheless repeated by his critics, was that the free man is *causa sui* (for his own sake), and that therefore it would be repugnant to his dignity to be ordered to the good of the community. De Koninck responds as follows:

> To the second part of the objection we reply that the proposition *liberum est quod causa sui est* must be understood not as meaning that the free agent is the cause of himself, or that he is, as such, the perfection for which he acts, but as meaning rather that he is himself, by his intellect and will, the cause of his act for the end to which he is ordered. One could also say that he is cause of himself in the line of final cause, insofar as he bears himself towards the end to which he is called as an intelligent and free agent, that is according to the principles themselves of his nature. But this end consists principally in the common good. The agent will be so much the more free and noble as he orders himself more perfectly to the common good. Hence one sees how the latter is the first principle of our free condition. The free agent would place himself in the condition of a slave if by himself he could not or would not

act except for the singular good of his person. Man retains no less his free state when, by his own reason and will, he submits himself to a reason and will which are superior. Thus it is that citizen subjects can act as free men, for the common good.[1]

Indeed, he argues that for a good to be truly common all must share in it. The common good is not the good of civil society considered as a quasi-individual; it is the good of the members of the community, and in fact their greatest natural good. This means that every member of the community must participate in the common good. In the following lecture De Koninck draws the rather strong conclusion from this that every member of a civil society must be a citizen. This conclusion seems too strong since one can participate in the common good by being a subject as well as a citizen, because obedience to the civil authority, as the minister of God, is ultimately obedience to God, "whom to serve is to reign."

The following lecture is, however, primarily concerned with showing that the family is ordered to preparing children to participate in the common good, and that the state therefore destroys itself when it usurps the functions of the family. The lecture is here published for the first time, transcribed from a typescript with handwritten emendations, probably written circa 1950.—*Editors*

* * *

I was asked to treat the present subject from the philosophical point of view. It is for this reason that I mention neither the sacrament of marriage nor the supernatural society which is the Church. Our viewpoint, however, is no less philosophical for being that of Christian philosophy. In fact, the chief basis for the present paper is none other than the Encyclicals of Pius XI: *Divini Illius Magistri* and *Casti Connubii*.

Of a family we say that it is good, when, faithful to the indissoluble union which they have vowed, husband and wife do all they can to provide their offspring with proper nourishment and education. This is the fundamental criterion, for the primary end of marriage

---

1. *Primacy of the Common Good* (Collins trans.), 70–71.

The End of the Family and the End of Civil Society

is the child; whereas the form and principle of the family consists mainly in the union of mind and heart between husband and wife, primarily in view of the child not only as to its generation, but even more so for the sake of its education to manhood. For this reason, whatever is characteristic of the married person must somehow be related to the child. Even the friendship of husband and wife (of which Aristotle has spoken so well in the *Ethics*) is intrinsic to marriage itself and must therefore be ultimately based on their union for the sake of the child whose education is the main reason for the indissoluble character of wedlock.

At this juncture a first difficulty may be raised against this doctrine. It seems that the end of marriage as well as the persons of husband and wife are altogether minimized if we confine them in the perspective of the child.

This objection may arise from the fact that on the one hand we seek in the family more than it is and on the other hand we would reduce the persons who make up the family to what they are insofar as they are members of this imperfect society, and correspondingly reduce their good to that which is theirs as members of such a society. For although the family is indeed a society in the strict sense of that term, it remains an imperfect one, as Pius XI states it in the Encyclical *Divini Illius Magistri*: "The family enjoys a priority both of nature and of right over civil society. Nevertheless, the family is an imperfect society, since it has not in itself all the means which are required for a perfect achievement of its end; whereas civil society is a perfect society, having all those things which are necessary to its proper end—the common good of our present life on earth. It is by virtue of this common good that civil society has pre-eminence over the family: only in the common weal can the family attain with security and propriety that temporal perfection which is its aim." Hence we should not expect to find within the confines of the family the fullness of the temporal good of man *qua* man.

What is this temporal good, which, absolutely speaking, is superior to that of the family? The same document replies: "It consists in the peace and security which the families and individual citizens enjoy in the exercise of their rights as well as in the greatest spiritual and material wealth that can be obtained in this life thanks to the

Integralism and the Common Good

concerted efforts of all." Note, particularly, that the temporal common good is not restricted to material wealth, but comprises spiritual goods, such as a wise legislation, not to mention "the arts and the sciences which make for the wealth and prosperity of civil society" (ibid.).

Because the family is an imperfect society which cannot reach even its own end outside the political community, both the latter and the former may tend, in practice, to transgress their respective limits. Nor are these limits always easy to define—even when we prescind from man's ordination to a common good far superior to that of civil society. However, the very fact that on the one hand the family is not self-sufficient in the pursuit of its own end, and that on the other hand the end of civil society is quite distinct from the former, may serve as the basis for a distinction to be made in the realm of civil society itself.

The primary end of the family is the education of the child to the maturity of manhood. This is an inalienable right of the family, since, as St. Thomas says: "the child is something of the parent."[2]

These words of the Angelic Doctor are quoted by Pius XI in the above-mentioned Encyclical. Yet, even here, "the family is not a perfect society which embraces all that is required for its own perfection." As Pius XI expressly points out: "the common good demands that the State promote the education and learning of youth in various ways," which must, of course, be performed with due respect for, and in conformity with, the innate rights of the family. The question is: how can the common good demand that civil society should share in promoting the good that is proper to the family? Must this be interpreted to mean that the common good of political society is subordinate to the good of the family? That the perfect society is subservient to the imperfect one? By no means; the contradiction is all too obvious. What, then, is the answer?

You may have noticed that in a passage already quoted from the Encyclical, the common good of civil society refers to the families and to the individual citizens: *"familiae singulique cives."* The same distinction is applied in the sentence which immediately follows:

2. *ST* II-II, q. 10, a. 12.

The End of the Family and the End of Civil Society

"The function of the authority which resides in the State is twofold: to protect and to further the family and the individual citizen, but not in the least by absorbing or replacing them." Family and individual citizen are not the same. Man is not born a citizen, the child is not as yet *causa sui*: in fact, the end of the family is to lead the child toward the status of *causa sui*. But until he has reached this status he belongs to the parent. "Prior to becoming a citizen, man must live, and this life he does not receive from the State, but from his parents. As Leo XIII declared: 'The children are something of the father; an extension, as it were, of the father's person; to be exact, they enter into and participate in civil society, not immediately by themselves, but through the domestic community in which they are born.... The authority of the father is such that it can neither be suppressed nor absorbed by the State'...." Hence, in this respect, the parent *qua* parent as well as the child are, normally, beyond the reach of the State. It is the parent as citizen who immediately, and by himself, enters into civil society. How, then, can the family concern the State? How can the common good demand that the State further the proper good of the family?

We have just pointed out that the good which the family pursues for the child is the status of *causa sui*, of being a free man: but this is precisely the primary condition of citizenship. The term of education is at the same time the very principle of civil society, which is an association of free men who seek their greatest good *qua* men in the common weal. It is therefore in the interest of civil society that its members be free men in the strict sense of the word: that they possess the education and learning essential to citizenship. That is why the common good of civil society must extend to the cradle of citizenship.

Obviously, the common good of civil society and the authority which resides in the government do not extend in the same manner to the family and to the individual citizen. Nevertheless, the end is the same in both instances. The end proper to political society is the common good of the citizen as such—of the freeman—"who can participate in deliberative or judicial office,"[3] whether directly or

---

3. Aristotle, *Politics* III.1.

indirectly. However, even in helping the family to achieve its own good—the perfection of the offspring—the State pursues this good only in virtue of, and for the sake of, the perfect human good which is proper to civil society.

Although the two have their principle and term in the same common good, we must distinguish the function of the State with regard to the individual citizen from its function in regard to the family. In protecting and helping the latter, the State meets a requirement which was already fulfilled to a degree in the pre-political stage of society. The needs of the individual family are such that it naturally seeks the facilities and security which result from inter-family cooperation. However, so long as the family turns to a larger group for the mere sake of its own good, not even the parents may be called free men and citizens in the true sense of these terms. Such persons do not as yet form a civil society. In this pre-political stage, social functions are merely social, confined as they are to the sole benefit of the family. The good of such a society is a certain common good, but it does not provide the *bene esse* which man is to attain as a citizen. It has more the nature of what is merely *useful* (*bonum utile*) and not strictly a common good. Social assistance, thus understood, is not political, since it is not yet practiced in view of the perfect human good. In fact, it is not even ordered to the true good of the family itself, which is a good to be achieved, not by *social* assistance alone, but by the assistance of *civil* society, i.e., in conformity with the perfect human good. This distinction, I fear, may reveal a sad state of affairs. The person whose concern is restricted to the individual good as such, *qua* a good that he may derive from association with others, does not deserve the name of citizen. For the same reason, a family which—though materially belonging to the civil community—is interested only in the kind of social assistance (but "more of it") which can be found in the pre-political stage of society, is not a good family: it does not pursue even its own true good—to make the child a free man is hardly the ideal that consistently governs its behavior. The citizen who, in voting, gives preference to the candidate from whose election he hopes to derive the greater personal good, forfeits his citizenship. It is only in a material sense that he acts as a free man, as a citizen proper.

The End of the Family and the End of Civil Society

And in voting for a man who promises a good for the family, which is harmful to the common good of the political community, the father turns against the family itself, and so against himself as a father.

If there is always the danger that the State may exceed the limits of its rightful power, there is an equal menace—resulting in a tyranny *sui generis*—in the family which seeks above all its own good. Such a good is of course no more than an apparent one. When the security of civil society is sacrificed to the material security of the family, the latter destroys its own true security. Perhaps there is no better criterion of the good citizen and the good family than the one which both St. Augustine and St. Thomas have quoted from Valerius Maximus: "The citizens of Rome preferred to be poor in a wealthy republic, rather than be wealthy in a poor republic."

This doctrine must not be interpreted to mean that the family or the individual citizen should blindly submit to whatever the government may plan or devise for them in the "name" of the common good. The child is subject to its parents, but neither the citizen nor the family are subjects to the State. Only under tyrannical government is the citizen reduced to the condition of subject—and he accordingly ceases to enjoy citizenship. When the State supplants either the family or the individual citizen, it has thereby destroyed itself as a civil society, for the latter is an association of citizens, and the citizen is by nature a free man. Again, it is the citizen that is attacked when the State assumes the authority of the father, since only the family whose rights are protected and whose needs are met in conformity with its own nature, can foster the child toward the status of free man.

9

The Mirror of the Benedict Option[1]

Edmund Waldstein, O.Cist.

One of the great sorrows that I encounter as a priest is the sorrow of parents whose children have abandoned the Faith. Their sorrow can be more bitter even than the sorrow of those parents who suffer the *fata aspera* of having to bury their children. To have given the gift of life, only to see that gift taken too soon, and to be able to give only the "unavailing gift" of funeral flowers, is a bitter fate indeed. But for those who have come to believe that true life is the eternal life of Christ, it is still more bitter to have brought a child to the waters of Baptism, hoping for that child to receive a share in the inheritance of infinite bliss, only to see that child trade the infinite good for the vain pomps of this world. If it were not for the hope of future repentance, this would be almost too much to bear. And yet, it is a sorrow that Christian parents have had to bear at all times. Children of believing parents have been abandoning the narrow way that leads to eternal life since the Church began. But the great falling away from the faith in Austria in the past five or six decades or so have given so *many* parents that sorrow. It is of course difficult to tell whether that is because hyper-modern culture has actually led more children astray, or whether it has simply made straying more obvious; previous generations of worldly children were perhaps better at pretending to their parents that they were still in a state of grace. When I tell such parents that I come from a family of eight children they often ask me whether all of my brothers and sisters are still practicing Catholics. And when I

---

1. A review of Rod Dreher, *The Benedict Option: A Strategy for Christians in a Post-Christian Nation* (New York: Sentinel, 2017).

The Mirror of the Benedict Option

answer affirmatively they invariably ask: "How did your parents do it?"

That question occurred to me again as I read Rod Dreher's *The Benedict Option*. Dreher's book is largely about the question of how parents can so live their lives that they can communicate the joy of life in Christ to their children. How can they avoid the pressures of a secular culture that seems ever more successful at drawing souls away? Dreher's book made me reflect on my own experience, and so this review will have a somewhat autobiographical character. Readers who find such an intrusion of the autobiographical boastful or self-absorbed need read no further; they are unlikely to like Dreher's book either, since he too illustrates his arguments from his own experience. My intention is not to hold up my own upbringing and family as an exemplar of perfection, nor to suggest that parents *must* do something similar to my parents if their children are to keep the faith—there are contrary examples—but simply to give an illustration of one possible answer to the question of how parents can help their children keep the Faith.

Dreher comes at the question from the perspective of someone who was once a mainstream, "conservative," American, political journalist. As one would expect, he thought that American culture was basically good, and that if only enough conservatives could get elected and roll back the interference of the liberal elites, the basic goodness of America would assert itself. But, he tells us, having children made him question this view. In his 2006 book *Crunchy Cons*, Dreher described how he came to see mainstream conservatism as a false alternative to liberalism. When push comes to shove, Dreher saw, American liberals and conservatives were both committed to liberating human desires in ways destructive to true human flourishing. Liberals worship the sexual revolution—so destructive of the family—while paying lip-service to a concern for regulating the economy in the interests of social equality and stability. Conservatives, on the other hand, pay lip-service to moral restraint in sexual matters, while extolling as "the holy of holies" a free market that is "destroying communities and turning us all into slaves of the economy." In reality, Dreher saw, mainstream American politics were a debate among different sorts of liberals. Naturally enough, this led him to an interest in the work of the philosopher Alasdair MacIntyre.

MacIntyre had long been arguing that modern liberalism sets the terms of contemporary political debate such that any quarrel or conflict *with* liberalism is transformed to a debate *within* liberalism. Political debate thus becomes a debate between "conservative liberals, liberal liberals, and radical liberals." Liberalism, according to MacIntyre, claims to provide a neutral framework in which all individuals can pursue the ends that they themselves consider to be good. But such supposed neutrality actually embodies an individualistic, subjectivist theory of the good "inimical to the construction and sustaining of the types of communal relationship required for the best kind of human life." He concludes that engaging in conventional modern party politics is counter-productive, since such politics is an institutionalized rejection of the tradition of the virtues that once fostered the sorts of human relations aimed at true human happiness. Participation in such politics transforms one into a liberal opposed to the true human good.[2]

At the end of his 1981 masterpiece *After Virtue*, MacIntyre suggested that the alternative to participating in liberal politics was to be found in the construction of "new forms of community" in which the true goods of human life could be pursued. Just as Benedictine monasticism was a new form of community that preserved the tradition of the virtues at the time of the barbarian invasions, so we are waiting for a new St. Benedict to begin a form of community that could preserve that tradition in our time of liberal hegemony. And just as Benedictine monasticism was the seed from which the culture of the Middle Ages was to spring, so might we hope that a new St. Benedict might be the seed for a new virtuous culture of the future. (I once cited this passage with approval in a lecture on rejecting modern politics.[3])

Dreher found MacIntyre's argument convincing, and at the end of *Crunchy Cons* he spoke of the "Benedict Option," as the choice of giving up the mainstream American conservative project, and turn-

---

2. See John Francis Nieto's similar argument in chapter 28.
3. See chapter 23.

The Mirror of the Benedict Option

ing attention instead to forming virtuous communities on a small scale. Now, after years of answering questions and objections to the Benedict Option on his blog, and of live blogging his own attempts at taking the Option, Dreher has given us a whole book on the idea. In *The Benedict Option*, Dreher gives a rough sketch of the ills of our liberal culture, together with a narrative of their genesis of a sort to which I am sympathetic.[4] He then examines Benedictine life to distill lessons from it for the "new St. Benedicts" of the Option. Benedict Option communities should learn from the monks that they have to have a life that is ordered to allow the development of virtue; a life focused on solemn liturgical prayer to God; a life of ascetic self-denial in small things to train the heart to fix itself on the goal; a life of stability that resists constant change and distraction; a life really lived in common with others whom one serves and by whom one is served, and from whom one can receive fraternal correction; a life of hospitality and charitable outreach to those outside the community; a life that embodies St. Benedict's sober moderation—neither too harsh nor too soft. Dreher then explores practical suggestions for living out such an option, illustrated by examples of communities whom he sees as already doing so to some degree or another.

Some critics have seen Dreher's book as too radical and alarmist. But Alasdair MacIntyre has criticized it for being on the contrary not radical enough. When asked about the "The Benedict Option Movement" in the Q&A to a recent lecture, MacIntyre claimed that it is still basically conservative—that is, that it does not really escape the liberal framework. To some extent MacIntyre's claim is surely justified. Dreher's arguments for abandoning the American conservative project focus not so much on the essential liberalism of the political framework, as on the fact that conservatives are unable to achieve the goals they ostensibly seek, because "the culture" is shifting beneath their feet. Clearly, from MacIntyre's point of view, this is not to get to the bottom of the problem.

---

4. See my response to Alan Jacobs, "In Defense of a Certain Kind of Story About the Origins of Modernity," *Sancrucensis*, January 14, 2015, https://sancrucensis.wordpress.com/2015/01/14/in-defense-of-a-certain-kind-of-story-about-the-origins-of-modernity/.

Integralism and the Common Good

And yet, it would be unfair to dismiss Dreher's whole book on those grounds. There is much that is truly sensible in Dreher's exploration of how Benedict Option communities can be formed that would be helpful to more consistent anti-liberals. Dreher's reading of the *Holy Rule* has its weaknesses. His understanding of the Benedictine attitude towards ordinary life seems to me to be closer to the bourgeois Puritan attitude analyzed by Max Weber than Benedict is. (I have explored the difference elsewhere.[5]) Dreher was once an American Protestant, and something of the "Protestant ethic" has remained with him. But for the most part the wisdom that Dreher gleans from St. Benedict is solid enough. Particularly notable is his discussion of education, which I take to be the heart of his book.

I am a Cistercian monk in a monastery that has been trying to follow the *Rule* of St. Benedict since its foundation in 1133. Every evening between supper and Compline at my monastery we have "recreation," which means that the silence of work and prayer is relaxed, and for 45 minutes we sit in a parlor and converse. Once when I was novice the conversation at evening recreation happened to turn to the pop musician Michael Jackson. I mentioned that I had never consciously listened to any of Jackson's music, and would not be able to recognize it. The (then) abbot looked at me in surprise, and asked, "Were you raised in a Cistercian monastery?" Obviously, I was not raised in a Cistercian monastery, and yet the question shows that my upbringing had incorporated some of the "monastic" elements that Dreher sees as fundamental to Benedict Option communities.

To be clear, we were never part of a community that tried to escape the "system" of capitalist neoliberalism through agrarian distributism, as some anti-liberal communities have. But then, Dreher never sets the bar so high. He envisions rather a sort of balance between integration into neoliberal society and withdrawal from it. The Benedict Option has been criticized for only really being an

---

5. See my blog-essay "Against the Overrating of Ordinary Life; or C.S. Lewis's Bourgeois Mind," *Sancrucensis*, November 1, 2016, https://sancrucensis.wordpress.com/2016/11/01/against-the-overrating-of ordinary-life-or-c-s-lewiss-bourgeois-mind/.

The Mirror of the Benedict Option

option for the middle classes and the rich, who can afford the leisure and stability that its practices requires. Workers, being at the mercy of the fluctuating labor market, are constrained to spend most of their time working, and often have to move to find jobs. But surely this is more a problem with unjust economic structures than with the Option itself. Certainly, my family was very privileged in this regard. My parents are academics, and my mother was able to stay at home and homeschool the children. We did move around a certain amount for the sake of my father's academic work. But we were always able to find like-minded families in our neighborhood.

Such like-minded families are very important lest the habits that one is trying to form in one's children are erased by peer pressure. Dreher's *beau ideal* of schooling is the small, classical private school, since such schooling naturally forms communities of families. He also discusses homeschooling as an option when no such school is available, emphasizing the importance to homeschoolers of finding an analogous community of families nearby.

Dreher sees the connection between the desire for God and the love of learning (in terms similar to those of Jean Leclercq). Education is a training of the heart in the pursuit of the good, the true, and the beautiful. Not a mere conveying of "information" or "content." But, as St. Benedict says of the monastic life, it is a path that can be narrow and difficult at first before the heart expands and one runs in the inexpressible joy of love. The human soul has to be trained to recognize the highest things, with which it is most deeply related. Popcorn movies are initially more accessible than Shakespeare. To be led to a love of the higher things generally requires both a negative and a positive principle. Negatively, it requires limits on the distractions of superficial "entertainment" that choke the soul in banality. And positively it requires teachers who are themselves full of love for the truth and beauty and goodness, and can therefore practice what Dreher calls "the ancient art of intellectual seduction."

In my family, we were not allowed to watch TV or listen to pop music. But much more important was the positive wooing of the heart with the good, and true, and beautiful. My father is a passionate lover of music, and spent much time listening to recordings of the great masterpieces of Monteverdi, Bach, Mozart, et al. His enthusiasm rubbed off on us children, so that by the time we were teenagers we would stand for hours in line to get good standing-room places at the Vienna State Opera. Both of my parents spent a lot of time reading books out loud to us. Not only when we were too little to read for ourselves, but even after. I remember having not only Tolkien and C.S. Lewis read to us, but also Charlotte Brontë, Daniel Defoe, and even Alessandro Manzoni. The books that my father read out loud to us after dinner made a particularly deep impression on my memory.

I was born in Rome, but we soon moved to Boston, Massachusetts, and then, when I was four years old, to South Bend, Indiana, where my father taught at Notre Dame. Every day we would go to Mass at 5:15 PM at the beautiful Sacred Heart Basilica at Notre Dame, meeting my father there, before returning home with him for supper, reading out loud, and evening prayers. As a little child I was often bored in church, as little children generally are. A colleague of my father's at Notre Dame, who also brought his children to daily Mass, would respond to them when they said that Mass was boring with the words: "Good. Mass isn't about you having fun; Mass is about God." In my case the way was narrow at first, and I was often punished for misbehaving, but slowly my heart began to be formed by the beauty of God's house. I recently returned to Notre Dame, and was struck by how much the basilica formed the horizon of memories.

We lived in South Bend till I was twelve (except for one year, when I was nine, which we spent in Tübingen, Germany). But when I was twelve, we moved to Gaming, in Lower Austria. There my family was part of the community of students and teachers centered on a former Carthusian monastery: the Kartause Gaming. The Kartause houses a catechetical institute, a study abroad program for students from Franciscan University of Steubenville in Ohio, and at that time it also housed the International Theological Institute, a theological graduate school at which my father taught, and which has since relocated to Trumau. My brothers and sisters and I spent most of our free time with the children of other teachers at the Kartause, and, as we got older, with students. I did also spend time playing soccer and watching televised soccer with local boys—especially altar boys from the local parish—but the older I got the less time I spent with them and the more time I spent with students from the Kartause, who were somewhat more distant from me in age, but much closer in their appreciation of art and literature and liturgy.

It was in Gaming that I really discovered the glories of liturgical worship. I served as an altar-boy for a Swiss priest, Don Reto Nay, who was at that time professor of Old Testament at the ITI. Don Reto was full of deep reverence for the mystery of the Holy Sacrifice. Even the Ordinary Form evening daily Mass with him in German made a deep impression on me on account of his connaturality with the mysteries. And then sometimes he would celebrate a sort of "reform of the reform" high Mass in Latin, *ad orientem*, with incense, candles, Gregorian chant, and polyphony. (He also celebrated the older form of the Roman Rite in the mornings, but I only went to that once or twice.) In Gaming I also discovered the glories of the Byzantine Rite. There were many Byzantine Catholics studying at the ITI, and a priest of the Ukrainian Greek Catholic Church celebrated Divine Liturgy regularly. (My younger brother, who may have been about eight or nine at the time, was so impressed by the Byzantine Rite that he once set up an altar in his room, and I found him singing pseudo-Byzantine chants to a statue of an Egyptian Pharaoh—a model that we had for art-history class—to which he was offering a sacrifice of breath mints: the Golden Calf is a perennial temptation, I guess.) The ITI students also sang the Akathist once a week with heart-rending beauty.

From Gaming I went to Thomas Aquinas College, a small "great books" school in California. The college and the community of families surrounding it have many of the features of a Benedict Option community. Moreover, many of the students at the College were themselves coming from various versions of the Option. There were many who had been schooled at small classical private schools, and many, many homeschoolers. The cliché about homeschoolers is that they are socially awkward losers and prigs. There were certainly some homeschoolers at TAC who fit the cliché. But many did not fit the cliché at all. And the same can be said of other versions of the Benedict Option: there are dangers, but many are able to escape the dangers.

Integralism and the Common Good

During the whole of my upbringing, my family was involved in the ecclesial movement Communion and Liberation ("CL," often referred to by the Italian names for those letters *ci-elle*, from which its members are called *ciellini*). Dreher explicitly mentions CL in his book (he refers to their economic organization *Compagnia delle Opere*), but CL seems to me less well described as a Benedict Option community than other communities in which I have been involved (such as the one around the Kartause Gaming, or the one around Thomas Aquinas College).

The founder of CL, Luigi Giussani, had thought deeply about the nature of modern society, and in his books he traces the loss of the "unitary mentality" of the Middle Ages in a way reminiscent of Dreher. There also many parallels between what Giussani says about education as formation of the heart, and Dreher's thoughts on education. And the emphasis on practical community in CL is exemplary of many of the sorts of things that Dreher talks about. CL is, however, a global movement, and thus its practical solidarity can have a further reach. When a brother of mine moved to Southern Italy to study architecture, he got in touch with the local *ciellini*, and decided to live with a group of CL students in a common apartment. There is something reminiscent of the solidarity of the early Christians in the solidarity of the *ciellini*. But the charism of CL is not really well described as "Benedictine." It is compatible with the Benedictine charism. The Abbot General of my own Cistercian Order is in fact a *ciellino*. But it is something different.

In his provocative book *Newman on Vatican II*, Fr. Ian Ker argues that in each age of the Church the Holy Spirit awakens movements within the Church that respond to the needs of the time. These charismatic movements assist the hierarchy, while being moderated and ordered by the hierarchy. Simplifying Ker's schema somewhat, one can speak of four great movements corresponding to four ages of the Church: the monastic movement, the mendicant friars, the Jesuits and other active orders, and the ecclesial movements typical of the decades following Vatican II.

First, the monastic movement beginning with St. Anthony Abbot, initially as a means of living the full radicalism of the Gospel in the Christian Empire, when the persecutions had ceased, and medioc-

The Mirror of the Benedict Option

rity was the great danger, but receiving its definitive form from St. Benedict who, in Newman's words, came "as if to preserve a principle of civilization, and a refuge for learning, at a time when the old framework of society was falling, and new political creations were taking their place." Benedictine monasticism was the foundation of the new Christian culture that arose out of the ruins of ancient civilization and barbarian chaos. For many centuries it continued to play a key role in European life, periodically reviving itself, as with Benedict of Aniane in the ninth century, the abbots of Cluny in the tenth and eleventh centuries, and the Cistercians in the twelfth.

But in the thirteenth century, with the growth of new towns and cities, the essentially rural nature of Benedictine life made a new kind of monasticism necessary: the mendicant orders, especially the Dominicans. The Dominicans lived in the cities, and practiced the new "scholastic" or scientific style of learning. They used the insights of philosophy to give clear, systematic expression to theological truths. The Dominicans still preserved many features of the monastic life, but reduced the amount of time spent in prayer and manual labor in order to give more hours to scholarly work and preaching.

And then in early modernity St. Ignatius of Loyola began a thoroughly practical form of religious life: the Jesuits. The Jesuits gave up the audible, public recitation of the divine office, leaving each Jesuit to pray the office soundlessly and by himself. They replaced the long hours of monastic prayer and lectio with highly efficient and concentrated meditations. And the efficient simplicity and interiority of their prayer life freed them for the ruthless, military efficiency of their exterior apostolate. There is, as it were, an ulterior motive to Jesuit contemplation; it is ordered to the apostolate. Is it not fitting that René Descartes was educated by Jesuits? The typically modern spirit of reflective interiority for the sake of efficient exterior action is the spirit of the Jesuits. In the wake of the Jesuits came many other religious orders devoted to external apostolates, to action, that is, rather than contemplation.

Finally, Ker argues, we have in our own time the rise of the new ecclesial movements. Many of these began already in the period immediately preceding Vatican II, but they found in Vatican II a welcome expression of their ideals. The ecclesial movements are often called "lay movements," but they really include members from all states of life. Thus in CL, for example, there are consecrated persons (the *Memores Domini*) and priests (the Missionaries of St. Charles Borromeo) as well as lay people. Ker argues that the new ecclesial movements embody the ecclesiology of *Lumen Gentium* that overcame the "clericalism" of the nineteenth century, that exaggerated the separation between the laity and the clergy and came close to identifying the Church herself with the clerical hierarchy.

I do think that CL embodies the teachings of Vatican II. CL embodies the "third way" between traditionalism and modernism that Pope John Paul II and Pope Benedict XVI saw in the council. And this is why, much as I love CL, and much as I owe to it, I don't "identify" with it. For I incline ever more to "traditionalism." CL has all the advantages of the attempted third way, but also all the disadvantages. While not being blind to the deep problems of modern culture, it has nevertheless a fundamentally optimistic attitude towards engagement with that culture. An attitude that stresses the signs of the desire for God that can be found at work even in the wasteland. This is manifested on a theoretical level by the enthusiasm that one finds within the movement for Henri de Lubac's questionable theology of grace, which identifies the natural desire for happiness with the desire for the supernatural end of the Beatific Vision. But it is manifested on a more concrete practical level as well.

Don Giussani was a man of great appreciation for the artistic treasures of the past, and wrote eloquently on Mozart and Beethoven. But at a CL meeting one is as likely to hear contemporary guitar music as the great composers. Giussani was close friends with Pope Benedict XVI, but Pope Benedict's project of a reform of the reform made little impression on liturgical practice in the movement. Going to Mass with CL people, one is likely to find an ordinary vernacular *novus ordo*. To the degree that I have moved more and more towards liturgical traditionalism, I have adopted a different approach. In politics too, there is no trace of "traditionalism" among the *ciellini*. Italian CL politicians tend to be post-war-style Christian Social democrats on the model of Alcide de Gasperi or Giulio Andreotti. This approach has its advantages of course. It

The Mirror of the Benedict Option

provides a readily applicable practical program in the current framework. But I think that it also has serious flaws. It opens one up to being co-opted by the liberal framework. As Pedro José Izquierdo has argued,[6] it is important to adopt an explicitly anti-liberal political principle in order to resist such co-opting. I am therefore a monarchist and an integralist, and would like to scrap the modern project of democratic politics altogether.

I remember once being asked by a sweet, young, Italian *ciellina* whether I felt more at home in Austria or America. I answered her that I always feel like a foreigner—like an American in Austria and like an Austrian in America. She then said that it was the opposite for her. She felt at home everywhere because "everywhere I am with Christ." A beautiful thought no doubt. I think that both thoughts are true. As Christians we must be strangers and sojourners on earth, with our hearts set on our heavenly Fatherland. But at the same time we must see that the Kingdom of God is also already among us. Both are true, and yet different members of the Body of Christ can put more emphasis on one or the other. Each of these has its advantages and disadvantages.

Ian Ker is right that our time is the age of the ecclesial movements with their optimistic dynamism in engaging contemporary society. But it is also a time of revival of the ideals of monasticism. Ideals of stability, and rich liturgical tradition, and uncompromising contempt for the vanity and pomps of this passing world. And Rod Dreher is right that elements of those ideals can be realized outside the monastery in the life of Christian families. "The Benedict Option" will not ensure that children keep the faith—the mystery of iniquity and the mystery of grace cannot be controlled by any strategy—but if my upbringing can be called "Benedict Option," then I do think that it can be a help.

In a comment on a review of *The Benedict Option*, Maclin Horton, once a co-editor of the defunct Catholic countercultural maga-

---

6. See Pedro José Izquierdo, "The Primary Political Question: A Response to Milco on Liberalism," *The Josias*, February 4, 2016, https://thejosias.com/2016/02/04/the-primary-political-question-a-response-to-milco-on-liberalism/.

zine *Caelum et Terra* (and the subject of a profile in Dreher's *Crunchy Cons*) wrote as follows:

> [T]his discussion was being held twenty-five years ago in the pages of the magazine *Caelum et Terra* and other places. We must withdraw—but we must remain connected. We must turn off the TV—but we mustn't turn our backs on the culture. We must form communities—but we mustn't isolate ourselves. We must be critical of technology—but we should use it when appropriate. We must find ways of educating our children apart from the proselytizing secularism of the state school systems—but we must not be overprotective. Etc. etc. etc. All these things have actually been going on in places like Steubenville, Ohio. The children of those talkers and experimenters are grown now, and the results have been mixed. Those having this conversation with such fervor now seem to be younger, and I wonder whether most of you can quite grasp how bitterly sad it is to see a young man named John Paul or a young woman named Kateri denouncing Christian "homophobia" and "transphobia" on Facebook. . . .

I don't deny that the results of the attempt to achieve the balance of which Horton speaks in my own upbringing are mixed—as helpful grumblers are always reminding me. But at least this much is true: my parents have been spared the bitter sadness of seeing me and my brothers and sisters fall away from the Faith. Words fail me when I try to express how grateful I myself am for having received that gift and not (as yet) lost it: I have found in it the pearl of great price and the treasure buried in the field.

10

Nature and Art in the Village

John Francis Nieto

We of the twenty-first century look for the village in legend and folk tale, to some extent in history and there, much more as we look back, less and less as we come forward. This is no accident, for reasons I will go on to point out. This fact and a few others make much of what I am about to say seem "abstract" and "ideal." Yet what I say here about the village is utterly "practical" and "realistic." Man cannot—I propose—have healthy familial life and just political order unless these take root and find support in village life.

At the same time, what I am about to say is not "immediately" practical. To live a true village life at this time is virtually impossible, is in most places illegal, and has been made ludicrously burdensome by the modern cult of convenience. Some few remote, impoverished places may still hide villages. Those wealthy enough can play "village." And heroic souls can strive to reestablish village life, but not, at present, without an unnatural and unhealthy dependence upon and interference from the modern, global "city-state."

My insistence upon speaking about the village "in its purity" does not arise from a refusal to face reality, from an unwillingness to appreciate what is good in things that are imperfect, or from a desire to depreciate the work of those who strive to live village life as well as they can, while I stand by only talking about village life. Rather, I want to encourage those interested in village life in two ways.

I want them to see how critical the village is to the whole human race. I also want to help them avoid the temptation to believe that the compromises necessary to any village in our day constitute improvements on the village. I would suggest that one cannot improve on the village. The village is one thing man has got right, or rather, *had* got right—albeit in many different ways.

For many reasons, we cannot hunt, sew, sing, farm, cook, dance, or wash clothes as could those who have lived in villages until very recently. We have exchanged such abilities for many advantages, especially long lives and material possessions. I propose here that the loss is much greater than the gain—in some sense it is infinite. I propose that we have lost the interaction with nature that allows us to cultivate our own, human, nature in a manner conducive to happiness—by which I mean true, human thriving and fulfillment—not merely living, but living well, the good life.

The basic claim of these remarks is that, while the village is not sufficient for human happiness, the village is necessary for such happiness. To defend the claim, I will do three things. First, I will briefly discuss the dependence of human social and political order upon nature. Second, I will compare the roles proper to the village and the city in achieving happiness. Third, I will argue that only in the village is man able to experience the natural world and within it, his own nature, in a manner that will fit him to found healthy cities and to live happily within them.

Now, when I was ten years old, my cousin Charlotte lived with us for several months. As she stood over the floor heater early winter mornings, she would often describe life growing up on an Indian reservation as well as her vagabond life as a hippie. I can still hear her hearty laughter as the warm air puffed up her flannel nightgown. Then one morning my mother asked her, "What do you hippies have against society? What's your criticism?"

I looked up at Charlotte's face. It had become serious and thoughtful. "We think society has got too far away from nature," she said. "Society is too artificial."

I cannot now recall whether their conversation continued; my thoughts had started on their own course. I felt sure immediately of two things. Society *had* separated itself too far from nature, though I felt less sure in what way it had done so and why. More fundamentally, I "knew," without yet seeing why, that a society could only remain healthy so long as it remained united to nature in the right

Nature and Art in the Village

way. The clearest image I had was of a hippie commune I had seen on television, where the members lived by raising goats and making cheese.

Now I have thought continually about these questions ever since. I struggled to express this in an essay written a few years later. "Man has become estranged," I began to write, and then I stopped. Should I say, "from nature" or "from *his* nature"? I thought about this some time. I went back and forth. I finally wrote succinctly, "Man has become estranged from nature." And I understood then and still understand the reality described by these words to mean this, that man, by surrounding himself with human contrivances and thus insulating himself from the natural world, has lost his understanding of that natural world to which he himself belongs. Precisely because man is a natural being and not artificial and man-made, he has at the same time lost his understanding of himself.

I have tried, therefore, most of my life to uncover that natural world that still lies hidden and masked all about us and thereby to find human nature and to understand how to fulfill its various powers, especially by those habits we have traditionally called art. In using this word I do not have the fine arts principally in mind. Yet I do not exclude them. First and foremost, I mean the habits of mind and body that make a man able to cultivate the material world. The habits that make him a farmer, a hunter, a seamstress or tailor, a cobbler, a house-builder, a doctor—that is, a medicine man. In the village where these arts begin to thrive, the fine arts also begin, in the embellishment of pots and jars, in the design of chairs and tables, in the cut of briar pipes, in placement of windows and doors and the thatching of a roof, in the songs and dances on summer evenings.

My search for human nature and its natural abilities led me first, through socialism and communism, to anarchism, which I professed from the age of eighteen to twenty-two. In some sense, during my years as an anarchist, I sought nothing more than the restoration of village life. But more penetration into my answers about human nature led me to abandon anarchism and the left. I had come to see, beneath the opposition of left and right, a deeper alliance. I will say almost nothing here about the reality and importance of their opposition. When it comes to questions of worldwide social order, to the choice between a world filled with villages and cities or a global order, granting a centralized, mechanized life to all its inhabitants, I have come to see the agreement between right and left as something more fundamental and more dangerous than their opposition. This agreement, to my mind, concerns precisely the understanding of man and nature that I have held since my tenth year.

Right and left agree that man cannot find his proper nature until he dominates nature in such a way as to free himself from the natural world. Sustainable domination would be preferable to an unsustainable domination. Still man must not only rise above it; he must rise out of it. Apparently, he must not only control and recreate the body nature has furnished him with, by making its properties and operations suitable to his desires. He must even escape the earth itself, must find some other planet fit for the "creation" and cultivation of a new "natural" world agreeing with the dictates of the sciences of chemistry, biology, and sociology.

This view, I propose, is the enemy of anyone who wishes to live in a village. The reason is quite profound. The principle I grasped at ten years old, first articulated distinctly by the Greek philosopher Aristotle and taken up by Catholic social teaching, belongs to the perennial wisdom that belongs commonly to the human race: man is naturally social and political. The most fundamental impulses of human nature call forth various "societies": first the family, then the village, and finally the *polis* or city (at least, in the true sense of that word).

Now, while still anarchist, I began to form an understanding of the village, of its distinction from and relations with the city. This understanding led me to suspect that the left, including anarchism, has neither the interest in protecting or establishing village life nor the ability to do so. My experience growing up in a highly developed capitalist commercial society had already led me to see the focus on consumption so necessary to this economy as hostile to the village and its proper relation to the city. Incidentally, I have since heard it claimed that before the rise of Dutch and English capitalism, households produced 95% of what they consumed. Today it would be heroic to produce merely 5% of what one consumes.

Nature and Art in the Village

So, first, I will look at the difference between village and city and the relations that follow this difference. Aristotle begins his book on political life by arguing that there are distinct orders of human society. These do not differ merely in size but rather in the order or rule proper to each society.

The distinction in order and rule follows from something more fundamental, the purpose or end that defines each of the societies. The family exists insofar as man naturally pursues what he needs for daily life: food, clothes, shelter, and thereby the nourishment and education of children.

In the village man aims at something above the daily needs. Here families support one another by providing, one for another, some aspect of their daily needs. This allows another order of fulfillment, one more proper to the village. Families can share, compare, and refine experience. Insofar as they obtain relief in the pursuit of daily needs, they can enjoy common recreation in music, poetry, and dance.

Yet there is something lacking. In the village, through its small size and its proximity to the extended family, justice cannot exist in its purest form, as something abstracted from the prudence of particular men and women. Nor can the village defend itself sufficiently. Villages come together into cities to obtain such justice in their exchanges and their common actions and common defense from enemies. Villages surrounding such cities also seek justice and safety from those cities. Cities therefore exist for the sake of peace in a very fundamental sense of the word.

Here in the city, however, man not only finds justice and safety but the full flourishing of his nature. Precisely insofar as peace frees him from constant attention to survival, man can pursue the good life. He comes together in families and villages to live; he comes together in cities to live well.

One might conclude from this understanding that the village is necessarily a passing phase in the development of social order. The village is a stepping stone, it may seem, to the city and passes out of existence once cities come about. I suspect this has led in one way or another to the view common in our time. Socialism and capitalism agree deeply that this is so. We now see economies founded on socialist principles employing capitalist principles and vice-versa, in a common effort to establish one political and social order throughout the modern state.

But this view misunderstands social order. The village looks to the city for safety, justice, and other excellences of human nature. But the city also looks "back" to the village for a prior fulfillment of human nature. And this fulfillment is necessary to the health of city life. In a similar way, both the city and the village depend upon families for something that neither can provide or cultivate.

The city looks to the village above all for cultivation of an understanding of nature and of man as a natural being. In the village man recognizes himself as a being that rises above the nature of his body, through reason's cultivation of the natural world, yet as one that remains a natural being in his body and its interactions with other beings of the natural world. In the city man can realize the highest aspirations of his spiritual nature, which most of all contributes to well-being. But in cities he can also misunderstand what constitutes living well. In the village man cannot delude himself with false conceptions of his relation to the natural world. There he necessarily concerns himself with living as it concerns the human body.

The ancient philosophers, so far as I can see, pay little attention to the dependence of the city on the village. They cannot imagine a world in which the village is a whim and a luxury. Industrialization and technology, especially as applied to agriculture, and the tremendous abundance that follow these developments, make the elimination of the village possible. In my understanding, its elimination is necessary to the view of man that arises from and corresponds to these developments, a false understanding of man freed from his dependence on nature. Man needs the village in order to maintain a proper understanding of human nature. Only while man sees himself as a natural being in a natural world can he properly conceive human happiness as the fulfillment of that nature.

Now, what makes the village capable of providing such an understanding of man? Answering this question demands elaboration of something I have already proposed, that the village is much closer to nature and to the family as the family arises from man as a natural being, as a certain kind of animal. At the same time, as in the family, life in the village provides man with a clear view of himself as an animal *of a certain kind*.

All animals necessarily feed upon plants and other animals. The higher animals take some kind of shelter and protect themselves from "the elements" and from natural enemies. Further, the higher animals all reproduce through the cooperation of male and female. In doing so, they complete and fulfill themselves insofar as each is male or female. Each species of animal has natural impulses by which its nature incites the members of that species to feed and reproduce and to protect itself and its offspring. The nature of each species conditions the manner in which that species pursues the goods involved in the survival of the individual and the species.

All animals—apparently even animals as simple as the amoeba and bacteria—use knowledge to pursue these goods. The most simple "smell" out their food and the toxins they must avoid and move toward or away, albeit erratically. Other animals use hearing and sight, together with smell, in various strengths and proportions, arising from and adapted to the overall structure of their bodies and the movement proper to those bodies.

Above these senses, one finds in some animals distinct operations of imagination and memory that allow them to pursue these goods in a manner that begins to rise above the limitations of place and time. While bacteria move in the general direction of their food, the ant and the bee find fixed routes to theirs and they can communicate knowledge of this route to fellow ants and bees. Many other animals can form a "map" of their territories used in hunting and reproducing. In raising offspring they often exercise the powers that form such "maps" in the offspring. Likewise, as one "ascends" through the higher animals, one finds that memory makes possible the storage of food, learning from experience, and even the rudimentary use of instruments. Hence, Aristotle speaks of each animal as having a kind of "prudence" proper to it, especially among the higher animals. In the highest animals, adults even "cultivate" this prudence in their offspring.

In the midst of the natural world, man quickly recognizes himself as distinct from other animals in the very fulfillment of his animal nature. Like all other animals, he pursues food and shelter for his survival as an individual and he produces offspring for the survival of the species. He uses his senses, his imagination, and his memory in performing these operations. Yet in doing so he transcends the limitations of place and time in a unique way.

Man pursues these goods through the use of reason. Reason involves an awareness of man himself and other natural beings he lives among not only as he finds each determinately in some place and time. Reason also considers each of these beings according to its *nature*. He asks *what* each is and strives to obtain the goods that he needs through his understanding of its being or *essence* and its nature.

Insofar as man's understanding of some essence and nature appears as the cause of the goods he pursues, that nature explains how to attain it. It appears as the *reason* in our reasoning about how to attain these goods. In this way our knowledge of what constitutes health allows us to attain health. Some understanding of what constitutes health is the *reason* we do the things we do in our pursuit of health. This knowledge will be more or less exact and complete, more or less appropriate to a man's particular needs. Yet always reason displays itself as a *universal* knowledge of many particular things.

For example, man has some conception of health, through which he pursues the things conducive to health. This understanding of health does not differ in differing places and times, except insofar as those places and times have some character that influences health. What is healthy in winter may not be healthy in summer; what is healthy in the north may not be healthy in the south. Yet health is in some way the same in summer and winter, in the north and the south.

This example concerns health as found in man and thus it suggests another. Man has a conception of health as a general property of all animal bodies. Just as he can make this conception proper to his own body, he can conceive of the health of the horse, the health of the dog, the health of the cow, and so on. We not only conceive of health generally; we also conceive of health as it belongs to each species of animal we encounter.

Each of these examples reveals two sides of reasoning: its

Nature and Art in the Village

abstractness and universality and the singular, material natural beings known in an abstract and universal manner. While reason never exhibits one of these sides without the other, in his reasoning a man is usually concerned with one more than the other. The philosopher and the scientist reason principally to know something universally, in all times and places. The farmer, the carpenter, the musician, that is, the maker and artist reasons to know some singular that he senses in the here and now. I will call these abstract and concrete uses or concerns of reason.

Now the more abstract concerns of reason—for at many levels one can distinguish the abstract and the concrete—"belong" in a certain sense to the city. Philosophy and science, the arts in their most refined and sophisticated state, especially as something taught in schools and especially the fine arts, all have an opportunity to flourish in the city. Again, the leisure available in the city makes it possible for philosophers to consider the existence and nature of God and other immaterial and spiritual beings. The religious worship that rightly follows the knowledge of such beings belongs in a particular manner to the city. For this reason, the Catholic Church bears the name, "City of God."

Still, the more concrete concerns of reason, especially those involved in the very use of the arts of farming, hunting, fishing, pottery, and so on, belong properly to the village. There the purposes of life can be pursued in a manner determined to the character and needs of particular men and women, particular families, and particular places with the climates and seasons proper to them. To some extent, the village even has some determination of what we call race. The Inuit or Eskimo peoples live a life that reaches toward the village. This life may not bring forth every possibility of man's various powers. But it reflects one way in which man's reason and his other powers can cooperate in the fulfillment of human life. This—in its own integrity—manifests man's nature in a way no other life, as lived by no other people, can.

Yet more important for human life "as a whole," the concrete, determined use of reason that is typical of the village, the use that is perfected in experience and art, remains so close to nature that man cannot forget that he is one of many animals, among many living beings, in a natural world that exhibits order. One critical order is that between man's own powers of knowing, sensing, and moving and the powers in animals and other natural substances.

Many aspects of these beings, such as their atomic constitution, the powers of their souls, the nature of DNA, and so on, become clear to us through the use of reason proper to cities. But some are known best in the village. There are things about the horse known best to the man who rides one. Much about the pig can be seen in the pork we buy in plastic wrapper or pre-cooked. The knowledge of these things belongs most of all to men in villages.

In cities, men easily lose the sense of themselves as natural beings. There great errors about reality arise: that things do not really exist outside me, that nothing can really be known, that all truth is relative, even the "noble" error that only God exists. Among the most important errors bred in cities in our time is the belief that non-living beings, mere matter, are the most real and fundamental of beings. On this view, life and spirit are hardly more real than an hallucination, if they exist at all.

Farmers may not delve into the speculations about God's nature, but they rarely fail to see that behind nature lies some divine being or divine beings working in and though nature to provide for all things, especially the living. They rarely fail to see that the most real being, the first being that causes all others, must be alive.

We see all around us the consequences of these views about reality and human nature. I will just point out two: our detachment from the earth expressed in fantasies about restarting the human race on another planet and confusion about the distinction between male and female. Both express a deep psychological inability to feel at home in this world. Such feelings must thrive in a human race divorced from nature.

Only villages can prevent man's embracing such errors. The modern philosopher Hegel imagined that various peoples and cultures scattered throughout the world exhibited the stages of political development. He thought further that this exhibition served reason's grasp of the nature of that development. By looking at those still living in more "primitive" stages we who live at the highest can see the "movement" that constitutes political "progress."

Nature and Art in the Village

Far more important I would say is the existence of villages around our cities. Only there can man observe himself as interacting with nature. There he survives through nature's powers working within himself and in other natural beings and by exercising his own powers. There he learns to feed himself, to clothe himself, and to amuse himself. There he discovers the ability to do these things within himself. He is capable of living together with others in the natural world. He can be happy on earth. Earth is his home.

Once the city has wholly dominated human life it become possible to have many goods but they almost always come from somewhere else. Our clothes come from China; our music and our dances come from Los Angeles or New York. We do not sing. We download songs. A generation has grown up that conceives of music as essentially something bought and sold. We live in a world in which folk music is an historical being, a world in which folk music is the product of a music industry.

I could speak at length about the nature of such errors and the order among them. Rather, let me conclude with an attention to one kind of error that manifests itself everywhere in our society. I will also point out the particular opposition of this kind of error to Christianity. The various errors I have in mind all involve fertility. Some of these are speculative but perhaps they are more frightening insofar as they are practical.

In some sense, T.S. Eliot announced this in one of the most important poems of the twentieth century, *The Wasteland*. Pope John Paul II had this in mind when he spoke of the culture of death. Almost every aspect of contemporary society manifests some contempt for fertility. Yet fertility is the work identified by Aristotle and even by Saint Paul as most proper to nature. Likewise, fertility is the work of nature which peoples have from time immemorial associated above all with God and the gods.

We see contempt of fertility and thus for nature in many ways. Most obviously, contraception attempts to prevent fertility in much of, if not most, sexual intercourse between men and women. Almost as a rule, women artificially make themselves infertile. While fathers stand by apathetic, women regularly chose to abort children. Paradoxically, they do so in the name of feminism, though fertility in some sense defines the feminine. Again, there are plans underway, the plans of cities, to control all seed, to own seed, to make seed no longer the work of nature but something essentially bought and sold. These have produced crops that bear no seed—should they accidentally do so, the corporation owns that seed and not the man who planted those crops. There are those who propose to "own" DNA, which seems to be nature's principal instrument of fertility. The same people hope to manage and control all livestock in the world—for purposes of health—though I have little doubt they will look closely at the reproductive powers of such livestock. I will speak metaphorically and point out the World Wide Web as an impediment to man's observation of nature and interaction with it. The internet has become an intellectual contraceptive. Man now dreams of a world in which the powers of life we find in nature belong to him—one more illusory fulfillment of the serpent's promise to Eve: You shall be as gods.

Perhaps some of you have recognized already what the Catholic must see as the most sinister aspect of this contempt for fertility. Our religion, with all its promises and hopes, relies upon the fertility of nature in its defining mystery, the incarnation of Jesus in the womb of the Virgin Mary. There we believe God worked in a manner that surpasses his usual operation in human conception both by instigating conception with his own active power without the instrument of male seed and by his Son taking on the human nature, the body and soul, formed in that act of fertility. Anti-fertility is a manifestation of the ancient enmity between the serpent and the Woman, between his seed and her seed.

In conclusion, let me point out one last aspect of the contempt of fertility in our culture. If the understanding of social and political order I have been developing since I was ten is right, the family is a kind of seed to the village and the village is a kind of seed to the city. The family and the village each expresses human nature in a manner disposed to a further, more complete and complementary expression of human nature.

This understanding appears in Euripides' tragedy, *The Trojan Women*. There Andromache speaks to Hecuba, the mother of her fallen husband, Hector. She says, "Hear me while I reason through this matter fairly." She then proposes how much better things are for the dead and for those never born. She expresses the view all too common today under names such as "nihilism," "pessimistic philosophy," and, quite expressively, "anti-natalism"—a movement opposed to birth itself.

But then Hecuba, the former queen of Troy, dreams that her grandson Astuanax, the son of Hector and Andromache, might one day rebuild the city. She also reasons through the matter: "This boy / my own son's child, might grow to manhood and bring back, / he alone could do it—something of our city's strength. / On some far day the children of your children might / come home, and build. There still may be another Troy." In a fine film based on the play, Hecuba adds, "One thought leads to another."

So the village leads to the city as two expressions of human reason working out human life here in the natural world. This is the reason villages no longer exist. Villages are the seeds of cities. The "global village," what Saint Augustine called the city of man, has no room for other, healthy cities, competing alongside it. If there were villages again, true city life, true political order, would once again arise. When there are villages, true cities will rise again. And we can trust that the God in whom the Father eternally generates his Son will bring forth from the earth these means of human happiness and fulfillment once again.

11

Urbanism and the Common Good

Nathaniel Gotcher

Society exists for the common good, the shared happiness of humans. The modern city, however, is characterized not by happiness but by violence and there is a sharp political divide between urban and rural citizens. The way we have organized our residential and commercial developments reinforces this reality: the city is in one place, the countryside in another, divided by "suburbs" developed with huge swaths of unproductive land. If the modern *polis* is fractured, is it any wonder our politics are just as fractured? If we are to make the common good central to our politics, we could do worse than look at how our cities are organized.

Cities have traditionally been organized to facilitate the everyday activities of the community. These activities include worship, exchange of goods, study, and recreation. Markets, where the exchange of goods took place, were often centrally located so that they were available to all. Temples (and later the church) were given prominent locations near the center of the city, making the worship of the gods (and later the one God) central to the lives of the citizens, both symbolically and practically. Those buildings and areas used most often were given greater attention and those buildings which symbolized the community and its identity were given places of honor. These material features of traditional cities were promoted out of necessity. Without the common sharing of space and resources, the economy would fail and so too would the city. This practical and public good of urban design is linked to the common good of a community, beneficial activity and happiness shared by all.

Urbanism and the Common Good

Cities in our day are so tied in to the global economy that it is unlikely that they will fail. Resources can be shared across oceans and continents in a matter of days; funds can be allotted instantly through the internet. While this can and does lead to very many good things (not least among them is the ease with which we can aid those starving or experiencing violence around the world), it has also all but abolished the necessity for citizens to share with each other the practical goods which promote a truly common good. Families (and even individuals) can survive and even thrive separately from those who live near them, as long as they have the funds to support their way of life. With enough personal wealth or property, we do not need the others in our community, at least not materially, as humans have in the past.

If traditional urbanism promoted the common good in addressing the practical necessities of city life, how should cities approach urbanism where those necessities no longer pertain? Cities, generally speaking, are made up of buildings and roads. Urban design focuses on where buildings and other destinations should be built and how best to get to them. Before proposing principles of urbanism that support the common good, we must know which buildings and spaces encourage the common life. The citizens of the modern world need, as humans always have, security and sustenance. To support these needs, a community must have certain building types and appropriate infrastructure. What this means will vary greatly between countries and even between neighboring cities, but the types remain the same.

The first and most fundamental type is housing. Houses provide immediate security to the citizens and give families a place in which to organize their personal lives so as to better participate in the common life of the city. Secondly, farm buildings and other buildings where food is grown, prepared, and stored for the sustenance of the citizens. All further urban development is built on this foundation. The production of tools for the everyday needs of the city's households and other manufactured goods require workshops. Storage buildings are necessary to keep these goods safe, and markets provide a place where these goods can be distributed and exchanged. These building types make up the basic layer of urban development; however, these building types only address the ordinary material needs of the citizens. The common good ultimately concerns the whole person, spiritual as well as material. The material needs provided by these buildings are essential to maintain a city, but without buildings which address the spiritual goods of the community, the city remains incomplete.

The human spirit must first of all be formed. To this end, a city should have schools where children are educated "in the arts and sciences for the advantage and prosperity of civil society."[1] This education allows the citizens to determine just and prudent action in the face of political uncertainty. A city thus needs a place set aside for careful political deliberation. Furthermore, a city needs places for artistic and scientific endeavors so that the human spirit might be elevated by the contemplation of truth and beauty. Finally, the city requires houses of worship so that the final end of the human person, union with God, is given a place of honor in society.

The arrangement of these buildings is the second half of urban design. There are three aspects of urban arrangement: number, proximity, and hierarchy. There must be a sufficient number of each building type so that every citizen is able to participate in the life of the city. Some needs, such as the storage and distribution of goods, are related and so their respective buildings should be built near each other. Also, the buildings which provide the daily needs of the citizens ought to be close to their houses so that travel does not dominate their lives. Those buildings which concern the human spirit should be given special attention in the design of the city. Streets, bridges, lighting and other infrastructure aid in the effective arrangement of a city.

All urban design decisions should weigh these considerations carefully. The arrangement of the parts of the city is an essential aid in the pursuit of the common good. The buildings and infrastructure of a city provide the necessary support for the security and sustenance of the citizens. Furthermore, they designate places for the pursuits of the human spirit. Scientific progress has brought us

---

1. Pius XI, *Divini Illius Magistri* 77.

many things: new and more efficient ways to grow food, faster transportation, and global trade among others. New urban forms are possible, and the organization of communities is more varied than ever. Despite this, human nature is the same, and cities should be designed to fulfill the common good, both material and spiritual.

III
ECONOMICS

12

Thomism and Private Property

W. Borman

St. Thomas raises the question of private property in the sixty-sixth question of the *Secunda Secundae*. The question under which the subsequent articles are organized purports to deal with the issues of theft and robbery. As always, Thomas recognizes that he must start right at the beginning and ask first: is it possible for people to possess things at all?

To this, Thomas answers with a resounding yes. God has what Thomas calls "sovereign dominion" over all created things according to His Will, but God has given over to man the stewardship of those things which man needs in order to pursue his good life, or, in Thomas's rather austere words, those things which are necessary for "the sustenance of man's body." From this, we can say that man has what Thomas calls "natural dominion" over things (in relation to God's sovereign dominion) and it is natural for man to possess things external to himself so that he can use them and labor over them in order to sustain his body.

It is important to remember the different meanings that Thomas acknowledges in his understanding of natural right, in *ST* II-II, q. 57, a. 3:

> [T]he natural right or just is that which by its very nature is adjusted to or commensurate with another person. Now this may happen in two ways; first, according as it is considered absolutely: thus a male by its very nature is commensurate with the female to beget offspring by her, and a parent is commensurate with the offspring to nourish it. Secondly a thing is naturally commensurate with another person, not according as it is considered absolutely, but according to something resultant from it, for instance the pos-

session of property. For if a particular piece of land be considered absolutely, it contains no reason why it should belong to one man more than to another, but if it be considered in respect of its adaptability to cultivation, and the unmolested use of the land, it has a certain commensuration to be the property of one and not of another man, as the Philosopher shows (*Polit.* ii, 2).[1]

It is clear that the natural right with respect to the possession of property is meant to be understood in the second sense, as Thomas says.

Returning to II-II, q. 66, a. 2, Thomas narrows his inquiry from the broad—whether it is *natural* for man in general to possess things in general—to the specific: whether it is *lawful* for a man to possess something *as his own*? Here, Thomas is responding to those who would claim that because all things are God's property, no man can really have ownership over anything. In support of this he quotes Basil and Ambrose, who condemn the rich who seize as their own things which rightfully belong as common goods to all. First, Thomas replies that private possession of things serves both practical ends (it induces men to labor with more care over things which are their own, it prevents the confusion of ownership and responsibility that is present when all things are owned in common) and spiritual/moral ends (the possession of private property allows people to be generous and to develop the virtues of giving to those in need).

Thomas then gives what is probably his most controversial statement in the question, and what might reasonably be considered a summary of his position on the nature of private property:

---

1. "Ius sive iustum naturale est quod ex sui natura est adaequatum vel commensuratum alteri. Hoc autem potest contingere dupliciter. Uno modo, secundum absolutam sui considerationem, sicut masculus ex sui ratione habet commensurationem ad feminam ut ex ea generet, et parens ad filium ut eum nutriat. Alio modo aliquid est naturaliter alteri commensuratum non secundum absolutam sui rationem, sed secundum aliquid quod ex ipso consequitur, puta proprietas possessionum. Si enim consideretur iste ager absolute, non habet unde magis sit huius quam illius, sed si consideretur quantum ad opportunitatem colendi et ad pacificum usum agri, secundum hoc habet quandam commensurationem ad hoc quod sit unius et non alterius, ut patet per philosophum, in II Polit." (*ST* II-II, q. 57, a. 3).

Thomism and Private Property

> Community of goods is ascribed to the natural law, not that the natural law dictates that all things should be possessed in common and that nothing should be possessed as one's own: but because the division of possessions is not according to the natural law, but rather arose from human agreement which belongs to positive law, as stated above. Hence the ownership of possessions is not contrary to the natural law, but an addition thereto devised by human reason.[2]

What Thomas is doing here is delineating the status of private property in relation to the laws (differentiating between the natural law and the human law), and making clear the significance of property both as a social or practical institution (which he derives from Aristotle and from several Roman jurists) and as a thing understood within the idealistic Christian-theological worldview (which he derives from multiple Christian sources, but primarily the Gospel writers and the early Church fathers). Speaking again on the same topic, in another section of the *Summa theologiae* concerning the natural law, Thomas writes that

> A thing is said to belong to the natural law in two ways. First, because nature inclines thereto: e.g., that one should not do harm to another. Secondly, because nature did not bring in the contrary: thus we might say that for man to be naked is of the natural law, because nature did not give him clothes, but art invented them. In this sense, "the possession of all things in common and universal freedom" are said to be of the natural law, because, to wit, the distinction of possessions ... [was] not brought in by nature, but devised by human reason for the benefit of human life.[3]

This helps to clarify for us what it means for Thomas for a thing to be either a consequence of the natural law or to be an invention of the human law. Natural law as well as natural right have both a primary and a secondary sense, and it is only in the secondary sense

---

2. "Communitas rerum attribuitur iuri naturali, non quia ius naturale dictet omnia esse possidenda communiter et nihil esse quasi proprium possidendum, sed quia secundum ius naturale non est distinctio possessionum, sed magis secundum humanum condictum, quod pertinet ad ius positivum, ut supra dictum est. Unde proprietas possessionum non est contra ius naturale; sed iuri naturali superadditur per adinventionem rationis humanae" (*ST* II-II, q. 66, a. 2, ad 1).

that private property is natural. Notice the contingent status of private property under this understanding—there is no absolute guarantee to one's particular possessions *directly from the natural law*, according to Thomas, but that which is provided by human reason. Moreover, the human laws which provide those guarantees do so "for the benefit of human life." Thus, property is not a natural right considered *absolutely*, but only *consequently* and as a result of natural reason.

---

3. "[A]liquid dicitur esse de iure naturali dupliciter. Uno modo, quia ad hoc natura inclinat, sicut non esse iniuriam alteri faciendam. Alio modo, quia natura non induxit contrarium, sicut possemus dicere quod hominem esse nudum est de iure naturali, quia natura non dedit ei vestitum, sed ars adinvenit. Et hoc modo communis omnium possessio, et omnium una libertas, dicitur esse de iure naturali, quia scilicet distinctio possessionum et servitus non sunt inductae a natura, sed per hominum rationem, ad utilitatem humanae vitae. Et sic in hoc lex naturae non est mutata nisi per additionem" (*ST* I-II, q. 94, a. 5, ad 3).

13

Aquinas on Buying and Selling[1]

Thomas Storck

In his *Summa theologiae* II-II, St. Thomas devotes two questions to unjust acts which are committed in buying and selling or lending.

The first of these questions (q. 77), divided into four articles, deals with fraud in the broad sense (*fraudulentia*), while the second (q. 78) concerns usury. A study of these questions reveals important differences not only between St. Thomas's teaching on injustices committed in economic life and the ethical attitudes common today, but differences in basic evaluations of the place of commerce in society. In order to make this clear, I will look at the first question, no. 77, setting forth first what Aquinas taught and then contrasting it with commerce and business ethics as these exist in a capitalist society.[2]

The first article of question 77 is, Whether someone can licitly sell something for more than it is worth? As is usual, St. Thomas first brings up some objections to his own opinion, which he will answer later on. The first is that civil law permits the buyer and seller to "deceive each other" and buy or sell for less or more than something is worth. The second is that common opinion endorses the idea of buying cheap and selling dear. (I omit his third objection, which deals with friends giving each other gifts.)

After offering the objections, Thomas gives his own considered opinion. He first briefly notes that to deceive a buyer in order to sell something for more than the just price is altogether sinful.

---

1. An earlier version of this article appeared in *The Distributist Review*.
2. For a discussion of question 78, on usury, see chapter 14.

But then he turns to the main question, where there is no actual deceit involved. In that case, he says, it is also wrong to sell something for more than it is worth: "to sell something more dearly than it is worth, or buy it more cheaply, in itself is unjust and illicit." But he instances an exception, the case where a buyer might need or want something greatly while the seller would be especially hurt by its loss. In such a case the seller can charge a premium since he may charge for the damage he will receive by selling the item as well as for its value. But note that Aquinas is not talking about price gouging following a natural disaster. His statement applies only when the buyer will suffer harm (*detrimentum* or *damnum*) by its loss. St. Thomas specifically says that a seller may not charge a buyer such a premium price unless he will suffer particular damage by selling it.

Then he proceeds to deal with the objections that were raised. To the first, that civil law permits buying cheap and selling dear, Thomas's answer is revealing. He states that human law must permit much that divine law will punish, but he also notes that civil law will demand restitution if the price deviates excessively from the just price, "*ultra dimidiam justi pretii quantitatem*," i.e., more than half again as much as the just price. St. Thomas notes, however, that a just price cannot be calculated with mathematical exactness, but is a "certain estimate, so that a small addition or subtraction does not seem to remove the equivalence of justice." With the second objection, that common usage allows such buying and selling, he simply states that "that common desire [to sell dear and buy cheap] is not natural, but is a vice, and therefore common to many who walk on the broad way of vices."

Let us then go on to St. Thomas's second article, Whether a sale is rendered illicit on account of a defect in the thing sold? He brings up three initial objections to the opinion. (I omit the first objection, which deals with goods whose appearances or qualities may have been altered by alchemy, as well as with the second, which deals with different measures being used in different localities.) The third objection is that it is unreasonable to expect a seller to be aware of all the defects in the thing he is selling, since "great knowledge is required which is lacking to most sellers."

Thomas then gives his opinion, which is that whether a defect arises from the quality or the quantity of the thing sold, a seller who knowingly misrepresents what he sells sins and is bound to restitution, as likewise a buyer sins and is bound to restitution if he purchases something for a lesser price than it is worth because the seller out of ignorance is not aware of its true value. And although a seller or buyer who out of ignorance charges or pays an unjust price does not sin, if he later discovers his error he is bound to restitution.

His reply to the third objection is simply that one does not expect a seller to know about the "hidden qualities" of the thing to be sold, but "those only by means of which it is rendered apt for human uses," such as whether a horse is strong or runs well, which "a seller and buyer are easily able to know." Then in his third article Aquinas asks, Whether a seller is obliged to reveal the defect of a thing sold? The first objection argues that since the seller does not compel a buyer to buy something and is not required to examine the buyer's decision to buy, therefore he may also assume the buyer's due diligence in examining the quality of the thing sold. The second objection states that it would be foolish for a seller to hinder a sale by pointing out a defect in the thing to be sold, quoting Cicero to the effect that it would be absurd for someone to advertise a house infested with pests for sale. (I omit objection three which deals with one's obligation to offer counsel or moral advice to someone else.) Then objection four argues that if a seller is not bound to reveal information he has about an impending drop in the price of a good (which usually would cause his own price to drop immediately), then neither is he bound to reveal defects in the merchandise to be sold which would likewise result in lowering the price.

Thomas answers with his own opinion, which is that a seller is bound to reveal faults which either make the item less valuable and would therefore lower its price, or defects which would result in some harm to the buyer. However, if the seller has already discounted the item on account of its defects, he is not necessarily bound to mention those defects if they are obvious, since in that case the buyer might demand an even greater discount.

Thomas replies to the first objection that a buyer cannot judge the quality of something if its defects are hidden, so that the comparison is invalid. As for the second objection, no one is bound to advertise something for sale mentioning only its defects, since the item may well have some good qualities as well. Then lastly, he answers the fourth objection, saying that a future event which will cause a fall (or rise) in prices is different from a present condition which does the same thing, i.e., that in strict justice one is not bound to reveal a future probable drop in price, but if a seller did give that information, or discounted his price, "he would be of very abundant virtue."

Then we come to the last article in question 77, Whether it is licit by engaging in business (*negotiando*) to sell something at a higher price than was paid for it? There are three objections adduced. (I omit the first and third objections which are basically arguments from the authority of certain Fathers of the Church.) The second objection argues that anyone who by his commercial activity sells a thing for more than he paid for it, necessarily either buys it for less than it is worth or sells it for more, and thus commits a sin.

In his reply Thomas distinguishes between various kinds of commercial activity. In the first place he mentions a "natural and necessary" sort "on account of necessities of life," and such exchange properly pertains not to businessmen (*negotiatores*) but to "*oeconomicos vel politicos*," i.e., to those who have some duty concerned with the welfare of the household or the political community, and this sort is praiseworthy. Then there is the kind of commerce engaged in for seeking gain, and this kind "is justly blamed because in itself it serves gain." But although gain in itself does not "imply anything morally good (*honestum*) or necessary, neither is it vicious or contrary to virtue in itself," provided it is done for a good end "and thus commerce is made licit." Thus gain may be sought moderately for the support of one's household or to help the poor or to provide for the common good, and the gain sought is simply a payment for one's labor (*stipendium laboris*).

In his reply to objection two Thomas notes that someone can licitly sell something for more than he paid for it if he made improvements in the item or because its price was higher on account of being exported to some other place or on account of the passage of time or on account of the risk he had in taking it to another place.

I think that anyone who compares the business ethics of St. Tho-

Aquinas on Buying and Selling

mas with those of today will be struck not only by the differences at specific points—e.g., not taking advantage of a buyer's ignorance—but on the whole approach to commercial life. But let us first look at some of the specific points before we raise more general considerations. At the very outset we are told that it is wrong to sell something for more than it is worth or to buy it for less than it is worth. This is surely one of the cardinal points at which capitalist economic thought is opposed to that of St. Thomas. For economics, as it has developed according to the spirit of capitalism, would reply not so much that Thomas's answer is wrong, but that the question itself is absurd. The phrase "more than it is worth" is meaningless. Prices are determined by a quasi-mechanical process which can be graphed in the familiar manner of neoclassical economics. It is true that under monopoly or other kinds of imperfect competition, firms can charge more than what economists consider the norm of marginal cost; still, in the end, something is worth whatever a buyer and a seller can agree on. No one forces a buyer to purchase an item, even at a monopolistic price. If a seller offers a product for too high a price, buyers will refuse to purchase it, and then (it is hoped) the self-correcting action of Adam Smith's invisible hand will intervene and the seller either lower his price or new firms enter the market—all in the long run, of course. And while there is some truth in this account of the operation of market forces, and while, under the rare and elusive condition of "perfect competition," the market price can sometimes even be an indication of the just price, it is merely an indication. Market forces are not the reason for a just price, even when they can be a sign of such a price. But in a capitalist economy, an economy characterized by the separation of ownership and work, many other factors must exist before we can begin to look at the market price as the just price. (One of the advantages of the distributist economic system proposed by such Catholic thinkers as Hilaire Belloc and G.K. Chesterton is that market prices would be more likely to be just prices, since no producer would be in a position to cut his labor costs so as to undersell his competitors.) Although the concept of "marginal cost" is of little use in the real world, still the idea that the price should reflect a firm's costs gets at the heart of a calculation of a just price. Of course, cost includes a just wage for the producer, and Aquinas's statement in article 4 that we just noted—that the profit of a merchant should be simply a wage for his labor—reflects this understanding.

The next two articles both deal with defects in products and the seller's duty to make these known to potential buyers. Here again we meet with a point of radical difference from capitalism. Not only is it generally held today to be stupid to reveal an unseen defect, but firms spend large sums on advertising and promoting products that are defective or harmful. In any case, if sellers today really revealed all the hidden defects in their products, I think it would change our buying habits quite a bit.

Thomas's fourth article gets to the heart of commercial life by asking whether it is licit for someone by engaging in business (*negotiando*) to sell something at a higher price than he bought it for, i.e., to do this as an occupation. He sets forth definite criteria for any increase in selling price over purchase price. If the seller has made improvements in the product, if on account of a change of place or time the price has legitimately risen, if he underwent risk in exporting it somewhere—all these justify selling something for more than one paid for it. But clearly there is no justification here for unlimited profits. Every increase in cost must be accounted for by some definite title. So although one may licitly engage in commerce, the gain should be payment for one's labor or risk.

We should also note the general attitude of St. Thomas toward commercial activity. Buying and selling which is for the sake of gain "is justly blamed (*juste vituperatur*) because it serves the desire for gain which knows no limit but tends into infinity. And therefore business (*negotiatio*) considered in itself has a certain baseness (*quamdam turpitudinem*) in so far as it does not imply of itself an honest or necessary end." With regard to the first point, that "business considered in itself has a certain baseness," there is ample confirmation of this in our own culture. Writing of New Left critics of American culture, the early neo-conservative scholar, Harry Clor, said in 1969,

> American society is said to be devoted to low, dull, and unexciting goals; it is said to be devoid of moral and spiritual inspiration. It is

moral mediocrity that is complained of. And this mediocrity is attributed to commercialism, a commercialism that produces an acquisitive, comfort-seeking, security-minded, and, hence, uninteresting way of life. This description of American life is no doubt exaggerated and oversimplified. But it is difficult, as well as unwise, to avoid the acknowledgement that there are some elements of truth in this description. In the United States a remarkable amount of attention is given to the accumulation and consumption of commodities. And we do not seem to mind being called a "consumer society." It does appear to be the case that for most Americans the pursuit of happiness has come to mean, in large measure, the attainment of economic security and the continual multiplication of the means for personal comfort and enjoyment.[3]

I would like to hope that any of my readers who are Christians, whether Catholic, Orthodox or Protestant, would without demur agree that a society devoted "to the accumulation and consumption of commodities" is hardly a model of what Christians should strive for. Apart from anything else, St. Paul's strictures in his first letter to Timothy ought to suffice to prove that point:

> If we have food and clothing, with these we shall be content. But those who desire to be rich fall into temptation, into a snare, into many senseless and hurtful desires that plunge men into ruin and destruction. For the love of money is the root of all evils; it is through this craving that some have wandered away from the faith and pierced their hearts with many pangs. (1 Tim. 6:8–10)

And further, as John Paul II wrote in *Centesimus Annus*, no. 36,

> It is not wrong to want to live better; what is wrong is a style of life which is presumed to be better when it is directed toward "having" rather than "being," which wants to have more, not in order to be more but in order to spend life in enjoyment as an end in itself.

And yet the fact remains, "In the United States a remarkable amount of attention is given to the accumulation and consumption of commodities." This is in a nation made up largely of people with some degree of Christian heritage and commitment, and which

---

3. Harry M. Clor, "American Democracy and the Challenge of Radical Democracy," in *How Democratic is America?* (Chicago: Rand-McNally, 1969), 105.

often likes to think of itself as one of the most religious nations on the earth. Any Christian critique of American culture which fails to comment on this "accumulation and consumption of commodities" and concentrates simply on (say) sexual misdeeds serves only to discredit any claims that might be made for the religion of Jesus Christ.

But there is one more general consideration which we must examine. St. Thomas speaks of that buying and selling which "is justly blamed because it serves the desire for gain which knows no limit but tends into infinity." Here is another important point to which little attention is given today. In order to understand it, let us look at a different passage, namely, ST I-II, q. 2, a. 1, ad 3. There Aquinas writes that "the appetite of natural riches is not infinite, because according to a set measure they satisfy nature; but the appetite of artificial riches is infinite, because it serves inordinate concupiscence. . . ." In other words, if we seek gain in order to fulfill our "appetite of natural riches," food, clothing, and so forth, whatever serves the necessities or reasonable conveniences of life, then this desire for gain has a natural end, a natural limit. We can eat only so much, we can reasonably keep only so many extra shirts or dresses in our closets. But not so with money, "artificial riches." Money very easily fits with "the desire for gain which knows no limit but tends into infinity." We can accumulate as much as we are able. We can receive gigantic salaries, as many CEOs do, money that many people would regard as a sufficient lifetime wage, yet which these receive year in and year out. It is truly incredible that in a country that so often claims to be Christian, such seeking after inordinate riches is tolerated, even defended and justified.

At least part of the reason that conservative Christians are apt to reactively defend such acquisitiveness is that many critics of such behavior are those who in other respects are hostile to Christian morality, e.g., in sexual matters. But Christians would do well to follow the example we saw above of Professor Clor, who was not afraid to admit that the New Left critics had a point. It is silly and ultimately self-defeating to refuse to acknowledge a truth that one's opponents advance. Rather, if our aim is to seek and defend truth, we should welcome it from whatever quarter it comes, and, if necessary, modify our own positions accordingly.

Aquinas on Buying and Selling

I have digressed somewhat from my original theme which was Aquinas's teaching on buying and selling. But I do not think that this digression was entirely useless. If we look at St. Thomas, or at Holy Scripture, or any other Catholic moral or spiritual writer, we shall see an attitude toward wealth and its acquisition which differs radically from that of a society "given to the accumulation and consumption of commodities," one that does "not seem to mind being called a 'consumer society,'" one in which "the pursuit of happiness has come to mean, in large measure, the attainment of economic security and the continual multiplication of the means for personal comfort and enjoyment." I imagine that some of my critics will accuse me of wanting to reduce our standard of living to that of penury, but I mean no such thing. Rather I think we might look to Pope Leo XIII's "frugal comfort" as our ideal. There is much more to life than material goods, and one cannot but pity those who do not realize that. In any case, St. Thomas lays down specific moral precepts for our business activity as well as setting forth what should be the goals of society as conceived by Catholic tradition. Anything less is unworthy of a Catholic, and indeed, of anyone else who claims to bear the name of Christ.

14

The Sin of Usury[1]

Thomas Storck

To the extent that usury is thought of or discussed today it is usually understood as the charging of excessive interest on loans, especially perhaps on a consumer loan as opposed to a business loan. Although the charging of high rates of interest is indeed a real social and political evil, this is not the classical understanding of usury. Rather usury, as that has been discussed for centuries in Catholic theology and condemned again and again by the Church, means the taking of *any* interest on *any* type of loan when it is taken simply by virtue of the loan contract. The most complete papal treatment of usury is found in the 1745 encyclical of Pope Benedict XIV, *Vix Pervenit*, the relevant portions of which run:

> The nature of the sin called usury has its proper place and origin in a loan contract [*in contractu mutui*]. This financial contract between consenting parties demands, by its very nature, that one return to another only as much as he has received. The sin rests on the fact that sometimes the creditor desires more than he has given. Therefore he contends some gain is owed him beyond that which he loaned, but any gain which exceeds the amount he gave is illicit and usurious.
>
> One cannot condone the sin of usury by arguing that the gain is not great or excessive, but rather moderate or small; neither can it be condoned by arguing that the borrower is rich; nor even by arguing that the money borrowed is not left idle, but is spent usefully, either to increase one's fortune ... or to engage in business

---

1. This chapter is an abridgment and revision of my article "Is Usury Still a Sin?," *Communio* 36.3 (2009): 447–74.

The Sin of Usury

transactions. The law governing loans consists necessarily in the equality of what is given and returned; once the equality has been established, whoever demands more than that violates the terms of the loan....

By these remarks, however, We do not deny that at times together with the loan contract certain other titles—which are not at all intrinsic to the contract—may run parallel with it. From these other titles, entirely just and legitimate reasons arise to demand something over and above the amount due on the contract.[2]

For most contemporaries this sounds odd and perhaps even contrary to reason, for does not a lender deprive himself of present money, and since he will receive the principal back only later, is it not simply just that he receive something over and above the principal to compensate him for the temporary loss? The short answer to this is No, for unless the creditor can point to some loss he will incur because he made the loan, or to some lost opportunity for gain, the mere fact of having made a loan does not give him the right to receive interest payments. We will look more closely at this below.

Historical background

In order to understand the argumentation of Pope Benedict, let us consider more fully the legal and theological framework which theologians and canonists for centuries employed when considering usury. In Roman law the contract known as *mutuum* governed the loan of something which was necessarily consumed in its use, and therefore the identical object could not be returned to the lender, only something of the same kind and amount.

> The subject-matter of the *mutuum* must consist of things that can be measured, weighed, or numbered, such as wine, corn, or money; that is, things which being consumed can be restored *in genere*.... From the nature of this contract the obligation is imposed upon the borrower to restore to the lender, not the identical thing loaned, but its equivalent—that is, another thing of the same kind, quality, and value....

2. Denzinger, 2546–50.

Integralism and the Common Good

With regard to the responsibility for loss, since from the peculiar character of the contract the right of consumption passes to the borrower, the latter is looked upon as the practical owner of the thing loaned, and he therefore holds it entirely at his own risk....[3]

The chief characteristic of the *mutuum* contract that differentiates it from any other type of loan is that the actual good borrowed is not returned but consumed or used up by the borrower. This is in contrast to the loan or rent of something which will be physically returned, such as a house or a car. In the latter type of loans, the same item that is loaned is returned to the lender, and because it is subject to wear and tear on account of its use by the borrower, compensation is justly due to the lender for this, beyond the return of the thing borrowed. But in a contract of *mutuum* there is no wear and tear on the item loaned and hence compensation for that does not enter into the contract. Any just title to interest must come from another source.

The Catholic Church manifested her opposition to usury beginning during the Patristic period, and gradually the reasoning of her theologians took on a more definite shape. The formulation by St. Thomas Aquinas is the classic and best example of these arguments. His most mature discussion of usury is in the *ST* II-II, q. 78.[4] I quote from the Respondeo from article 1, which contains his theory in a nutshell.

> I answer that to receive usury for money loaned [*mutuata*] is in itself unjust, because that is sold which does not exist, by which clearly an inequality is constituted which is contrary to justice. For the evidence of which it must be known that there are certain things the use of which is the consumption of those things; as we consume wine by using it for drinking or we consume wheat by using it for food. Whence in such things the use of a thing ought not to be computed separately from the thing itself; but to whomever is granted the use from that fact itself is granted [possession

---

3. William C. Morey, *Outlines of Roman Law*, 2nd ed. (New York: G. P. Putnam's, 1914), 355–56.
4. See also the *De Malo*, q. 13, a. 4.

The Sin of Usury

of] the thing; and on account of this in such things through the loan [*mutuum*] ownership is transferred. If anyone therefore wishes to sell separately the wine, and again wishes to sell the use of the wine, he would sell the same thing twice, or he would sell that which does not exist; whence clearly he would sin by injustice. And by a similar reason he commits injustice who loans [*mutuat*] wine or wheat seeking to be given two recompenses; one indeed the restitution of an equal amount of the thing, the other, on the other hand, the price of the use which is called usury.

Let us formulate Thomas's argument in a slightly different way so as to show that it is not unreasonable, and in fact makes perfect sense. Money is certainly the most common example of something loaned at *mutuum*, but not the only one. As we saw, St. Thomas based his argument on the more general class of consumptible things. And I think that if we look at ordinary consumptibles, such as food or drink, we might be able to look at the question afresh and understand the Church's doctrine better. Let us consider the following analogy.

Suppose we have a small businessman who owns a catering service, catering food and drink, and let us suppose further that any supplies which accompany the food and drink are disposable, plastic forks, paper napkins, etc., so that there is nothing which he provides to his customers which he must reuse and which are thus subject to wear and tear. Now what may he licitly charge his customers for? For the replacement cost of the food and drink and the other disposable supplies. In addition, he may charge each customer for a share of the overhead of his business, such as rent, utilities, his delivery van, wages for any employees, and for a salary for himself, which may be defined as a "return for his labor of organization and direction, and for the risk that he underwent."[5] But as regards the food and other consumptibles which he provides, it is hard to see how he can charge a customer for more than the amount purchased. If he furnishes 100 bottles of wine, the caterer may charge what it will cost him to replace a similar kind and amount of wine. Anything additional which he charges a customer

---

5. John A. Ryan, *Distributive Justice*, 3rd ed. (New York: Macmillan, 1942), 176.

Integralism and the Common Good

must come from one of the other titles I just mentioned—costs incident to the running of his business and wages for his employees and for himself.

This last is what is generally called profit, a term that is often used loosely and inexactly. As we see here, Msgr. Ryan reduces it to the proprietor's labor, plus his entrepreneurial abilities and risk. It is not an open-ended invitation to charge as much as the market will bear, but rather there must exist some title of justification such as Ryan enumerates. Looked at in this way the limiting of the reimbursement for the consumptibles sold seems obvious. Of course the caterer cannot charge for 110 bottles of wine if he delivers only 100. His profit, in reality his salary and compensation for risk, etc., is not gained by expecting more in return than what he supplied of the product, but rather is paid for in its own right.

The application of this to loans of *mutuum* can easily be seen. Someone in the business of making loans could justly take expenses from customers. In the Middle Ages there existed institutions called *montes pietatis*, lending institutions created to provide an alternative to usurers, sponsored by local governments or the Church. The *montes* were non-profit institutions, but they charged interest to cover their expenses, including salaries of their staff. But according to Msgr. Ryan's analysis no business is profit-making in the sense that it can justly seek the widest profits it can obtain. The owner can seek a fair "return for his labor of organization and direction, and for the risk that he underwent." Although one cannot calculate such returns with mathematical exactness, neither can one maintain that they have no theoretical limit. And even if one did argue that there should be no limit on such a return for labor, skill, and risk, still that is not the same as saying that usury for the lending activity itself may be exacted, for we have seen that the entrepreneur can require only the same amount of the consumptible good as he has provided, "the equality of what is given and returned," as Benedict XIV taught.[6]

---

6. Another way of looking at this example which yields the same conclusion is to regard a *mutuum* of money as a *sale*. As in the case of the caterer who provides 100 bottles of wine and receives as part of his total payment the price of the 100 bottles,

The Sin of Usury

Of course our caterer receives immediate or nearly immediate payment for his expenditure on food and other consumptibles. A loan of money, however, is generally paid back after a period of time, or gradually during such a period. Is not the lender entitled to some compensation on account of this delay? No, for "the mere time differential by itself does not cause a difference in value. There must be added the possibility of earning a profit in the intervening time period."[7] That is the meaning of the words of Pope Benedict XIV, that "We do not deny that at times together with the loan contract certain other titles—which are not at all intrinsic to the contract—may run parallel with it. From these other titles, entirely just and legitimate reasons arise to demand something over and above the amount due on the contract."

Historically the chief parallel titles were *lucrum cessans* and *damnum emergens*. The former is the loss of opportunity for gain—say an opportunity of becoming a partner in a business venture—which someone might forgo by making a loan, and the latter is some actual damage which he might incur by not having the funds available which he had loaned. But it is crucial to recognize that the mere fact of making a loan does not equate to the right to repayment of more than the principal. Unless the lender will suffer financial harm because he has loaned the funds, or for some other special circumstance, there is nothing in the loan transaction itself that entitles him to any interest payment.

Application of usury theory to contemporary economies

If it is the case that the "law governing loans consists necessarily in the equality of what is given and returned," then several questions suggest themselves which we will consider in this last section. In the first place, we have to ask what effect the intrinsic evil of

---

no more and no less, if we look at money loaned as a sale of money we see that the price of $100 is obviously $100. Any other just charges come from the same titles as the caterer had, overhead expenses, wages, etc. For the product provided one can charge only what it is worth, which in the case of money is its face value.

7. Heinrich Pesch, *Lehrbuch der Nationalökonomie/Teaching Guide to Economics*, translated by Rupert J. Ederer (Lewiston: Edwin Mellen, 2003), 5:200.

usury should have on the moral conduct of the Christian. Is there anything that Christians should do or avoid in their financial or economic behavior as a result of the sinfulness of usury? Secondly, what meaning does usury have in an economy hopelessly enmeshed in all kinds of interest-bearing transactions as a matter of course and without a thought as to any justifying title? Since even in the Renaissance lawyers found ways around the prohibition of usury by drawing up contracts that authorized repayment of more than the principal under various complex formulas,[8] and theologians could be found who sanctioned these contracts, are we committing the Church to a ridiculous anachronism, a relic of the past? Are we hankering after a silly formalism in order to justify something that it is easier and more honest simply to call interest on a loan?

In regard to our first question, the praxis of the Church beginning at least in the first half of the nineteenth century was to presume that some justifying title to interest probably exists in most cases in the context of a modern finance economy. This point of view was embodied in the (now abrogated) 1917 *Code of Canon Law* which restated the doctrine of *Vix Pervenit* while allowing in practice for the taking of interest under other titles.[9] Thus no one can be condemned for taking the legal or customary rate of interest on a loan, provided that that is not excessive. The Church is assuming

---

8. For example, the *contractus trinus* or triple contract, a three-fold contract made between two business partners, the first of whom was the active partner and the second inactive. The first part of the contract stipulated that the first partner manage the enterprise, say a trading voyage, and the second supply some or all of the funding. The second part of a *contractus trinus* stipulated that the active partner insure the inactive against loss, and by the third part the silent partner paid for this insurance by taking a return which was less than the expected profit of the enterprise, say 4% on his investment, against an expected return of 8%, but which was guaranteed even if the enterprise miscarried.

9. Canon 1543 of the 1917 *Code of Canon Law* ran, "If a fungible thing is given to someone in such a way that it becomes his and later is to be returned only in the same kind, no gain can be received by reason of the contract itself; but in the payment of a fungible thing, it is not in itself illicit to contract for the gain allowed by law, unless it is clear that this is excessive, or even for a greater gain, if a just and adequate title be present." There is no comparable canon in the 1983 *Code*.

The Sin of Usury

that parallel titles which justify interest exist in the vast majority of cases, and that even if in some cases they do not, it is better for the sake of consciences to ignore that fact than to attempt the probably hopelessly complex task of disentangling the various elements of the contract.

This does not mean, however, that in today's economy the question of usury is dead. We should recall that interest on a loan is justified only when some opportunity for legitimate gain is forgone or some loss sustained. The extrinsic titles were never given official approval except as compensation for lost opportunities for investment earnings, and therefore "they can never be advanced as a justification of a general loan system based on motives of profit."[10] But one can hardly justify taking interest on the ground that one is forgoing another lost opportunity for taking interest! The lost opportunity must be of some other sort, such as a partnership or business expansion. Moreover, while it is certainly correct to point out that today there is usually opportunity for productive investment, and that therefore those who put money out at *mutuum* but would otherwise invest it are entitled to claim *lucrum cessans*, this reasoning does not always hold. For in cases of depression or recession "the profit expectations of businessmen are likely to be so low that they would not employ men and machines on new investment projects even if you let them borrow temporarily at a zero interest rate."[11] In such cases "some savings will follow the sterile path of debt-financed consumption, with eventual repayment at the expense of current consumption."[12] In other words, in such situations a lack of consumer demand makes spending on productive investment unprofitable, so it is likely that someone putting money out at *mutuum* is not truly forgoing investment profit, because no profit is to be had for the time being. Thus when there is excess savings with no outlet for profitable use, it is hardly in accord with justice or the

---

10. John P. Kelly, *Aquinas and Modern Practices of Interest Taking* (Brisbane: Aquinas Press, 1945), 33.
11. Paul Samuelson, *Economics*, 9th ed. (New York: McGraw-Hill, 1973), 336.
12. John F. Cronin, *Economics and Society* (New York: American Book Co., 1939), 131.

common good to reward those who choose to loan by giving them a rate of interest based on a merely hypothetical opportunity cost.

Likewise it also seems hard to justify *lucrum cessans* for those who have no real intention of making investments, simply because such opportunities are normally available to all. What of ordinary savers who desire to put their money into insured savings accounts at banks or credit unions and who because of inexperience or fear of loss have no desire to invest in business ventures, even to buy shares of stock or mutual funds? They are not undergoing a real loss of investment income on account of their loan of money to the bank, since otherwise they might have simply hidden the money in a mattress. I do not see how the merely theoretical possibility that they could make gains from investments applies to them, since they are too risk averse to do so. Can they licitly claim interest on bank accounts and under what title? I think there is a reason for thinking such interest just, but it is not one of the extrinsic titles that theologians approved. It is the mere fact of inflation. "He who receives a loan of money . . . is not held to pay back more than he received by the loan"[13]—but with our ability to monitor the level of inflation in an economy, we realize that money simply left alone, as in a mattress, will usually diminish in value. Therefore payment for inflation for money deposited in a bank or credit union seems just.

In the sixteenth century and thereafter the zeal for economic justice in Catholic Europe began to wane, and lawyers and merchants increasingly sought ways around the usury prohibition, such as the *contractus trinus*. But if instead of that, men's souls had been animated by love of God and neighbor, or even fear of judgment, what might have been done—or what could be done now? Let us look briefly at a few financial practices and institutions which Christians might promote on behalf of justice.

The whole Christian doctrine of property with its responsibilities of ownership which the modern world has forgotten is wrapped up in this question of money and the taking of interest thereon. If I am in possession of money, I am in possession of something that is vital

---

13. *ST* II-II, q. 78, a. 2, ad 2.

The Sin of Usury

to the society in which I live. I, as a Christian, therefore, have very definite responsibilities with respect to the ownership of that money. Christian morality knows of no theory of an unqualified and unconditional ownership of property of any description. Property must be used according to its true end and purpose and in the case of money that true end and purpose is as a means of exchange. Therefore, the wrongful withholding of that money from circulation for the purpose of making a profit by waiting is a misuse of property.[14]

Such a doctrine of money is akin to what Paul VI teaches about property in *Populorum Progressio*:

> Private property does not constitute for anyone an absolute and unconditioned right. No one is justified in keeping for his exclusive use what he does not need, when others lack necessities.... If certain landed estates impede the general prosperity because they are extensive, unused or poorly used, or because they bring hardship to peoples or are detrimental to the interests of the country, the common good sometimes demands their expropriation. (nos. 23–24)

Clearly expropriation of funds that are being used merely in idle usury should be a last resort, and normally the law will use financial incentives and penalties to direct such funds toward uses more in accord with the common good. But no Catholic need be afraid to acknowledge that "the public authority, in view of the common good, may specify more accurately what is licit and what is illicit for property owners in the use of their possessions."[15] A Christian society, then, by outlawing true usury completely, and by forbidding or discouraging the kinds of contracts that during the Renaissance helped undermine the usury prohibition among both theologians and merchants, would seek to direct money toward its proper use. Some form of credit union, akin to the *montes*, would be adequate for providing financing for non-productive consumer loans. The demand for commercial credit could be satisfied either by merchants diverting funds from investments, and licitly claiming *lucrum*

---

14. Kelly, *Aquinas and Modern Practices of Interest Taking*, 46–47.
15. Pius XI, Encyclical *Quadragesimo Anno* 49.

cessans, or by some form of commercial credit union run by associations of businesses or by occupational groups (guilds).

Catholics should have as lively a sense of the demands of the moral law relative to the economy as they do relative to sexuality or war.

> In the Middle Ages, it was taken for granted God's law applied to the totality of life. The idea of a double standard of morality, with a strict code for private life and a minimum of moral obligation for business and public life, is an innovation based on philosophical and religious individualism of the eighteenth century.[16]

However far we are today from a Christian society or a Christian economy, the goal "to impress the divine law on the affairs of the earthly city"[17] is always imperative. As with most of Catholic social morality today, our first task is one of education and formation, since very few Catholics are aware of the existence of these doctrines or of their binding character. This may seem of little consequence, but as with all our efforts in this life, this is part of making the world a more perfect offering to the Sacred Heart of Jesus who will one day renew all things in himself.

---

16. John F. Cronin, *Catholic Social Principles: The Social Teaching of the Catholic Church Applied to American Economic Life* (Milwaukee: Bruce, 1950), 43.

17. *Gaudium et Spes* 43.

15

Robin Hood Economics

Edmund Waldstein, O.Cist.

Once, when the Sheriff of Nottingham's men came across Robin Hood deep in Sherwood Forest, he was kneeling before an altar, hearing Mass. Robin waited until the holy sacrifice was over before turning to fight them. The old ballads consistently describe Robin as a pious and faithful Catholic, scrupulously chaste, who was said to have heard three Masses every day before breakfast. In fact, Robin's band of merry men is described as following a quasi-monastic rule. They shared a common purse. And according to the sixteenth-century play *The Downfall of Robert, Earle of Huntingdon,* based on older ballads, they even took a vow of chastity: "Thirdly no yeoman following Robin Hoode / In Sherewood, shall use widowe, wife, or maid, / But by true labour, lustfull thoughts expell."

Nevertheless Robin loved to rob the abbots and priors of England's rich, feudal monasteries: "From wealthy abbots' chests, and churls' abundant store, / What oftentimes he took, he shar'd amongst the poor." Those monasteries practiced a certain kind of poverty—they held everything in common, and each monk was to receive only what was necessary from the common stock—yet, corporately, they were rich landowners, and their abbots and priors were influential lords.

The monasteries gave much to the poor, providing a kind of social security. (Indeed, the dissolution of the monasteries by Henry VIII was to lead to a social crisis.) Yet to Robin Hood they were on the side of the rich who take an unfair share of the crops produced by peasants. The only religious whom Robin seemed to like were the mendicant friars, such as Friar Tuck, who were the proponents of a new interpretation of religious poverty, in which there was to be no corporate wealth.

The world described in the Robin Hood ballads of the fifteenth century, when the feudal system was in its post-Black Death decline, is obviously very different from our own world of global capitalism. And yet, Robin Hood can in some ways be a spur to reflection on our own situation.

The implicit foundation of Robin Hood's stealing from the rich to give to the poor is the perennial Christian teaching that the goods of the earth are given by God for the sustenance of all human beings. This is the principle that modern Catholic social teaching calls the "universal destination of goods," and it issues an urgent challenge to us in our own time.

As a Cistercian monk, I find that Robin's contempt for the monasteries of his time raises questions for me about the relation of my monastic community, with its communal sharing of goods, to the wider economic order. This is a question that any community of believers that tries to live like the early Church in Acts 2:44–45 will have to ask: How can we interact with the wider economic system that surrounds us without becoming complicit in the injustices of that system?

JESUS's injunctions on giving freely and without expectation of return fulfill and complete the teachings of the Old Testament. God gave the earth to all humankind. To give to those in need, therefore, is an act of justice, rendering to them what they are due as those to whom God has given the earth.

After the conversion of Constantine, as more of society became Christian and being Christian became less a countercultural choice, the Fathers of the Church were very concerned with correcting wealthy Christians who had lost sight of this principle and were withholding their wealth from those in need. Saint Basil the Great in the East and Saint Ambrose of Milan in the West were particularly insistent on the point. Thus, Basil addresses the rich man in Luke 12:18, who says "This is what I shall do: I shall tear down my barns and build larger ones. There I shall store all my grain and other goods and I shall say to myself, 'Now as for you, you have so many good things stored up for many years, rest, eat, drink, be merry!'" To this man Saint Basil retorts, "Tell me, what things are yours? Where did you take them from? Did you give them being?" The grain that has grown does not really belong to the rich man; it is for those who need it. Similarly, Saint Ambrose preached a sermon on the story of King Ahab's coveting of Naboth's vineyard in which he addressed himself directly to the rich citizens of Milan with searching questions: "How far, O rich, do you extend your mad greed?... Why do you cast out the companion whom nature has given you and claim for yourself nature's possession? The earth was established in common for all, rich and poor. Why do you alone, O rich, demand special treatment?" It is unjust, Ambrose thinks, for the rich to claim the fruits of the earth for themselves exclusively, when that bounty was given to humankind in common.

In the light of these teachings of Scripture and the Church Fathers, the scholastic theologians questioned whether the possession of private property in any sense can be justified.

Saint Thomas Aquinas argued that while the use or *enjoyment* of goods always has to be common, in the sense that each person only gets to use or consume what they need, the system of *producing* goods can be private, in the sense that each person can dispose of what they produce. In fact, he gives reasons why it is conducive to a peaceful and just society for there to be private property in that qualified sense. He thinks that people tend to work harder when they have responsibility for what they produce. He gives the example of a household in which there are too many servants: in this case, some of them will not bother to work for the common store, since they can depend on the others to work for them: "Every man is more careful to procure what is for himself alone than that which is common to many or to all: since each one would shirk the labor and leave to another that which concerns the community, as happens where there is a great number of servants." The experience of the socialist regimes of the twentieth century confirms Saint Thomas's insight here.

He also argues that things are more orderly when there is private property, whereas confusion would result from communism. The idea seems to be that needs are more efficiently recognized and met when each person has responsibility for what he produces.

Integralism and the Common Good

Nevertheless, Saint Thomas holds that the *use* of goods has to remain common. By this he means that each person can only justly keep what he needs to live and appropriately fulfill his role in society. A person who has a representative role in society (the ruler, for example) will need a certain magnificence to fulfill that role, but even here there is a limit. And each person is bound to give away *all* of his superfluous goods to those in need. This is the principle now known in Catholic theology as the "universal destination of goods."

A consequence of this principle is that when someone is in urgent need, he may take goods away from someone who has more than enough without committing the sin of theft. This is the justification of the "Robin Hood Principle" of "stealing" from the rich to give to the poor. It is not really stealing if the poor are in real need, and the rich are living in real superfluity. In the Rhineland, this kind of "stealing" is called *fringsen* after Cardinal Frings, the Archbishop of Cologne, who instructed his flock to "steal" coal from the coal yards of the railway companies when they were dying of cold after the Second World War.

Modern Catholic social teaching, beginning with Pope Leo XIII in the nineteenth century, developed the principle of the universal destination of goods and applied it to the problems of modern economies. Thus, Pope Pius XI thought that the government has the duty of regulating private property to rectify unjust distribution. "When the State brings private ownership into harmony with the needs of the common good," he wrote in 1931, "it does not commit a hostile act against private owners but rather does them a friendly service; for it thereby effectively prevents the private possession of goods, which the Author of nature in His most wise providence ordained for the support of human life, from causing intolerable evils." In 1952 Pope Pius XII taught that the universal destination of goods required prosperous countries to receive needy migrants from poor countries.

The actual phrase "universal destination of goods" was coined by the Second Vatican Council: "Whatever the forms of property may be, as adapted to the legitimate institutions of peoples, according to diverse and changeable circumstances, attention must always be paid to this universal destination of earthly goods." The council hinted that in a globalized economy, traditional means of realizing the principle would sometimes have to be changed. Pope Paul VI developed this insight in the encyclical *Populorum Progressio*, in which he emphasizes that the connections that have arisen between peoples of different parts of the world imposes responsibilities on those who live in rich countries. We cannot be content to live in superfluity when there are children starving in poorer parts of the world.

WHILE the Catholic Church continues to hold Saint Thomas's position that a limited kind of private property can be just, nevertheless she has also always held that it is more perfect for Christians to live in communities in which not only the distribution, but also the production of goods is common. It has usually been thought that while absolute community of goods is not beneficial for society at large, it is very beneficial indeed for monastic communities. As monks we have dedicated ourselves to living as a sign of the Heavenly Jerusalem that is to come. We do not marry and are not given in marriage; we submit to the obedience of a rule and an abbot; we hold all things in common.

Since the beginnings of the monastic movement in third-century Egypt, it has been held that community of goods is closely connected to celibacy and obedience. Without the freedom from worldly care that comes from celibacy (1 Cor. 7:33), and without the discipline of obedience, the community of goods would not be beneficial. And without community of goods, and care against any superfluous wealth, celibacy and obedience would become lax. One of the things that I find fascinating about communities such as the Bruderhof is that they seem to provide a counterexample to this ancient wisdom, insofar as they have obedience and community of goods without celibacy.

My own monastery, Heiligenkreuz Abbey in Austria, lives according to the rule of Saint Benedict of Nursia. Saint Benedict is emphatic. "Above all," he writes,

> this vice of private property has to be cut out of the monastery by its roots. Let no one presume to give or accept anything without

the abbot's orders, nor to have anything as his own. Not anything at all: neither book, nor writing-tablet, nor pen; nothing whatsoever, since he is not even allowed power over his own body and will. But let everyone look to the abbot of the monastery to receive what is needful. Nor can they keep anything which the abbot has not given or allowed. Let all things be common to all, as it is written: "no one said that any of the things which he possessed was his own" (Acts 4:32).

Saint Benedict wants his monks to live from the work of their own hands, and to be generous in sharing the goods they produce with the poor and with travelers. He recognizes that the monks will sometimes have to sell their goods in order to buy others which they cannot produce themselves. But he commands them to sell them at their true value, so that the purpose of the transaction is exchange rather than profit: "And in the prices themselves, let not the vice of avarice creep in, but let things always be sold somewhat cheaper than by worldly persons, that in all things God may be glorified."

Saint Benedict's form of monastic life turned out, perhaps unexpectedly, to be what we would now call an economic success. The efficient division of labor achievable by a community living under a vow of obedience meant that monasteries were good at producing goods. The principle of always selling at cheaper prices than non-monastic producers turned out to be an effective means of attracting buyers.

Yet there was a danger latent here. Many monasteries became very rich, and their great stores of goods had a corrupting influence on monastic discipline. This problem was compounded in the Middle Ages, as monasteries came to be integrated more and more into the feudal system. Often monasteries came to rule over feudal lands, and over the serfs who worked those lands. In the eleventh century in the great French monastery of Cluny the monks spent almost the whole day in prayer. They no longer lived from the work of their *own* hands, as the rule commanded, because they had serfs to work for them. Not surprisingly, the serfs sometimes resented their monastic overlords, and thought that they took an unjust share of the produce of the serfs' labor.

My own order, the Cistercian order, was founded partly in reaction to that problem. The Cistercians wanted to return to a literal observance of the rule, living from their own manual labor. Nevertheless, even in the Cistercian order, the greater part of the manual labor was soon done by the illiterate "lay brothers" (peasants who had entered the monastery) while the educated "choir brothers" (recruited from the gentry) were more engaged in intellectual labor—copying manuscripts, teaching, writing theological treatises—and in more frequent formal prayer. Moreover, when they were given lands to found a monastery, the people giving the lands would often relocate the serfs who had been there before. My monastery was founded in 1133 when Saint Leopold III, margrave of Austria, donated some of his feudal possessions for our foundation. In the woods behind our monastery one can still see a few stone walls belonging to a village whose inhabitants were relocated when our monastery was founded. I often wonder what the serfs who lived there thought when they had to leave their home. Later on, the Cistercians, too, ruled over peasant inhabitants in their territories.

TODAY, my monastery still has many of the lands that were given to us in the Middle Ages, and we live principally from the timber, grain, and wine grown on them. A few monks still work the land, but on account of various necessities through the centuries, most of the monks now "work" as parish priests in nearby parishes, or as teachers in our theological college (as I do). But this means that most of the work in our forests, fields, and vineyards is now done by wage labor. Our workers and employees like to quote the old saying, "life is good under a crooked staff"—meaning that clerical masters (symbolized by the pastoral staff or crozier) are more lenient than lay ones. In fact, we try to follow Catholic social teaching in treating those we employ; we pay them a living wage, and so on.

But this sometimes leads to difficult situations. For example, we used to have a sawmill to process the timber from our forests. If we could have worked the sawmill entirely with the labor of monks, it would have been profitable, but since we had to employ wage laborers, and since we paid them a living wage, it could not compete with the large-scale sawmills run by competitor corporations. Eventually, after losing money on the sawmill for several years, we decided to close it down. It was a difficult decision, and the difficulty arose from the almost inevitable necessity of interacting with the larger capitalist system that surrounds us. The system has its own dynamic, which is hard to escape.

According to the principle of the universal destination of goods, *all* superfluous goods belong by right to the poor. But the difficulty comes in determining what really is superfluous. The human heart is devious, and skilled in self-deception. It is perhaps easier for communities to judge objectively about this than individuals. But even in communities one can find what Eberhard Arnold, cofounder of the Bruderhof, called "collective egoism."[1]

My own experience of living out community of goods in the monastery has been a liberating one. Since I receive everything that I need from the monastery I am free to devote myself to prayer, to teaching theology, and to my other duties. But I must admit that Robin Hood would probably disapprove of me. Although my monastery tries to give away as much of our income as possible, nevertheless we monks live fairly comfortable lives, with good food and warm rooms. Saint Benedict lists the necessary things that a monk should receive from the abbot: two cowls, two tunics, sandals, shoes, a girdle, a knife, a pen, a needle, a handkerchief, and a writing tablet. I'm afraid that in addition to cowl and tunic I have coats, jackets, socks, skiing equipment, and so on. That writing tablet has now become a laptop. I am even given a monthly allowance of pocket money for buying books, chocolate, and other luxuries.

But, of course, whether Robin Hood would approve of us or not, we are grateful for the good things that God gives. The primary purpose of monastic poverty is not to despise the gifts that God has given to humankind, but to conform ourselves to Christ. There is a time for fasting and doing penance, but there is also a time for feasting, and using the goods of the earth to express joy. "For John came neither eating nor drinking, and they say, 'He has a demon'; the Son

---

1. "From Property to Community," *Plough*, May 19, 2016, www.plough.com/en/topics/community/church-community/from-property-to-community.

of Man came eating and drinking, and they say, 'Behold, a glutton and a drunkard'" (Mt. 11:18–19). This was a lesson that the early Cistercians had to learn. In the early years of Saint Bernard's monastery at Clairvaux, the monks were unwilling to eat anything that tasted good. But when William of Champeaux, the Bishop of Châlons-sur-Marne, visited them, he taught them to accept their food with thanksgiving: "You will be safe in doing so, for through God's grace it has become fit for you to use. On the other hand, if you still remain disobedient and incredulous, you will be resisting the Holy Spirit and so be ungrateful for his grace."

In the old ballads, Robin Hood is famous for his generous woodland feasts. So on this point at least, he and the bishop would have seen eye to eye.

16

The Needy Immigrant and the Universal Destination of Goods[1]

Edmund Waldstein, O.Cist.

The current debates on immigration between liberal globalists on the one hand and populist nationalists on the other raise fundamental questions about the nature of political community and solidarity. Neither side offers satisfactory answers to these questions. Immigration naturally raises such fundamental questions, since the extent to which new members are admitted to a community varies widely depending on how that community understands and sustains its own internal unity. Thus a nomadic tribe, living in easily breachable tents and depending on close bonds of trust, will approach the integration of strangers differently than a city-state with stone houses, locking doors, speculative philosophy, and law courts.

The vast numbers of persons currently fleeing the incessant wars in the Levant or economic hardship and disruption in the global south (disruption caused in part by the dynamics of the globalization of neoliberal capitalism), and trying to enter the prosperous and relatively stable countries of Europe and North America, have thus brought the debates between nationalists and globalists to a head. The globalists favor a liberal immigration policy, not only out of compassion for the needy, but also as a means to the destruction of the remnants of homogenous national cultures, in order to make

---

[1]. A letter replying to this article, as well as the author's response to that letter, may be found at *The Josias*, on March 11, 2017, https://thejosias.com/2017/03/11/letter-on-the-needy-immigrant/.

way for a fully liberal, multi-cultural future. The nationalists, on the other hand, favor protectionist immigration policies, often with callous disregard for the needs of refugees and migrants.

In this essay, I do not propose a complete solution to the questions raised by the globalist-nationalist debate, nor do I offer a complete account of an immigration policy from the perspective of Catholic Social Teaching. Rather I offer first a brief sketch of the origins of both nationalism and secular globalism, origins which call their respective ideas of solidarity into question. And second I explain an important principle of natural law as expounded by Catholic Social Teaching that has to be constantly insisted on in the current debate. The principle is that wealthy countries have obligations toward needy migrants that stem from the universal destination of goods.

The debate between globalism and nationalism is in many ways reminiscent of a debate raised in ancient philosophy by the conquests of Alexander the Great: is man a political animal or an imperial animal?[2] That is, does the nature of man limit him to the small-scale communal life of the ancient city, in which he can know most of his fellow citizens, and a solidarity based on friendship can bind the community together? Or does the universality of reason rather incline him to hold, as Plutarch put it, "that his friends and kindred should be the good and virtuous [of all mankind], and that the vicious only should be accounted foreigners"?

The Christian Middle Ages were, to some extent, able to achieve a synthesis of those two ideals. Christendom was ideally a universal community in which all the baptized were considered friends and fellow-citizens of the City of God, and only Muslims and Jews were considered foreigners. The whole of Christendom was united by the authority of the Pope, who entrusted the temporal sword to the emperor. But that order was subsidiary, with many common goods pursued at the lower levels of kingdoms, duchies, counties, abbeys, towns, villages, etc.

---

2. "Empire II: Herodotus, Aristotle and Jokes," *Sancrucensis*, March 25, 2012, https://sancrucensis.wordpress.com/2012/03/25/empire-i-herodotus-aristotle-and-jokes/.

Integralism and the Common Good

Medieval Christendom was always fraught with tensions—between spiritual and temporal powers as well as between various temporal authorities—and it began to break down at the turn of the thirteenth and fourteenth centuries. The conflict between King Philip the Fair of France and Pope Boniface VIII was in part a conflict between the old ideal of Christendom and the emerging strong territorial monarchies. The new monarchies transferred many of the claims of the Church on to themselves—thus the French monarchy was seen as a "mystical body" headed by the King, and those who died for France were seen as martyrs.[3] The classical idea of *patria*, the fatherland, which had previously been applied either to the Heavenly City, or to the village where one was born, was now applied to the Kingdom of France. This had in part to do with the rediscovery of Aristotle's *Politics* in the thirteenth century. Aristotle's teaching on the *polis* was now applied to the Kingdom, seen as a complete society arising from natural inclination, and thus receiving its authority from God through the natural law, rather than through spiritual power.

Thus began the development of the modern nation-state, whose severance from the ideal of Christendom was solidified in the seventeenth century at the Peace of Westphalia. The nation-state combines the worst features of political and imperial communities. It lacks the advantages of a small community founded in friendship and mutual trust among citizens actually living a common life, but preserves the communal egoism and hatred of outsiders typical of such small communities. It lacks the capaciousness and ability to unite many nations typical of ancient empires, but has all of their militarism and *libido dominandi*. The absurd spectacle of modern "imperialism" (abusively so-called) shows a form of human solidarity that lacks the most important political goods, and replaces the pacific goods of empire with endless unjust wars of conquest.

It cannot be denied that such nation-states were at times able to serve the common good to some extent, and one cannot fail to

3. See chapter 5 of Ernst Kantorowicz's enduring classic *The King's Two Bodies: A Study in Mediaeval Political Theology* (Princeton, NJ: Princeton University Press, 1997).

praise the heroism of such true patriots as St. Joan of Arc. But on balance the rise of the nation-state seems to have brought more harm than good. The ever more idolatrous political theologies and ever more internecine wars of self-sacrifice with which nation-states have tried to bolster their internal solidarity culminated in the horrific slaughter of World War I and World War II.

After the horrors of the World Wars of the twentieth century, a new ideal of global solidarity founded in a secular, liberal conception of human rights came to the fore. This aridly rationalistic global liberalism cannot, however, provide true universal solidarity, which can only be found in the Social Kingship of Christ.[4] Thus we are left with the current situation in which the heirs of Enlightenment rationalism press their unrealistic dream of a secular end of history against the no less ugly heirs of the ideals Philip the Fair, Henry VIII, Cardinal Richelieu, and Bismarck. Much depends on how this struggle will end. In the meantime, however, it is important to try to follow the natural law as best we can in the present situation.

An important precept of the natural law, perennially taught by the Church, is the obligation to help refugees and needy immigrants. This obligation is inextricably linked to the principle of the universal destination of goods. In an address to American bishops cited in his Apostolic Constitution *Exsul Familia Nazarethana*, Pope Pius XII taught the following:

> The natural law itself, no less than devotion to humanity, urges that ways of migration be opened to these people. *For the Creator of the universe made all good things primarily for the good of all.* Since land everywhere offers the possibility of supporting a large number of people, the sovereignty of the State, although it must be respected, cannot be exaggerated to the point that access to this land is, for inadequate or unjustified reasons, denied to needy and decent people from other nations, provided of course, that the

---

4. "Secularized Fraternity or Solidarity and the Failure of the European Union," *Sancrucensis*, June 24, 2016, https://sancrucensis.wordpress.com/2016/06/24/secularized-fraternity-or-solidarity-and-the-failure-of-the-european-union/.

public wealth [*publicae utilitati*], considered very carefully, does not forbid this.⁵

In this passage Pope Pius traces the natural law demand for allowing the immigration of the needy of other parts of the world into a polity to the principle that "the Creator of the universe made all good things primarily for the good of all." This is a perennial principle of Catholic Social Teaching: "the universal destination of goods." One of the most famous witnesses to that principle was given by St. Ambrose of Milan in *On Naboth*:

> It is not one poor man, Naboth, who was slain; every day Naboth is struck down, every day the poor man is slain. Seized by this fear, the human race is now departing its lands. Carrying his little one, the poor man sets out with his children; his wife follows in tears, as if she were accompanying her husband to his grave. Yet she who mourns over the corpses of her family weeps less because she [at least] has her spouse's tomb even if she has lost his protection; even if she no longer has children, she at least does not weep over them as exiles; she does not lament what is worse than death—the empty stomachs of her tender offspring. How far, O rich, do you extend your mad greed? "Shall you alone dwell upon the earth?" (Is. 5:8). Why do you cast out the companion whom nature has given you and claim for yourself nature's possession? *The earth was established in common for all, rich and poor*. Why do you alone, O rich, demand special treatment?⁶

External things such as food, fuel, and shelter, and also the land which is necessary for the production of such things, are given by God to the whole human race for the sustenance of life. The tradition recognizes that private property is lawful insofar as it is conducive to such sustenance (see *ST* II-II, q. 66, a. 2), but those who have property beyond their needs owe it to those who are in need. Thus St. Thomas teaches that *"fringsen"* (to use the post-war German term for taking from the superfluity of others when one is oneself in need) is permissible:

---

5. Text from http://www.papalencyclicals.net/Pius12/p12exsul.htm, emphasis added.
6. Text from http://hymnsandchants.com/Texts/Sermons/Ambrose/OnNaboth.htm; emphasis added.

Needy Immigrant and Universal Destination of Goods

According to the natural order established by Divine Providence, inferior things are ordained for the purpose of succoring man's needs by their means. Wherefore the division and appropriation of things which are based on human law, do not preclude the fact that man's needs have to be remedied by means of these very things. Hence *whatever certain people have in superabundance is due, by natural law, to the purpose of succoring the poor.* For this reason Ambrose says, and his words are embodied in the Decretals: "It is the hungry man's bread that you withhold, the naked man's cloak that you store away, the money that you bury in the earth is the price of the poor man's ransom and freedom." Since, however, there are many who are in need, while it is impossible for all to be succored by means of the same thing, each one is entrusted with the stewardship of his own things, so that out of them he may come to the aid of those who are in need. Nevertheless, *if the need be so manifest and urgent, that it is evident that the present need must be remedied by whatever means be at hand* (for instance when a person is in some imminent danger, and there is no other possible remedy), *then it is lawful for a man to succor his own need by means of another's property,* by taking it either openly or secretly: nor is this properly speaking theft or robbery.[7]

Pius XII's teaching on immigrants is a specific application of this general principle. Wealthy countries that have a superfluity of external goods owe a share of those goods to the needy who flee less fortunate countries on account of war or unemployment or hunger. This is a matter of justice, not merely of voluntary generosity.

Pope Pius XII of course recognizes that a country needs to preserve its common good. The demands of justice in a concrete situation will depend in part on the demands of the common good. And of course the common good includes the social bonds in a society on which its internal unity and peace depend. Thus the demands of the common good will vary depending on what sort of social bonds are necessary to hold a particular society together: the very point at issue in the globalist/nationalist debate. But one thing is certain: it is not acceptable for a wealthy country to frame immigration policy

---

7. *ST* II-II, q. 66, a. 2; emphasis added.

exclusively in terms of "what benefits us." The wealth of the world has been given to the whole human race, and we owe the needy a share in it.

IV
POLITICS

17

A Note on the Legitimacy of Governments

Daniel Lendman

In general we consider something to be legitimate when it is operating in accord with the laws and rules which properly govern that thing. In this way, we say that a person acts legitimately when he operates in accord with the laws of the state in which he dwells. This is perhaps the first meaning of the word. However, states likewise have a legitimacy or illegitimacy by which they must be measured. Since Locke, many have seen that legitimacy as something "derived from the consent of the governed." Some, such as Max Weber with his notion of *Legitimitätsglaube*, exclude all normative criteria for legitimacy and reduce it to a set of beliefs that a people have about their government.[1] Such notions, however, are (finally) excluded when one turns to the teachings of the Church summarized well by Pope Saint John XXIII, "Since God made men social by nature, and since no society can hold together unless some one be over all, directing all to strive earnestly for the common good, every civilized community must have a ruling authority, and this authority, no less than society itself, has its source in nature, and has, consequently, God for its author."[2] Political legitimacy, therefore, must be derived from God.

Now, the legitimacy of a government is necessary to determine if one is to act in due obedience to said government. Legitimacy of a

---

1. Cf. Max Weber, *The Theory of Social and Economic Organization*, ed. Talcott Parsons (New York: Free Press, 1964), 382.
2. John XXIII, Encyclical Letter *Pacem in Terris* 46; cf. Leo XIII, Encyclical Letter *Immortale Dei* 3.

government must be determined by a rule or law that is the measure of that government, and cannot be determined by something which is measured or ruled by the government. Further, the legitimacy of something must be judged according to its proper operations; but the proper operation of a government is care for the common good through legislation, and enforcement of legislation, etc. Therefore, if a government enacts legislation or enforces legislation in a manner that is violation of the rule or law by which said government is duly measured, that government, insofar as it acts thus, acts illegitimately. Therefore, the proper measure and rule for governments of nations/states is the eternal and divine law as manifested in natural law,[3] since the manifestation of what is according to divine law (outside of Revelation) is made present in the natural law. Therefore, to the extent that a government violates natural law in its legislation and decrees, it makes itself illegitimate.

Currently, in the United States of America, the question of "gay marriage" has come before the Supreme Court in such a way that the decision of the court will likely determine, in a somewhat definitive and permanent way, whether gay marriage becomes part of "the law of the land."[4] Such a decision is of grave importance to the legitimacy of the government. Marriage, while duly and reasonably encouraged and in some way regulated by the state, nevertheless is not subject to political deliberation. Marriage is a "pre-political" institution.

By pre-political, what I mean is that marriage must be assumed by just and legitimate governments as a principle on which just and healthy societies must depend. In this way, it is much like the principle of the inherent dignity of human life.[5] A government cannot legitimately authorize murder. To the extent that it does, it shows itself to be illegitimate. So also, a government cannot legitimately authorize marriage that is not between one man and one woman. To the extent that it does, it shows itself to be illegitimate.

---

3. Cf. St. Thomas, *ST* I-II, q. 94, q. 95, and q. 96, a. 5.
4. This essay was published in May 2015. The following month, the Supreme Court in the case *Obergefell v. Hodes* held in a 5-4 decision that all states must grant same-sex marriages and recognize such marriages granted in other states.—Eds.

A Note on the Legitimacy of Governments

To the extent that a government is illegitimate, its decrees and legislation have no authority. The reason for this is that all authority is derived from God.[6] Authority, therefore, is only possessed when one adheres to the eternal law as expressed by the natural law. Violation of the natural law, therefore, shows that one has forsaken one's source of authority and that, consequently, one has no authority at all. What this means is that by declaring two men or two women to be married, the U.S. government would manifestly be acting against natural law such that it has no authority to recognize marriage at all. All its decrees and legislation regarding marriage are justly and necessarily to be held in contempt. Marriage as a legally recognized institution will be utterly meaningless in the United States.

The frightening and sobering considerations that follow hard on the heels of the above argument concern when a government becomes wholly illegitimate such that its citizens become duty-bound to establish a new government. Already we see that the United States government has shown itself illegitimate in questions of religion by rejecting the due influence worship of God ought to have in society; it is illegitimate in questions of life through its sanctioning of abortion; and now, apparently, soon it will show itself illegitimate with regard to marriage.[7] How many pre-political societal principles must be violated before the government is rendered wholly illegitimate?

There is some, hope, however. In the past, the United States government showed itself to be in some measure illegitimate with its sanctioning of a race-based institution of slavery and then segrega-

---

5. There are also a-political questions that are similarly not properly subject to political deliberation. An example of such a question that nevertheless has been a frequent object of political deliberation in the United States is the theory of evolution. While it is conceivable that such questions could legitimately be discussed in a political context if they pertain to the common good, nevertheless, this would be a sign of a societal malady, and should be avoided as much as possible.

6. Rom. 13:1 and Mt. 28:18; cf. Leo XIII, *Diuturnum Illud*.

7. My focus here is on domestic matters, but one could likewise include unjust wars and other illegitimate activity in foreign countries in this list, but this would involve larger discussions about sovereignty, etc.

tion. Through much effort, these gross violations of natural law were overcome. It seems right, therefore, that all citizens of the United States should see themselves duty-bound to strive with all their might to bring their government back to legitimacy. There can be no peace under an illegitimate government. What is more, there *should be no peace* under an illegitimate government. These sobering and frightening reflections should instill fear in the hearts of our leaders and all citizens. When a government is no longer acting legitimately and forfeits its authority, this is precisely when mob-rule or tyrants take control.

18

The Duties and Rights of Subjects Toward the Civil Power

Tommaso Maria Cardinal Zigliara, OP[1]

Editorial Note

Cardinal Zigliara was a prominent Thomist philosopher and theologian in the latter half of the nineteenth century. Among many other accomplishments, he was closely involved with the preparation of the Leonine edition of the Angelic Doctor's *Opera Omnia* (the first volume of which contains his synopses and annotations on St. Thomas's *Organon* commentaries[2]), and assisted in preparing the encyclicals *Aeterni Patris* and *Rerum Novarum*. This present excerpt is taken from the Cardinal's widely circulated manual, *Summa philosophica* (14th ed., 1910), vol. III, *Philosophia moralis*, lib. ii, cap. II, art. 7. *De officiis et iuribus subditorum erga politicam potestatem*, 251–61.[3]

ARTICLE SEVEN
On the Duties and Rights of Subjects with Respect to Political Power

I. Duties and rights in general. Often has it been said that society ought to be conceived after the manner of an animated organic body, or, as I might better say it, after the manner of a human individual. Therefore, just as it is necessary that in the individual the

---

1. Translated by Timothy Wilson.
2. See http://archive.org/stream/operaomniaiussuio1thom#page/n11/mode/2up.
3. See https://archive.org/stream/summaphilosophico3zigluoft#page/250/mode/2up.

members should aid and support themselves, and all be at once submitted to the soul; so it is necessary that citizens, who as members compose a social body, should love themselves with greater love, mutually maintain and sustain themselves, and obey authority—authority, which is as it were the soul which vivifies the social body and preserves it in unity. But on the other hand, the civil authority ought sedulously to be intent on guarding the unity of the social body, in that manner, and with those means, which we have indicated above when treating of legislative authority.

II. First question. These things generally having been touched upon, the first question concerns the duties of subjects with respect to legislative power; that is, whether subjects are held *from conscience* to be subject to laws given by the sovereign for the rule of society. But that the question might rightly be understood, note that laws are divided into *moral* and *penal*: the first are those, the transgression of which is *culpable*; but the second sort adjudge transgressors not to fault, but to some punishment to be suffered. Because, therefore, obligation, concerning which at present we speak, arises only from law as it is precisely human, if this law be exclusively penal, it is manifest that a transgressor indeed incurs punishment, but not fault. I say, if it is exclusively *penal*: for generally speaking, the intention of a human legislator is not directed solely to punishment, but he wills also to oblige the citizens morally to the observance of laws: whence generally speaking, human laws ought to be retained as moral-penal, unless the contrary should for some other reason be clear. Concerning moral laws, therefore, the question is whether they oblige citizens in conscience. I respond:

III. Human laws: 1° if they are just, oblige citizens in conscience;— 2° but they do not oblige PER SE, if they are unjust;—3° yet these are able to oblige PER ACCIDENS, so long as they be not contrary to divine laws. St. Thomas proves this proposition, with respect to all of its parts, in IIaIIae, q. 96, art. 4, by means of the following brief and lucid argumentation.

First part. Laws are called just *from the end*, when they are ordained to the common good; and *from the actor*, when the law

Duties and Rights of Subjects Toward Civil Power

given does not exceed the power of the one giving it; and *from the form*, when according to equality of proportion there are imposed upon the subjects burdens with a view to the common good. Man, considered as a citizen, is a part or member of society; but a part, if it be considered as a part, is ordained to the good of the whole: and hence it is, that the very nature of a part imports a certain diminishment, when it is necessary to preserve the whole. Therefore, if human laws are just, they oblige citizens in the forum of conscience, by that principle by which they are obliged to the good of society.

Second part. Now laws are unjust in a twofold way. *In one way*, through contrariety to a human good; and this, either *from the end*, just as when a President imposes laws which are burdensome to the subjects, not pertaining to the common utility, but more to his own cupidity or glory; or *from the actor*, as when someone promulgates a law exceeding the authority committed to him; or *from the form*, e.g., when burdens are dispensed unequally upon the multitude, even if they are ordained to the common good. Considered in this way, human laws are more violences than laws: because as Augustine says in Book I of his *De libero arbitrio*, ch. 5, n11, *That seems not to be a law, which is not just*. Wherefore such laws do not oblige *per se* in conscience, because no man is held in conscience to visit injustice upon another.

Third part. Nevertheless, if thereafter there should arise scandal or disturbance of public order, although unjust laws in conscience do not oblige *per se*, as has been said; yet because a citizen is obliged not to scandalize little ones, and not to disturb public peace, for this reason is he held, in external actions, not to make resistance to the aforementioned laws. In this case, therefore, and on account of this unique reason, "a man ought to cede even his own right, according to Matth. V, 41: *If a man contend with thee in judgment, and take away thy coat, let go thy cloak also unto him. And whosoever force thee one mile, go with him other two.*"

Fourth part. "In another way, laws are able to be unjust through contrariety to a divine good, as the laws of tyrants inducing to idolatry, or to any other thing whatsoever which is contrary to the divine law; and such laws [not only do not oblige in conscience, but more] it is in no way permitted to observe them: because, as is said in Acts V: *It is necessary to obey God, rather than men,*" as has been said above.

IV. Second question. But the preceding conclusion opens the way to another and most grave question, that is, of *resistance* to the unjust laws of sovereigns, and consequently, to yet another question, concerning resistance to a sovereign, who is placed at the head of a society to rule and govern. Is there in the subjects a right of resisting the unjust laws of sovereigns, and consequently the Tyrant himself, and of expelling him, lest he rule longer in the society which he oppresses? Behold the question, the solving of which requires that we proceed cautiously and step by step: for from its false solutions, either too much is allotted to the sovereign, or too much is conceded to the subjects; or, either the tyranny of the sovereign is justified, or the treason of the subjects.

V. First preliminary note. Resistance, generally taken, is opposition to the activity of another subject: morally taken, it seems to signify the same as disobedience: for then another is morally resisted when obedience is refused to him. But there is *passive* and *active* resistance; *passive*, if the subject suffers violence, but his will is not prevailed upon, as in the martyrs; *active*, if he repels inflicted violence with violence.

VI. Second preliminary note. The question is not concerned with passive resistance. For if human laws are just, they oblige in the forum of conscience; therefore that citizen is culpable, who even passively makes opposition to those laws; but much more is he culpable, if he actively resists the executive power of the laws themselves. And the same is absolutely to be held however much a given law may seem to be of dubious justice: for in this case, it does not pertain to the citizen to judge of the law, because it does not pertain to him to make provision for the common good, but to the sovereign. If, finally, a law is manifestly unjust *by contrariety to a divine good*, since in this case a man is held from conscience not to obey, passive resistance is not only licit, but also commanded, as with St. Thomas we have said in the final part of the thesis, and as we are taught from the example of the martyrs. Briefly. Passive resistance is to be adjudicated from the morality of the law. Therefore, the entire question is concerned with active resistance, and with respect to laws manifestly unjust, whether contrary to the common good of society or contrary to a divine good, by which resistance the executive, and consequently the legislative, power is so resisted that violence is visited upon it by the subjects. It is asked, whether this resistance is licit? With one mouth do all toadies of *popular sovereignty* proclaim the affirmative part, who place the true subject of political authority in *democracy*, as they say, or in the multitude. Wherefore, they proclaim unjust laws that are not pleasing to them, so that they arrogate to themselves the right of stirring up the multitude and of rising up against legitimate sovereigns. What, therefore, should be thought in this matter, we shall say little by little.

VII. On the tyrant. Tyrant, τύραννος, signifies the same thing as king or sovereign, one who has fullness of power over his subjects; whence at first it was accustomed to be taken in a good way, as may be seen in the books of the *Politics* of Aristotle, in the *Miltiade* of Cornelius Nepos; in which sense Virgil, *Aeneid* VII, 265–66, says: *Let him come, let not his face shudder at friends.—The part of peace, for me, shall be to have touched the right hand of the tyrant,* that is of Aeneas.—But in the progress of time, the name of *tyrant* acquired a perverted sense, that is, for signifying sovereigns who, abusing the powers of rule through arrogance, ruled, not by right and equitable laws, but by force and a certain wantonness of soul (cf. *Lexicon latinum,* etc., *in usum Seminarii Patavini,* Tyrannus). In this sense, the nature of the tyrant is described by Tully, in *De amicitia,* cap. XV: "For this is the life of tyrants, in which, without doubt, there is able to be no faith, no charity, no confidence of steadfast goodwill: all things are always suspected and in turmoil: there is no place for friendship."

VIII. On the tyrannical regime, and on tyrannical usurpation. Tyrant, taken in its unfavorable signification, commonly is distinguished into tyrant *by rule* and tyrant *by usurpation.* He is called tyrant *by rule*, who legitimately took up the principate in some society, but governs through laws manifestly unjust; he is called tyrant *by usurpation*, who *through ambition or in some other illicit manner secured power*, as St. Thomas says in lect. 1 on Rom. 13.

IX. On resistance against a tyrant by usurpation. "He who through violence steals dominion is not truly effected the prelate or ruler; and thus when the means are present, one is able to remove such dominion: unless perhaps he should presently be effected a *true* ruler, whether by the consensus of the subjects, or by the authority of a superior." This St. Thomas writes, *In II Sent.*, dist. XLIV, q. 2, art. 2: from which it is manifest, in the first place, that a tyrant by usurpation is able to become a legitimate ruler, as all agree. But the question is not concerning this.

Again, we are able to consider the tyrant by usurpation in a twofold manner, namely *in the act of usurpation*, that is, *in the act of war* unjustly inflicted on the state; and after the usurpation already has been completed, namely when, the state having been pacified, the tyrant is in control and draws up and promulgates laws not *by right*, but *in fact*, he yet is not had as a legitimate ruler.—In the act of usurpation, the tyrant is an unjust invader; and thus, just as an individual person is able to repel force with force, so *a fortiori* the Respublica, upon which force is visited, is able to repel force with force and kill the tyrant: and I say the Respublica, or the citizens, not by private authority, but by the public authority, whether express or tacit, of a legitimate ruler; or of those who legitimately carry on its successions: for it pertains, not to the private judgment of citizens, but to the public authority to judge concerning the common good of the Respublica.—St. Thomas speaks to this sense, in the place cited above, in the response to the fifth objection: "When someone steals dominion for himself, the subjects being unwilling or even coerced to assent, and *when there is no recourse to a superior, through whom a judgment might be able to be made concerning the invader*; then he who slays the tyrant for the liberation of the country is lauded and receives a reward."

But if the tyrant already is in control, yet in fact is not a legitimate ruler, absolutely speaking, the oppressed Respublica, or the legitimate ruler, if he exists, has the right against the tyrant, and through force is able to expel the unjust invader of the Kingdom. I say *absolutely speaking*: for if the tyrant should not be able to be expelled without great public calamities, and without the utmost detriment to the Respublica, neither is the legitimate ruler able to move against the tyrant, but the latter is patiently to be borne: because the ruler is to be procured for the good of the Respublica. Therefore, if the legitimate ruler were to make war upon the tyrant only amid the utmost ruin of the Respublica, he would provide not for the Respublica, but for himself; and thus in another way, when he would oppose the tyranny, he himself truly would incur the mark of tyranny. In this hypothesis, therefore, the legitimate ruler retains the right, but the exercise of his right is suspended.

But with respect to laws which are promulgated by the dominating tyrant, and which look to the *external* ordering of the Respublica, these words wisely are given by Francisco Vitoria, *Relection. theol.*, Relect. III *De potestate civili*, no. 23: "Since the Respublica is oppressed by the Tyrant and is not of its own right, it is neither able to promulgate laws, nor execute those previously given; if it were to not be obedient to the Tyrant, the Respublica would perish besides. Certainly it seems that laws, *which are agreeable to the Respublica*, oblige, even though they be promulgated by a Tyrant: not indeed because they are given by a Tyrant, but from the consent of the Respublica, since it is more pious that laws given by a Tyrant be observed, than that none be observed. And certainly it would be unto the clear ruin of the Respublica, if rulers, who do not have just title, should occupy a kingdom, that there should be no judgments, nor that malefactors should in no way be able to be punished, or coerced (since the tyrant is not a legitimate judge), if his laws do not oblige."

X. On resistance against a tyrant by rule. But the question chiefly is agitated concerning the tyrant by rule: namely, whether *active* resistance is licit in subjects against the tyrant, such that either he may be despoiled of the kingdom by the subjects, or even punished by death. In this question to be solved, the teaching of the Catholic Church ought to be kept in mind. Therefore in the Council of Constance, session VIII, and in the *Constitution* of Martin V, *Inter cunctas*, there is condemned this proposition, which is the seventeenth of the forty-five articles of Wycliffe: "Peoples are able, according to their own will, to set aright delinquent Rulers."—And in session XV by the same Fathers, and from Paul V, Constitut. *Cura dominici gregis* of 14 January, 1615, there is proscribed this teaching: "Any tyrant is able and ought licitly and meritoriously to be killed by any vassal or subject of his, even by means of secret plots, and subtle flatteries, or adulations, notwithstanding any past oath or confederation made with him, the sentence or mandate of any judge not being hoped for."—Cf. Roselli, *Ethica*, ult. q., art. 5, where he also refers to the definitions of the Fifth Council of Toledo.—Tyrannicide, therefore, perpetrated by private authority, is illicit and to be detested: but from this, [does it follow that] any active resistance whatsoever to a tyrant is illicit?

XI. First opinion. In this difficult question which is to be solved, therefore, various opinions are proffered by writers. Without doubt, wicked rulers are bestowed by God upon degenerate peoples, according to Osee XIII, 11: *I will give thee a king in my wrath*; and Job XXXIV, 30: *Who maketh a man that is a hypocrite to reign for the sins of the people*. From all these things St. Thomas wisely concludes, in *De regimine principum* I.6, that the fault of the people must be put away, so that the plague of tyrants might cease.—Nevertheless, all these things do not justify the Ruler. *Woe to the Assyrian!*, it is said in Isaiah X, 5; and the Assyrian was the rod of the wrath of the Lord sent to a deceitful nation, and against the people of the wrath of the Lord (ibid., v.5–6). But "when the Lord shall have performed all His works in Mount Sion, and in Jerusalem, I will visit the fruit of the proud heart of the king of Assyria, and the glory of the haughtiness of his eyes" (v.12). The question therefore remains intact.

XII. Second opinion. It is said secondly, that tyrannical oppression is to be endured patiently, just as infirmities, and just as all the other evils with which the life of men is afflicted in this world. But by this response the question is changed, not resolved. For we ask about justice, and the response is about patience. Moreover, there is a distinction between the evil of tyranny and the other evils: for these latter are inflicted by God, with whom there is for us no right; but subjects have the strict right that they be governed rightly by a Ruler, and thus they suffer *unjustly* by a tyrant, who is most culpable, even though God may permit that he exercise his tyranny, as has been said above. Finally, that the injustices of men ought patiently to be borne, I most willingly admit, but patience does not destroy the faculty in the one suffering of claiming his right; and if this is true among individual citizens it will be at least equally true in a republic in respect of the ruler. The question therefore remains.

XIII. Third opinion. Wherefore, others say that with citizens there is the right of protesting, of appealing, and of employing other similar means. This is very charming indeed. But: 1° The tyrant who, through laws *clearly* unjust (for if the reader well recalls, we speak exclusively of this hypothesis), destroys the common good and does away with the rights of the citizens would much more certainly prevent the citizens from legally claiming their rights. And in this case? The difficulty returns, the solution of which we seek.—2° There can be danger in delay: think if a tyrant should with certainty hand over the Respublica to a foreign dominion, or draw up laws unto the manifest ruin of the citizens, and other similar things: in which cases, either he is to be resisted, or to be yielded to. Is resistance licit? If it is not licit, then ridiculous is the right to a Ruler with respect to right rule in society which is granted to the citizens; if it is licit, then there is granted to the subjects some right which is not the simple right of protesting, appealing, etc.—I assert, therefore, the strict duty of first employing all peaceful means so that the tyrant might retreat from laws manifestly wicked and clearly destructive to society; but I do not see the question solved, in the hypothesis in which those means are inefficacious.

XIV. Fourth opinion. In the fourth place it is animadverted, that resistance to a tyrant heedlessly begets greater evils for society. For either armed resistance does not prevail, and *the tyrant, being provoked, rages more*, as St. Thomas says in *De regimine principum* I.6;

or it prevails, and as the holy Doctor notes in the same place, "from this there often come forth the most grave dissensions in the people, whether while resistance is made against the tyrant, or while, after the casting down of the tyrant, the multitude is divided into parties about the ordering of the regime. It also happens, that sometimes when the multitude expels the tyrant with the help of someone, he, power having been received, seizes the tyranny: and fearing that he might suffer from one that which he did to another, he oppresses the subjects with a heavier servitude.—This reason, which is confirmed by experience, is valid. For in order to expel a lesser evil, reason dictates that a greater evil ought not to be induced which is especially unto the ruin of society. And hence it is that if a tyranny is not excessive, it ought to be tolerated, because between two inevitable evils, the lesser evil is chosen.—However, we think that some things ought to be said in addition.

XV. Offensive resistance and defensive resistance. This distinction is necessary, although it may import a certain violence to the word, for *resistance* seems to signify defense, not offense. I call offensive resistance *inflicted force*; I call defensive resistance, repulsed force. Let us illustrate the thing by example. In an act of unjust aggression, he who is unjustly invaded *repels force with force*; and this is *defensive* resistance; but beside the *act* of unjust aggression, he who would attack an enemy, anticipating his aggression, *would not repel force with force, but would inflict force*, although he would do it in order to forestall aggression. This second resistance I call *offensive*.

XVI. OFFENSIVE resistance by subjects against a tyrant by rule is absolutely illicit. The reason adduced in the *fourth opinion* chiefly proves this our conclusion, which is confirmed with the following argument. Subjects, as subjects, inflicting force upon a tyrant, administer authoritative judgment upon the tyrant, and thus subject him to their own private judgment. But this is entirely illicit: for although the tyrant, not by force of authority (for this is *per se* to the good), but by his own ill will, enforces tyranny, he is yet the ruler *by authority*, and thus is juridically superior to the subjects, and is not subject to them. Therefore offensive resistance against a tyrant by

Duties and Rights of Subjects Toward Civil Power

rule is entirely illicit.—Add, that a tyrant by rule *abuses* the right of ruling. But from the abuse of a right, the *right* is not lost. A tyrant by rule, then, abusing the right, always has the right of ruling. But it is illicit to despoil someone of his right by private authority. Therefore absolutely illicit are the rebellions of subjects who undertake to remove a King, or punish him with death.

Against excessive tyranny, therefore, St. Thomas proposes three remedies in *De regimine principum* I.6.

1. "If it pertains to the right of some superior to provide the multitude with a king, a remedy against the wickedness of a tyrant may be expected." But most of all does this right of defending the rights of peoples pertain to the Church, that is, to the Vicar of Christ, the Roman Pontiff: whatever those quarrelsome men should prate to the contrary, who, being subjects, affect the liberty for justifying rebellions, but when ruling, enforce tyranny to sustain the sovereignty of the State.

2. "If it pertains to the right of the multitude to provide itself with a king, an established king can, not unjustly, be deposed, or his power checked, by the same, if he tyrannically abuses regal power. Nor should it be thought that such a multitude, deposing a tyrant, acts unfaithfully, even if the multitude had previously subjected itself to the same tyrant in perpetuity: because he merited this, not comporting himself faithfully in the rule of the multitude, as the office of the king demands, so that that which was appointed to him by the subjects is not retained."—Note the words of St. Thomas, *if it pertains to the right of the multitude*; as if he should say: if the right of judging and disposing of the person of the king (e.g., if such be fundamental laws of the kingdom) pertains to the multitude. It is therefore a simple hypothesis which the Angelic Doctor poses, lest he should omit some member in his disjunctive argumentation; but he does not say that this condition is always shown to be true: indeed, by the nature of the hypothesis he supposes in fact that the contrary can be granted, as is commonly granted.

3. "But if no human help is able to be had against a tyrant at all (*according to the two preceding hypotheses*), then recourse ought to be had to God the king of all things, Who is a help in times of tribulation. For it is within His power, that He might turn the cruel heart

of a tyrant to gentleness, according to the words of Solomon, Proverbs XII, 9: *The heart of the king is in the hand of God, whithersoever He will He shall turn it."*

XVII. Against excessive tyranny, DEFENSIVE resistance can be licit. I say against excessive tyranny: for, as St. Thomas emphasizes in *De regimine principum* I.6, *if there be not an excess of tyranny, it is more useful to tolerate a moderate tyrant for a time, than to be entangled in many dangers by acting against the tyrant, which dangers are more grave than the tyranny itself,* and which dangers the citizens are thus held to shun, lest the good of the Respublica be endangered.— These things being declared, the thesis is proved. It is commonly conceded that passive resistance to laws manifestly unjust is licit for subjects. Hence St. Thomas, in IaIIae, q. 96, art. 4, ad 3, speaking *of a law which imports an unjust burden upon the subjects, to which the order of power divinely given does not extend itself* (as they are *laws onerous to the subjects and not pertaining to the common utility, but more to the cupidity or glory of the legislator, or laws given above the power committed* to the same legislator), affirms that *in such things a man is not obliged to obey the law, if he is able to resist without scandal or greater detriment.* All of these things we have noted above in n. III with the same Angelic Doctor.—It is therefore certain that there is in subjects the right of resisting passively, that is, of not obeying the aforementioned tyrannical laws. But just as the tyrant abuses the legislative power, so can he abuse the *executive* power, and do violence to the subjects, that they might be subject to tyrannical laws. Therefore, the right, which in this case is in the subjects, passively of not obeying a tyrannical legislative power, gives to them the right of resisting the violence of the tyrannical executive power, repelling force with force, in which we have said *defensive* resistance to consist: otherwise, the right of passive resistance would be absurd if it could not be defended from an unjust invader. In which case, there is no resistance to authority, but to violence; not to right, but to the abuse of right; not to the sovereign, but to an unjust aggressor against a proper right in an act of aggression.

But in this matter, one ought to proceed in an orderly fashion. For according to those things which we have proved above (49, V), the immediate elements of civil society are not individuals, nor families, but *Municipalities* or *Provinces*, which are perfect societies (to which, consequently—unless other fundamental laws should be in force, society being bereft of a legitimate sovereign—belongs the right of electing a new sovereign, not to the *multitude* or *people*) and which are means between the civil power and families. To *Provinces*, therefore, or *Municipalities*, which have the true authority in respect of families, and not to individuals or families, does it pertain to employ defensive resistance and to repel, with united powers, the violence of a tyrant. But if even the Provinces or Municipalities, in place of protecting and defending the subjects, should become instruments of social tyranny, then tyranny is to be withstood in passive resistance alone, and they ought to desist from defensive resistance, not because of a defect of absolute right, but on account of the certainty of greater evil. In this case, therefore, *recourse ought to be had to the Lord, the king of all things, Who is a help in times of tribulation,* as we have said above with St. Thomas.

19

The Illegitimate State as Chastisement

Gregory de Rivière-Blanche

The Josias's publications regarding legitimacy have raised several interesting questions about the legitimacy of modern states. One point that has come up repeatedly in the various contributions is whether a Catholic ought to obey an illegitimate government.[1] In discussing this question, Daniel Lendman has assumed that the illegitimate state is necessarily at variance with the divine will.[2] For our part, we shall show that, to the contrary, the illegitimate state may be an expression of the divine will as a chastisement sent by God to a sinful people. We suggest, therefore, that the Catholic should consider this point when examining his relationship to an illegitimate government.

Aquinas addresses this very question in his discourse upon the thirteenth chapter of Romans, in which Paul says:

> Let every soul be subject to higher powers: for there is no power but from God: and those that are, are ordained of God. Therefore he that resisteth the power, resisteth the ordinance of God. And they that resist, purchase to themselves damnation. For princes are not a terror to the good work, but to the evil. Wilt thou then not be afraid of the power? Do that which is good: and thou shalt have praise from the same. For he is God's minister to thee, for good. But if thou do that which is evil, fear: for he beareth not the sword in vain. For he is God's minister: an avenger to execute wrath upon him that doth evil. Wherefore be subject of necessity, not

---

1. We accept Aquinas's definition of a tyrant: a ruler who pursues his own good over the common good. *De regno* [hereafter, *DR*], lib. 1, cap. 4. In our view, illegitimacy and tyranny are the same thing.
2. See chapter 17.

The Illegitimate State as Chastisement

only for wrath, but also for conscience' sake. For therefore also you pay tribute. For they are the ministers of God, serving unto this purpose.[3]

Paul is speaking of the pagan Roman emperors and the obligations of the Christians in Rome to those emperors. Paul's teaching here sits alongside earlier Scriptural teaching regarding rulers,[4] including the words of the Lord in St. John's Gospel: "Thou shouldst not have any power against me, unless it were given thee from above. Therefore, he that hath delivered me to thee, hath the greater sin."[5]

Aquinas begins by noting that Paul is responding to the belief in the early Church that the freedom granted by Christ included freedom from temporal powers.[6] Paul responds that every soul is subject to higher powers—that is, temporal rulers[7]—because those powers are established by God. Aquinas demonstrates this point elegantly:

> For whatever is said in common of God and creatures, comes to creatures from God, as in the case of wisdom: all wisdom comes from God (Sir. 1:1). But power is said of God and of men: God does not abandon the powers, since he is powerful (Job 35:5). Hence, it follows that all human power is from God. . . .[8]

Aquinas next shows that the order of ruler and ruled is implicit in the power God gives to temporal rulers. He argues,

> God made all things through his wisdom, for it says in a psalm: *in wisdom have you made all* (Ps. 104:24). But it is the function of wisdom to dispose things in order. . . . For if the power of rulers is from God and nothing is from God without order, it follows that

---

3. Rom. 13:1–6.
4. E.g., Prov. 8:15–16; Dan. 2:21; Sir. 10:4.
5. Jn. 19:11.
6. *Super Epistola ad Romanos*, cap. 13, lectio 1, n. 1017. (Section numbers and translations are taken from the Aquinas Institute edition.)
7. *Super Rom.*, cap. 13, lect. 1, 1017–18.
8. Ibid., lect. 1, 1021: "Quicquid enim communiter de Deo et creaturis dicitur, a Deo in creaturas derivatur, sicut patet de sapientia, Eccli. I, 1: *omnis sapientia a Domino Deo est*. Potestas autem de Deo et de hominibus dicitur. Iob c. XXXVI, 5: *Deus potestates non abiicit, cum ipse sit potens*. Unde consequens est, quod omnis humana potestas sit a Deo."

Integralism and the Common Good

the order whereby the lower are subjected to the higher powers is from God.[9]

This is a crucial point: if a ruler has power from God, then virtue demands that the ruled obey him. "And they that resist, purchase to themselves damnation."[10] Aquinas explains how the resisters "purchase to themselves damnation." First, those who resist authority that they should obey incur punishment from God (i.e., eternal damnation), as Dathan and Abiron did when they resisted Moses and Aaron.[11] Second, those who resist authority also incur punishments imposed by the temporal authorities themselves.[12] However, Aquinas notes that, "against this is the fact that the apostles and martyrs seem to have resisted rulers and authorities and did not receive damnation from God as a result but rather a reward."[13] He resolves the apparent contradiction easily:

> The answer is that the Apostle is now speaking of one who resists a lower power as established by God. But the divine order requires that a lower power not be obeyed in opposition to a higher one, as even in human affairs a governor is not obeyed against an emperor, nor a bailiff against a king. And every human power is set under the divine power, so that no human power should be obeyed against God, as it says in Acts: *we must obey God rather than men* (Acts 5:29).[14]

---

9. Ibid., 1024–25: "Deus omnia per suam sapientiam fecit, secundum illud Ps. CIII, 24: *omnia in sapientia fecisti*. Est autem proprium sapientiae ordinate omnia disponere.... Si enim potestas principum, inquantum talis est, a Deo est, et nihil est a Deo sine ordine, consequens est, quod etiam ordo, quo inferiores potestatibus superioribus subiiciunutur, sit a Deo."
10. Rom. 13:2.
11. *Super Rom.*, cap. 13, lect. 1, 1027.
12. Ibid.
13. Ibid., 1028: "Sed contra hoc videtur esse quod apostoli et martyres principibus et potestatibus restiterunt et ex hoc non damnationem a Deo sed praemium acquisiverunt."
14. Ibid.: "Sed dicendum est ex quod Apostolus hic loquitur de eo qui resistit potestati inferiori, secundum quod a Deo ordinata. Habet autem hoc divina ordinatio ut potestati inferiori non obediatur contra superiorem, sicut etiam in rebus humanis ut proconsuli non obediatur contra imperatorem, nec balivo contra regem.

The Illegitimate State as Chastisement

Having shown that resistance against the temporal powers brings both eternal and temporal damnation upon the resistor, Aquinas turns to the statement,

> For princes are not a terror to the good work, but to the evil. Wilt thou then not be afraid of the power? Do that which is good: and thou shalt have praise from the same. For he is God's minister to thee, for good. But if thou do that which is evil, fear: for he beareth not the sword in vain. For he is God's minister: an avenger to execute wrath upon him that doth evil.[15]

He connects the first part of this statement with the very purpose for having rulers, which is to create the fear of punishment that is the only thing that governs some individuals.[16] This part also supports Aquinas's statement earlier that those who resist authority incur damnation, for, if rulers punish bad conduct and one is punished, then one is acting badly.[17] The key to avoiding punishment (and obtaining rewards) from a ruler is simply to do what is good.[18] Aquinas shows, too, that this principle applies to wicked rulers, arguing that wicked rulers are also a terror to bad acts. He even goes so far as to say that wicked rulers will produce good results for the just, even if the just are oppressed.[19]

Aquinas turns to the second part: "For he is God's minister to thee, for good. But if thou do that which is evil, fear: for he beareth not the sword in vain. For he is God's minister: an avenger to execute wrath upon him that doth evil."[20] He explains this directly:

> This is clear in regard to the proper order of rulers. For they are under the authority of God, the supreme ruler, as his ministers: *because as ministers of his kingdom, you did not rule rightly* (Wis. 6:4). But the ruler and the magistrates work for the same end: *like*

Et omnis potestas humana sub potestate Dei ordinatur et nulli potestati humanae est contra Deum obediendum, secundum illud Act. V, 29: *oportet obedire magis Deo quam hominibus.*"

15. Rom. 13:3–4.
16. *Super Rom.*, cap. 13, lect. 1, 1030.
17. Ibid.
18. Rom. 13:3; *Super Rom.*, cap. 13, lect. 1, 1032–33.
19. Ibid.
20. Rom. 13:4–5.

the magistrate of the people, so are his officials (Sir. 10:2). Therefore, just as God works for the good of those who do good, so also do rulers, if they perform their office rightly.[21]

In other words, because God works for the good of those who do good, so too do rulers, who are ministers of God in their rule. Now, coming to our point, Aquinas says:

> Furthermore, even wicked rulers are God's minister for inflicting punishments according to God's plan; although this is not their intention: *ah, Assyria, the rod of my anger, the staff of my fury . . . but he does not so intend* (Is. 10:5). *Behold I will send, and take all the kindreds of the north, says the Lord, and Nabuchodonosor the king of Babylon my servant: and I will bring them against this land, and against the inhabitants thereof, and against all the nations that are round about it* (Jer. 25:9). And also because such wicked rulers sometimes afflict good men, God permitting, who profit thereby; *for we know that in everything God works for the good with those who love him* (Rom. 8:28).[22]

One can understand this argument in the light of the previous point. God works for the good of those who do good, and he may do so through his ministers. Likewise, God punishes those who do wicked things, and he may do this through his ministers, too. However, the ruler need not understand that he is one of God's ministers. He may think that he is acting for his own ends or according to his own design.

---

21. *Super Rom.*, cap. 13, lect. 1, 1034: "Quod quidem manifeste patet, quantum ad debitum ordinem principem. Sunt enim sub regimine Dei, quasi supremi principis, tamquam ministri ordinati. Sap. VI, 3: *cum essetis ministri regis illius*, et cetera. Ad idem autem tendit minister et dominus. Eccli. X, 2: *secundum iudicem populi, sic et ministri eius*. Et ideo sicut Deus operatur in bonum his qui bonum agunt, ita et principes si recte ministerium suum impleant."

22. Ibid., at 1034:5: "Sed et mali principes ministri Dei sunt, secundum ordinationem Dei ad inferendas poenas, licet hoc sit praeter intentum eorum; secundum illud Is. X, 5: *assur virga furoris mei, et baculus ipse in manu mea est. Ipse autem non sic arbitrabitur*. Et Ier. XXV, 9: *assumam universam cognationem Aquilonis, et Nabuchodonosor regem Babylonis servum meum, et adducam eos super terram istam, et super habitatores eius*, et cetera. Et quia tales mali principes, interdum, Deo permittente, bonos affligunt, quod in bonum eorum cedit, secundum illud supra VIII, 28: *diligentibus Deum*, et cetera." See also *DR*, lib. 1, cap. 7.

The Illegitimate State as Chastisement

Lendman has argued that "authority, therefore, is only possessed when one adheres to the eternal law as expressed by the natural law. Violation of the natural law, therefore, shows that one has forsaken one's source of authority and that, consequently, one has no authority at all."[23] We now see that this is not correct: God may give authority to a tyrant in order to punish a sinful nation just as he gave authority to the Assyrians to punish Israel.[24] God sends punishments not for the sake of punishment, but to spur the people to repentance and reconciliation. Gregory the Great explains, "For we are become at variance with God by sin. Therefore it is meet that we should be brought back to peace with Him by the scourge, that whereas every being, created good, turns to pain for us, the mind of the chastened man may be renewed in a humbled state to peace with the Creator."[25] In other words, God sends a wicked nation a tyrant so that the nation might repent of its sins and be reconciled to God.[26]

Furthermore, Lendman suggests strongly that once a government loses legitimacy, its citizens are no longer subject to it, or, at the very least, ought to treat its decrees with contempt. (Which is essentially saying the same thing.) However, when a tyrant has been sent by God as a chastisement, its citizens are still subject to him. We have seen that "the order whereby the lower are subjected to the higher powers"[27] is implicit in the very power of rulers. Thus, if God has sent a tyrant to chastise a sinful people, the divine order holds that the citizens are subject to the tyrant. Aquinas calls rebellion against this order contrary to virtue.[28]

One might object at this point, however, that this means that a Catholic is bound to obey a tyrant even to the point of violating the

---

23. See chapter 17.
24. Is. 10:5.
25. *Moralia in Job*, lib. 3, no. 15: "Per culpam quippe Deo discordes exstitimus; dignum ergo est ut ad pacem illius per flagella redeamus; ut cum unaquaeque res bene condita nobis in dolorem vertitur, correcti mens ad auctoris pacem humiliter reformetur." (Translation by John Henry Parker.)
26. See also Is. 10:20–21.
27. *Super Rom.*, cap. 13, lect. 1, 1025.
28. Ibid.

divine law. An Irish citizen might be required, one might say, to acknowledge, one way or another, one of the new same-sex "marriages." This is not the case. Aquinas, citing the example of the martyrs, reminds us that we must obey God rather than men.[29] When the tyrant's decrees are opposed to the divine law, the Catholic obeys God against the tyrant as one obeys an emperor against a governor.[30] But this does not mean that the governor has no authority whatsoever: he simply has less authority than the emperor. Furthermore, Aquinas also reminds us that God works all things, even tyranny, to the benefit of the just.[31] In particular, Aquinas notes that those who patiently suffer persecution win praise.[32]

The tyrant as a chastisement sent from God demonstrates clearly the difficulty in linking legitimacy with authority. A tyrant certainly does not pursue the common good and is, therefore, illegitimate. However, a tyrant may well have authority from God because God wills to punish a sinful nation through the tyrant. The Catholic, therefore, should not necessarily assume that the illegitimate government is completely without authority because it no longer pursues the common good.

The Catholic, instead, should consider very seriously the state of his nation and whether it is possible that God has sent the tyrant as a chastisement to the nation. Lendman discusses the United States and the apparently forthcoming legalization of same-sex "marriage." It is apparent that large numbers of Americans support any number of objectively gravely sinful acts, ranging from abortion to no-fault divorce to same-sex "marriage." Worse than that, many of these citizens view those acts as fundamental rights, implicit in the United States Constitution. (There are, of course, many serious sins championed by the political right, though those sins are harder to summarize in a word.) Is it beyond belief that God would send such a country a tyrant to spur it to repentance? Of course not.

29. Ibid., 1028.
30. Ibid.
31. Ibid., 1034.
32. Ibid., 1033: "Verificatur hoc etiam de malis principibus, quorum iniustam persecutionem, dum boni patienter sustinent, laudantur. Iac. V, 11: *ecce beatificamus eos qui sustinuerunt*."

20

Catholics and the Ethics of Voting

Joshua Kenz

The main purpose of our civic actions must be the promotion of the common good. Voting becomes a duty when the common good or the good of religion demands it: "It is the duty of all citizens who have the right to vote, to exercise that right when the common good of the state or the good of religion and morals require their votes, and when their voting is useful."[1] It is important to note the second qualifier "when useful." It is fully possible that a vote might be useless—say, if all candidates were equally wicked and no write-ins were allowed.

But whom must we vote for? Well, we must choose good candidates. What makes a candidate good? Those are good "who with strength of mind, in a Christian spirit, and skill in bearing affairs, exhibits knowledge of political matters and sufficient eloquence."[2] They must be upright and capable and have a strong backbone. Obviously, the eloquence necessary in a county clerk may be different from that needed in a Senator, but it must be sufficient for the position they are running for.

There are several possibilities that may arise in elections. One possibility is that all the candidates, or least those with the greater support, are worthy candidates. In this case, one is free to choose whomsoever is to their liking, based perhaps on agreement over matters of prudence. Another possibility is that only one candidate

---

1. Henry Davis, S.J., *Moral and Pastoral Theology* (London: Sheed & Ward, 1938), 2:90.
2. Dominic M. Prümmer, O.P., *Manuale theologiae moralis* (Freiburg im Breisgau: B. Herder, 1923), vol. 2, §608.

Integralism and the Common Good

among the "viable" is worthy. In this case you have a grave moral obligation to support the worthy candidate, even if you disagree with him on minor matters.

But what if there are no worthy candidates, or if the only worthy candidate is "unviable"? Then the moral analysis is tougher. If there is a worthy candidate, then although he might "not be elected on account of a plurality of contrary votes, nevertheless it profits much at least by a choice that shows what is the will of good citizens."[3] The grave obligation to support worthy candidates remains, and mere lack of viability does not excuse. If there are no worthy candidates, then one may abstain.

Now one can in good conscience leave it there. One is never required to support an unworthy candidate. However, one *may* support such a candidate for grave reasons. But we must distinguish between two sorts of unworthy candidates. The first sort is, perhaps, morally upright, but lacks experience, or eloquence, or some other faculty by which to govern, legislate, etc. effectively. We may say that such is "negatively unworthy" in that he lacks what is befitting the office, but does not present active harm. Against a candidate that is an enemy of religion, or who threatens the common good through the promotion of immoralities or war or any other wicked policy, there may easily be grave enough reason to support the candidate that is lacking only in aptitude. But this is easy because one is not cooperating with, advancing, promoting or complicit in any moral evil by this act. One is simply choosing an imperfect good—a Gomer rather than the Andy they should like.

The question is much harder when it is a question of supporting a candidate who is "positively unworthy," whether due to moral character, being an enemy of religion and morals, etc. Here, a vote for him is a cooperation in evil. Now, if one shares the evil intent, clearly one sins and is formally complicit in the evil. But what if one does not share the intent? There are two types of cooperation here: immediate and mediate material cooperation. In immediate cooperation, one does not share the intent of the evil act, but one does contribute to circumstances that are essential for the evil act to hap-

3. Ibid.

pen—for example, were I to lease a building knowingly to Planned Parenthood. This is never justified, save maybe under extreme duress (e.g., opening a door to let a robber in because he has a gun to your head).

But when one contributes only to the morally licit circumstances that are not essential to the evil action, the cooperation is mediate material and *may* be morally licit. The liceity of the action depends on multiple factors. The long and short of it is this: the graver the evil, the more causally removed one must be, and the greater the good one must be intending. In a Presidential election, e.g., an Elector is more causally proximate than a voter in California who elected him.

Is the avoidance of evil, i.e., stopping an even worse candidate, by itself grave enough reason? No, because in mediate cooperation you are contributing to circumstances that are themselves good for a good reason, despite the non-essential aid it gives an evil act. That another candidate is even worse may be reason, after one has examined the issue of moral cooperation, to go ahead and vote that way, but it is not reason itself. The principle of "choosing the lesser evil" is not a valid way of determining what is morally right. It universally is only held by Catholic moralists in the case of a perplexed conscience, i.e., when there appears, albeit wrongly, only immoral options to the conscience. In that case, lacking time and ability to solve the perplexity—i.e., by figuring out another option or else seeing that one is not actually immoral—if one must choose, then one should choose what appears to be the lesser evil. But we already established that one need not vote for an unworthy candidate, and that there is already an always moral option here, so no conscience is perplexed. One can vote only if there is some good to be accomplished and not merely evil avoided. One is not forced, then, to choose the "lesser evil." To choose under that rationale is to choose evil and to sin.

I offer here an analogy to illustrate.

Say you have some land, but you cannot make the payments on it anymore. The bank makes a deal with you—sell it by November 9th and give them the money you owe them, or on November 9th they sell it, and after fees and what is owed, you get what is left. Now say that the bank is going to sell the place to the most debauched line of strip clubs. You, of course, oppose that. So you look for a better buyer. But say that the only buyer that you can find will open an adult video store instead. So you have an option... "minimize the evil" and enable the existence of the adult video store, or do nothing and let the bank enable the existence of something worse. Clearly, in Catholic morality, your option must be not to accept the buyer. You may pray and hope for a last minute alternative, but you cannot enable the adult video store in order to minimize harm. The reason is that it would be immediate material cooperation. You are not enabling the strip club, but rather, however sadly, failing to prevent it since no moral means were available to you.

Now think about the election. This analogy is apt in one way, though defective in another. Certainly if there be an argument for Trump, it is not immediate material cooperation, but mediate material cooperation. But it is apt in this way... if your entire reasoning is "I vote for Trump because he is not Hillary" or some belief that "I have to choose the lesser evil," a doctrine that is not determinative of the moral good, you are like the seller that becomes complicit in promoting evil, in order to minimize evil.

Remember, there is only an obligation to use all reasonable moral means to stop an evil, and sometimes there are no such means. Yet people feel pressured to have to do something, anything. That is a trick of Satan.

If you think that there is a contribution to the common good that Trump will make and that it is proportionately grave enough to justify material cooperation in whatever ill you think he will likely cause, then you have a case that he is a moral means, and the "worse-ness" of Hillary would be an added reason as to why one might choose it. But if that is not the case, then you are faced with an immoral choice no matter how much worse Hillary would be— it is excluded even before considering her. In which case, while you may re-examine Trump in light of the common good, you must reject temptations that come from scaremongering and the villainization of Hillary. You must reject the idea that you should set aside your conscience because you "have to do something."

When man relies on himself alone, all comes to naught. Maybe the lesson here is to stop trusting in our political contrivances and stratagems. Cursed is he who places his hope in man, saith the Lord. Maybe it is good that you are bereft of some voting option to choose in order to battle Hillary; then maybe you will learn to see in it the vanity of human affairs and turn to the Lord.

We are supposed to minimize our cooperation in evil. One might see proportionate reasons in Trump himself (and not merely in comparison to Hillary) to hold one's nose and vote for Trump; I disagree, but I am not talking to those people, who may well be in good conscience. Rather, I am talking to those that keep repeating calls to violate conscience (sin), or to choose the lesser evil (sin). Those avenues are traps of the devil. Instead, inform your conscience rather than violating it, and always remember that the first precept of the natural law is, "do good, shun evil," not "do alright, minimize evil."

Charles De Koninck asked:

> Why does one not require, as a matter of principle and as an essential condition, that the leaders of society be men who are good purely and simply? How can one admit that a bad man might make a good politician? To be sure, it is not new to see subjects governed by bad men, men to whom one does nonetheless owe obedience in those things which pertain to their authority. What is new however is the manner of accepting and defending them.[4]

SOURCES: Dominicus Prümmer, *Manuale theologiae moralis*, v. 2; Henry Davis, SJ, *Moral and Pastoral Theology*, v. 2; The United States Conference of Catholic Bishops, *Forming Consciences for Faithful Citizenship*; Benedictus Merkelbach, *Theologia moralis generalis*, v. 1; Heribert Jone, OFM Cap. and Urban Adelman, OFM Cap., *Moral Theology*; St. Thomas Aquinas, *De Veritate*, q. 17, a. 4, ad 8, *ST* II-II, q. 62, a. 2, ad 2, *ST* III, q. 82, a. 10, ad 2; Adolphe Tanquerey, *Synopsis Theologiae Moralis and Pastoralis*, v. 3; Charles De Koninck, *On the Primacy of the Common Good*.

---

4. *On the Primacy of the Common Good* (Collins trans.), 69.

21

Is Man an Individual?

Ian Bothur

A popular tendency of the modern mind is to regard the human person as a mere individual; as something like an atom of the human species, existing completely in itself and for itself. This tendency is not only the hallmark of the liberal tradition, but is implicit even in the most popular "alternative" political philosophies of today. Compounding this problematic notion is the now centuries-old influence of modern natural science, whose practitioners tend to pursue creation's deepest mysteries by simple division.[1] These influences tend to seep even into Church documents. *Gaudium et Spes*, for example, defines the "common good" as "the sum of those conditions of social life which allow social groups and their individual members relatively thorough and ready access to their own fulfillment."[2]

Community itself thus seems to be defined by the Church as a totality of individuals. However, as the pastoral constitution later qualifies, "the common good embraces the sum of those conditions of the social life whereby men, families and associations more adequately and readily may attain their own perfection."[3] Here, the ultimate aim of political society is made quite clear; human perfection. The individualist tendency can thus be avoided if we understand man's existence to be inseparable from the order of which he is a part. If man is a creature ordered to perfection, he is therefore

---

1. Natural science does regularly achieve many interesting findings with respect to the order of natural bodies; not just the very small subdivisions of matter.
2. *GS* 26, §1.
3. *GS* 74, §1.

Is Man an Individual?

ordered to society. And insofar as man is ordered to society, he is not an individual in the sense that he is "self-sufficient"; rather, the substantial unity which characterizes each man's existence must exist within a unity of order by which he enjoys communion with others.

Individual

Common use of the term "individual" hides within it two distinct concepts: the first is the unity of a particular thing; the second is the thing as distinct from other things. With respect to unity, an individual is that which cannot be divided while remaining the same thing (i.e., the literal meaning of the term).[4] Of course, every physical thing is divisible, but once, say, a cow is divided in half, it would cease to be a cow and become two sides of beef. With respect to the thing's distinction from other things, an individual is discrete and separate: this individual cow is distinct from the herd, because this cow is not any other cow.

What causes a thing's unity is not what causes its separation from others, as Aristotle notes. Formal cause is responsible for unity. Thus, so long as the form is preserved, so also the individual: if my left hand were removed, it would cease to be my hand, but the remainder of my members would remain one body, because they are still united in my soul. We can therefore say that unity is a formal, immaterial quality of a thing. It is a thing's material cause, however, which distinguishes one individual from another within the same species. Formal cause is enough to distinguish a cow from a horse, but when I say "this cow is not that cow," I do so with regard to what the cow is made of. Two distinct cows contain two distinct collections of matter. That is, it is matter that *allows* forms that are the same in species to be multiplied in number, just as wax allows the one form of a signet ring to be multiplied in many seals.

So, "individual" refers in one sense to formal cause and in another sense to material cause. Individuality, then, allowing for both senses to be taken together, is a term by which we can know a thing's

---

4. Thomas Aquinas, *Super Sent.* I, d. 24, q. 1, a. 1.

essence, the composite of substantial form and determinate matter.⁵ To adequately understand a thing at all is to intuit its essence, and therefore, when speaking of things as they really are, each sense of "individual" must be understood with reference to the other.

Person

In contrast to cows, each man is not *merely* an individual, but a *person*; "an individual substance of a rational nature." With this distinction, it would seem that human beings are individuals in one sense, and persons in another. It is on this distinction that Jacques Maritain famously posits his brand of "Thomistic personalism." In his work, *The Person and the Common Good*, Maritain offers a summary of the distinction between "individuality" and "personality":

> [S]uch are the two metaphysical aspects of the human being, individuality and personality, together with their proper ontological features. [...] [W]e must emphasize that they are not two separate things. There is not in me one reality, called my individual, and another reality, called my person. One and the same reality is, in a certain sense an individual, and, in another sense, a person. Our whole being is an individual by reason of that in us which derives from matter, and a person by reason of that in us which derives from spirit.⁶

In speaking of individuality as the material aspect of man, Maritain must be speaking of "individual" in only one of the senses described above; that by which a thing is distinct from others of the same species. Personality, however, describes an individual of a rational nature. Hence, the determining characteristic of personality is rationality. But man is rational by virtue of his soul, his formal cause, which is the unitive aspect of a thing's individuality. So, perhaps Maritain means to use "personality" to denote the unitive aspect of an individual and "individuality" the distinguishing aspect.

---

5. Thomas Aquinas, *De Ente et Essentia*, trans. Armand Maurer (Toronto: Pontifical Institute of Mediaeval Studies, 1968), IV.iii, p. 36.
6. Jacques Maritain, *The Person and the Common Good*, trans. John J. Fitzgerald (New York: Charles Scribner's Sons, 1947), 3.

Is Man an Individual?

It is clear, in any case, that he does not refer to "individuality" in the unitive sense. In omitting this sense, he leaves only the material; and without reference to form, the purely material is unintelligible. Moreover, because all non-rational living things are individuals with a formal and material cause, they are not purely material, but neither are they persons.

The inherent problem with Maritain's distinction is that it is made at too low of an order: the distinction between individual and person is a useful one, but man is more properly understood in his *individuality* as a discrete unity of substantial form and determinate matter. But rationality is a specific attribute of formal cause and hence proper to man as a species; it is not enough to distinguish between individual men. Therefore, individuality is not purely material, but involves even man's rational nature.

Man is best understood in his *personality* as a being in a unique, rational relation to being. Thus while matter (whatever particular material his soul informs) is the *principle* or *beginning* of the distinction of one man from another, that beginning allows for spiritual differences. Although his intellect is specifically the same as the intellect of another man, his subjective apprehension of the world entails a unique, personal relation to the true and the good. Personality is therefore founded on individuality, but it goes beyond it. What distinguishes personality from individuality is not rationality per se, but the particular relation of a subject to the objects of his intellect and will.

Order

Of course, things do not subsist as embodied essences or definitions, but as sharing in a certain nature, which entails not just the formal and material causes of a thing, but its final cause as well.[7] Simply put, a thing's final cause is that for the sake of which it acts. In other words, it is the impetus of a thing to attain its end, which is its own perfection.[8] It is with respect to final cause that we under-

---

7. Aristotle, *Physics* II.8, 199a12.
8. Perfection is synonymous with completion or the fullness of its own being.

stand the good; that is, whatever is good for a thing is good insofar as it is the end, the final cause.[9] It is also with respect to final cause that we can give an account of natural activity: whenever a thing acts, it acts for its final cause, to attain its own perfection.[10]

It is perhaps with respect to nature that *order* can most easily be understood. A thing that is perfect is also said to be well-ordered. Likewise, a thing that is lacking in some perfection is disordered. Things that are capable of activity are disordered if their actions do not pertain to their final cause. In one sense, then, to be disordered is to fail in being. To exist as a creature is to exist in order; to be absolutely disordered is not to exist at all.[11]

There are different kinds of order. Most generally we can say that order is a relation of before and after (priority and posteriority) of many to one beginning or principle. For example, the points on a line have relations of before and after to each other in comparison to the beginning point of the line: this is the *order* of the points on a line. Each of the four causes (matter, form, agent, and end) can be called a beginning or principle, and so there is an order corresponding to each of the causes.[12] The most important cause is the final cause, the cause of causes, and so the most important kind of order is the relations of before and after that many things or actions or parts have among themselves in comparison to their final cause.[13] To understand or to produce order is proper to intelligence, hence we can say that things are ordered by the activity of an intelligent principle that governs or moves them toward their end.[14] Ultimately, all things are governed by the Eternal Law of God, and it is in this Law that all creation is ordered.

As activity entails final cause, and final cause implies order, all natural activity participates in the order of the Eternal Law. Man,

---

9. Aristotle, *Physics* II.3, 195a26.
10. Thomas Aquinas, *De Veritate*, q. 22, a. 1.
11. Thomas Aquinas, *ST* I-II, q. 52, a. 1.
12. Thomas Aquinas, *ST* I, q. 5, a. 3. I am grateful to Pater Edmund Waldstein for help with the general account of order.
13. Thomas Aquinas, *In Ethica* I, lect. 1.
14. Thomas Aquinas, *De Veritate*, q. 22, a. 1.

Is Man an Individual?

however, acts according to his own free choice by virtue of his intellect and will. Thus, man's participation in the Eternal Law is not diminished by his freedom, but is of a higher order than that of lower creatures, because in participating in the order of things to God, man first orders things to himself.[15] For example, when a cow eats grass, the grass is ordered to the good of the cow, because it is in the nature of cows to eat grass. But when a man eats a cow, it is not because it is in man's nature to eat cows, but because it is in man's nature to apprehend the good with his intellect and to decide how he might best pursue that good. In short, man can act by his own intellect as from a principle, rather than by the design of nature, and so governs lower things according to himself.

Of course, man's intellect is not absolute, but is a participation in the Divine Intellect as its ultimate formal and final cause. Man's mind does not render things intelligible; rather, things are intelligible insofar as they have a formal cause received from God. And as the knowledge of truth is the perfection of the intellect, and God is Truth, God Himself is the ultimate end of man's intellect.

Unity

Order implies the unity of the many ordered. When a cow eats grass, the substantial form of the grass ceases to exist and its matter is incorporated into the cow. But as both cow and grass exist, one is ordered to the other (formally in one sense and individually in another), and from this relation arises a "unity of order." Thus, with respect to the same order, many things are said to be one.[16] This unity is not merely a semantic one, as one might call a pile of rocks "one." Rather, a unity of order is necessary for the perfection of the individuals it contains. Our cow cannot exist without grass, and so long as it remains malnourished for want of it, it is imperfect. Moreover, grass can exist well enough without cows, but not without a variety of other things. In fact, investigation into the order of any

---

15. The free participation of rational creatures in the Eternal Law is the Natural Law.
16. Thomas Aquinas, *ST* I, q. 39, a. 3.

individual ultimately reveals the order of the whole universe in which it exists. Thus, St. Thomas calls the whole universe a unity of order.[17]

St. Thomas calls unity of order "the least of unities,"[18] but only with regard to the proximity of the principle by which things are made one. For example, an individual animal has unity by virtue of a formal principle, which is in a sense identical with the animal and cannot be separated from it. But the universe has unity insofar as all things are ordered for an extrinsic principle, which is God.[19] Hence, substantial unity is a "stronger" kind of unity than unity of order, but it does not follow from this comparison that unity of order is not a "real" unity. Rather, substantial unities necessarily participate by their nature in a unity of order.

Man finds his perfection in knowing and loving God, and therefore he is ordered to direct union with Him. It is precisely because man has an intellect and will that he is ordered to such a noble end. These same powers of his soul also enable man to order things lower than him to his own end (and what serves man is therefore elevated into a higher participation in the order of creation).

Persons are ordered to God, but as political animals by nature, they find their natural perfection in community with other persons. Man is ordered to participate in human society not only out of expedience; rather, he cannot attain his natural end without living in community. That man is a political animal follows from the ordering of social relations by his own reason; a reason that reaches its fullest power in the use of language, which is itself a socially acquired trait.[20] Furthermore, even a person who has attained perfection, who has no use for society, nevertheless delights in the goodness of others and is inclined to do good to them.[21]

---

17. Thomas Aquinas, *Quodlibet* VI, q. 11.
18. Thomas Aquinas, *SCG*, Bk. 2, ch. 58, n. 5.
19. Thomas Aquinas, *De potentia*, q. 3, a. 16, ad 2.
20. Aristotle, *Politics* I.2, 1253a3–17.
21. Thomas Aquinas, *ST* I-II, q. 4, a. 8.

Is Man an Individual?

Conclusion

We conclude that there are at least four ways in which every human being, as an individual, necessarily exists within a unity of order. First, every individual has his being as part of the order of the universe. In all his actions (even breathing), he is dependent upon other things for his existence. It is not his choosing that makes it so, but his very nature which determines what is good for him; what is necessary for the perfection of his being. Second, every individual human being is a person who bears a unique relation to other things by virtue of his rational nature. Each person actively participates in the order of creation by imposing order upon things to serve his own needs and ultimately to assist him in attaining his own perfection. Third, persons are, by virtue of their rational nature, capable of entering a unity of order with other persons. As man is a political animal by nature, society is necessary for man's perfection not only as a prerequisite to meet his material needs, but as the proper operation of human perfection. And finally, the ultimate end of every individual is communion with God; man's nature is part of this order, even though he is by nature incapable of attaining it.[22]

Therefore, Man is an individual part of a unity of order. Outside of this order, he is nothing.

---

22. *ST* I-II, q. 5, a. 5, ad 1; I-II, q. 3, a. 8.

22

Logos and Leviathan: Leonine Perspectives on Democracy

Zachary Thomas

> Must the political order be derived from a cosmic model (or, at any rate, from an external, transcendent reference point), or are there valid and effective substitutes? Can unaided humanity, through the mobilization of its faculties, create a sacred, or at least a myth, powerful enough to convey a model? If the answer to these questions is no, we must ask then: Can a community exist without the sacred component, by the mere power of rational decisions and intellectual discourse?
>
> Thomas Molnar, *Twin Powers: Politics and the Sacred*

In the ancient world, legitimate political forms ranged across a wide spectrum in which "rule of the people" was only one of many political forms conducive to the common good—and a very unfavorable one at that. But today, "democracy has become almost a synonym for legitimate government, for the rule of law."[1] Pundits declaim that democracy ensures freedom and fair government, while a new colonialism seeks to spread "democratic values" to every corner of the world. If we are clued in to the reductive tendencies of modern thought, we should be wary of such absolute claims. In fact, with a little digging, we discover that the democratic ideology of modernity is built upon a novel philosophy and cosmology. Early moderns like Hobbes, Locke, and Rousseau sought to

---

1. Edmund Waldstein, "The Politics of Nostalgia" (see the following chapter). All of the subsequent citations of P. Edmund are taken from that essay.

replace the worldview of Christian religion with their own, and in the process created new philosophies and myths that still legitimize modern political forms. A democracy bedizened with the false hopes of Enlightenment scripture becomes a Leviathan irreconcilable with church teachings; if it is disengaged from this unfruitful union, however, and defended under the aegis of Catholic Logos theology, it may be the political form most well adapted for securing the common good of modern nations.

We will first explain the nature of government according to the classical and Catholic understanding. Then, we will trace the discarding of this image in the early modern period. Finally, we will suggest how democracy might be disengaged from its current anti-Logos framework and put to good use in a Catholic political order.

1. The discarded image: a Logos-oriented politics

A. *The classical cosmos*

Edmund Waldstein succinctly explains the classical understanding of law, that discarded image of the cosmos upon which the Catholic Church has largely built its social teaching. Classical Greek thought, as found in Plato and Aristotle, presupposes that there is an "objective good that is knowable by human reason." Today the term "objective good" seems to denote a vague notion of reason, but it was more colorful for the Greeks. In broad terms, it meant nothing less than *the total harmonious order of the universe*. They saw the "cosmos" as a marvelous hierarchy of things each tending towards the perfection of a unique principle called nature. Nature is the essence of a thing, its ordering principle, the plan or purpose of its birth, unfolding, and consummation. Nature uses its powers to perfect itself in fruitful interaction with other natures. A horse, for example, is born from its mother, grows to maturity by eating grass, propagates its species, and dies: it has fulfilled its nature in the grand scheme of the cosmos.

Man too has a nature struggling to work itself out, and it is a *rational* nature. Man's unique identity consists in his ability to *know* his own objective good and also comprehend something of the order of the cosmos. But there is a problem:

The problem is that there are different powers in the human soul; there are the senses (touch, taste and so on) and then there is reason. The senses know a limited kind of goodness, and from this kind of knowledge come certain passions such as hunger and thirst and lust. Only reason knows the complete good, wherein happiness really lies, and *understands* it as good.[2]

In other words, there are competing powers within man, and it is reason's job to order those powers to man's true good: man must be educated. Reason must "train the human soul ... to help produce a harmony among its different parts.... This harmony is called virtue."[3]

But Greek virtue was not "moral" in the Kantian sense, a self-actualizing quest for self-mastery. Rather, it presupposed a real *participation* in the order of the cosmos, an order that does more than give man a static model from which to work out his own perfection. Plato's world of forms did serve that exemplary function, but in a much more religious sense, the forms were the real source of perfective power. There was a "givenness" about Greek virtue, a sense of being drawn up into a mysterious cosmic dance. As Waldstein explains:

> The order of the whole universe is what Charles De Koninck calls "the good of the universe" and "God's manifestation outside Himself." Man as the micro-cosmos can reflect this order in his own person through virtue. This is why virtue can be identified with happiness—because virtue is a participation in that order which is the greatest image of the divine beauty and goodness.

Seen in this light, communion among men is a crucial part of this great order. Since personal virtue is not really individual but rather a participation in a cosmic pageant, a virtuous community shows an even greater participation in the cosmic order. This is how Aristotle argues the point: "Even if the end is the same for a single man and for a state, that of the state seems at all events something greater and more complete, whether to attain or to preserve; though it is

---

2. Ibid.
3. Ibid.

worthwhile to attain the end merely for one man, it is finer and *more godlike* to attain it for a nation or for city-states."[4]

St. Thomas Aquinas took up the insights of Plato and Aristotle, and fashioned a Christian notion of the common good. He argued that "order is what God principally intends in creation: every individual creature reflects some aspect of God's glory, but it is the order, the harmony, the beauty of their unity, that most perfectly reflects the creator."[5] Something in the sum total of perfected beings is also god-like. Waldstein continues: "It is good for man to realize the order of the universe in his own soul but it is *more godlike* for him to realize it in the state ... the community of men reflects God more than an individual man, just as the universe reflects Him more perfectly than any one creature."

We are finally ready to discuss the role of law. Since the goal of community is to manifest the divine order, law has the principal function of "producing this unity of order, both in the individual soul, and more especially in the community." In other words, all law aims at the perfection of man's nature within the context of a community. It is illegitimate otherwise: "legitimacy on this view does not depend on the 'consent of the governed' given through democratic rituals, but rather it depends on the objective good."[6]

B. Authority in the Catholic state according to Leo XIII

The discussion must inevitably pass to practical matters, to the forms of government in which this harmonious order can be instantiated. Pope Leo XIII's social encyclicals provide a coherent Catholic teaching about the nature and forms of political authority, its relation to religious authority, as well as the proper relationship of the citizen to this authority.

It is first to be remarked that Leo is not opposed to any benign form of government in principle: "Catholics, like all other citizens, are free to prefer one form of government to another precisely

---

4. *Nicomachean Ethics* I.2, 1094b, emphasis added.
5. Waldstein, "Nostalgia."
6. Ibid.

because no one of these social forms is, in itself, opposed to the principles of sound reason nor to the maxims of Christian doctrine."[7] In fact, Leo is largely indifferent to the form or the means by which authority is constituted, so long as the source of authority be rightly conceived:

> There is no reason why the Church should not approve of the chief power being held by one man or by more, provided only it be just, and that it tend to the common advantage. Wherefore, so long as justice be respected, the people are not hindered from choosing for themselves that form of government which suits best either their own disposition, or the institutions and customs of their ancestors.[8]

Leo immediately goes on to explain this right conception of authority:

> But, as regards political power, the Church rightly teaches that it comes from God, for it finds this clearly testified in the sacred Scriptures and in the monuments of antiquity; besides, no other doctrine can be conceived which is more agreeable to reason or more in accord with the safety of both princes and peoples.[9]

The pope does not go on to suggest some sort of divine right of political leadership; rather, he makes a metaphysical argument about the nature of political authority. Man cannot find perfection except in society; thus society is part of nature and willed by God. But every association of man needs a ruling authority, or else there will be mere anarchy. No man has in himself the authority to constrain the will of others; that power resides only in God. Thus, all political power comes from heaven, and "it is necessary that those who exercise it should do it as having received it from God."[10] In other words, society is one of the instruments God has ordained for the perfection of man's nature; over and above individual reason, God constitutes social authority as a necessary means for man's per-

---

7. Leo XIII, Encyclical Letter *Au Milieu des Sollicitudes* (1892), 14.
8. Leo XIII, Encyclical Letter *Diuturnum Illud* (1881), 7.
9. *Diuturnum* 8.
10. Ibid., 11.

fection. Authority, in this view, most emphatically does not arise from the will of the people, even if they are the efficient cause of its peculiar shape. Rather, it is from God and for Him.

From this metaphysical principle, it follows that the social organism must acknowledge its source by offering *public worship* to the true God: "For men living together in society are under the power of God no less than individuals are, and society, no less than individuals, owes gratitude to God who gave it being and maintains it and whose ever-bounteous goodness enriches it with countless blessings."[11] In fact, Leo calls it a "public crime to act as though there were no God"; it is "one of [government's] chief duties to favor religion, to protect it, to shield it under the credit and sanction of the laws."[12]

Any wholly natural and metaphysically consistent society, therefore, must acknowledge its dependence on God and explicitly enforce the laws of the Church. To do otherwise is to undermine the very nature of human society. In fact, Leo argues that unless the state acknowledges God, its authority will lack any sure stability.[13] The doctrine of social contract is bound to lead to contempt for authority and an incessant revolutionary spirit. On the contrary, the Catholic doctrine will cause citizens to love and obey their rulers, and rulers to love and serve their citizens.

To summarize traditional Catholic teaching on the nature of political authority: society is the normal means ordained by God for the perfection of men's souls, and its right ordering puts it in consonance with the rest of the cosmic order. Thus, authority takes its legitimacy from its place in this divine plan. Legitimate authority acknowledges this dependence on God, and orders the state according to the laws of the true religion.

II. Leviathan: liberty and authority in modern political thought

What we have described is the Logos-oriented politics of the clas-

---

11. Ibid., 6.
12. Leo XII, *Immortale Dei* (1885), 6.
13. See, for example, *Immortale Dei* 32: "A State from which religion is banished can never be well regulated."

sical and Catholic tradition. Government is the art of moving men and communities toward their final end in God, who has instituted governments for this very purpose. For government to work, laws must be drawn in accordance with the objective good, citizens must respect legitimate authority, and the true religion must be enshrined.

Now we turn to modern political philosophy. Modernity prides itself on being objective, practical, and this-worldly, but as we examine its roots in the early modern period, we will find that it too rests on hidden, theocratic foundations. Its cosmology is, of course, not so rich as the antique, but it nevertheless exists as an a priori, mythological backdrop to modern political thought. The modern predilection for democracy must be understood as the necessary corollary of an erroneous cosmology that divinizes man.

Continuing trends of late medieval nominalism and humanism, the early moderns developed a novel conception of human freedom that, as Waldstein argues, was "disengaged from the good." This development had several aspects. The first was philosophical. Late medieval nominalists scorned the delicate synthesis by which Thomas and the ancients had knitted nature to the divine, and offered a radically simplified cosmic image: Essences became disconnected from ends; the symphonic cosmos became a mundane world of individual objects moved by the arbitrary will of God. Humanism ushered in the next stage when, poring over rediscovered treasures of pagan literature, humanists imbibed the classical sensibility of the glories of human accomplishment. They began to exalt what they perceived to be the infinite indeterminacy of the human will, its capacity to achieve nearly anything.[14]

But if humanism retained some affinity with the old virtue tradition, early moderns who followed the Reformation radicalized the concept of freedom, stripping from it any connection to the good. In the emerging view, man's dignity consists above all in *being unimpeded*. Freedom is no longer *what is accomplished*, but the con-

---

14. Concerning humanism, it is important to note that it began as a deeply Catholic movement. Its unofficial manifesto, Mirandola's *De Hominis Dignitate*, could seem an idolization of human will. But for Pico, man's perfection is still deeply connected with God and grace.

dition of accomplishment: a radical autonomy, the absence of any restraint on the will.

Another aspect was political. As post-Reformation nations were racked with internecine religious conflict, it became convenient to argue

> that the objective good for man is *too hard to know, too difficult to agree about*, that in order to avoid the bloodshed of religious wars, it is necessary to limit politics to the care of a bare minimum of peace necessary to allow for the non-violent coexistence of persons with different views of what the true good is.[15]

This is the thrust of Locke's *Letter Concerning Toleration*.[16] Whatever theoretical consensus remained to Europeans concerning some common objective good was destroyed in this final political development. From then on, politics decided not to concern itself with religion or any sort of claims about the objective good. Or so it thought. As Michael Hanby has argued, the liberal state makes an implicit metaphysical claim: by denying God any role in the polity, it posits "that a thing's relation to God, being a creature, makes no difference to its nature or intelligibility. Those are tacked on extrinsically through the free act of the agent."[17] In this denial, modernity effects the apotheosis of man in a new mythology.

This apotheosis has a long history, including those steps discussed above, but took a great leap in the Scientific Revolution. Encouraged by pioneers like Francis Bacon and Galileo, early modern thinkers discarded Aristotelian conceptions of the universe for more empirical methods. Most importantly, they redefined motion, the concept underlying all classical cosmology. In ancient physics, motion was an interior, teleological phenomenon directing natures

---

15. Waldstein, "Nostalgia."
16. For more on Locke, see Jeffrey Bond, "Locke's Doctrine of Toleration: A Contract with Nothingness," published in three parts at *The Josias*, May 14, 15, and 16, 2015; cf. https://thejosias.com/2015/05/14/lockes-doctrine-of-toleration-a-contract-with-nothingness/, with other links given there.
17. Michael Hanby, "The Civic Project of American Christianity," *First Things*, February 2015, http://www.firstthings.com/article/2015/02/the-civic-project-of-american-christianity.

toward their ends; in modern physics, motion becomes a mere external happening, the blind action of material forces whirling objects around *per inane quietum*. This divorce from final causes leads to a new way of seeing and relating to the natural world. If the old world functioned organically, as a sort of garden of natures growing in participatory being towards fruition in God, the new world is a machine, a collection of empirical objects jostled here and there in space according to fixed laws of nature.[18] Man is no exception. His natural activity, deprived of a final end in God, becomes the autonomous working of his own nature. Thus, man "attains his end," or in the new metaphor "functions most efficiently," when he enjoys that power most characteristic to him, the law of reason.

On this basis of mechanistic physics, early moderns built an edifice of mechanistic politics. Throwing out the organic metaphors, early moderns conceived the state in terms of a vast mechanism of forces checked and balanced against one another. For example, Hobbes's systematic political treatise *Leviathan* takes as its theoretical foundation a mechanistic epistemology. In his account, man is not even really free, but like a floundering ship, is carried this way and that by his passions, which are in turn merely determined responses to external stimuli. Like atoms in the void, men bump into each other constantly in a state of incessant war. The only way to peace is for an absolute sovereign to be invested with all power of coercion. Hobbes's sovereign stands like a lid on a kettle, tasked with keeping the effervescent passions of his people from boiling over into civil war.

Locke's views are more pertinent to the discussion of democracy. Like Hobbes, he begins by considering a state of nature. Before society, however, man is also in a state of war (though endowed with a more respectable rational faculty than Hobbes allows). Society is joined not for moral improvement, but for physical protection against predatory raids and a guarantee of more economic prosperity than was attainable in the state of nature. Locke's ethos is that of

---

18. It is also ripe for exploitation. Man is no longer the steward of the nature-garden, but a mechanic whose powers give him unrestricted domination over the other machines.

Logos and Leviathan: Leonine Perspectives on Democracy

a very reasonable gentleman, and he often seems to invoke some sort of natural law; but he too ultimately deploys mechanist metaphors to explain the working of his system. Explaining the necessity of majority rule, he quite bluntly appeals to the physical principle of inertia according to which the lesser force must always yield to the greater.[19] Locke's state too is an engine, and human beings are its cogs. And like an engine in a factory, its end is only the production of material prosperity.[20]

If Locke and Hobbes gave to modern political thought its theoretical matter, Rousseau composed modernity's mythological form. Surprisingly, underlying the new rationalist philosophy about man's nature, there stands a veritable myth: the state of nature. This myth, in its various forms, underlies and legitimizes the political project of each of these thinkers.[21]

According to Rousseau, men were born into a paradisiacal state of absolute self-sufficiency and contentment. Far from needing the help of other men, he wandered through warm forests eating plentiful food, hardly meeting other men. He was entirely sustained in a

---

19. E.g., "For when any number of men have, by the consent of every individual, made a community, they have thereby made that community one body, with a power to act as one body, which is only by the will and determination of the majority. For that which acts any community being only the consent of the individuals of it, and it being necessary to that which is one body to move one way, it is necessary the body should move that way whither the greater force carries it, which is the consent of the majority; or else it is impossible it should act or continue one body..." (John Locke, *The Second Treatise on Government*, ed. Tom Crawford [New York: Dover Publications, 2002], 44).

20. Of course he pays lip service to the natural and divine laws, but even as he invokes these laws he limits them explicitly to practical measures ensuring preservation.

21. There is no difficulty in the myth coming to light after its philosophical and political expressions. Some orthodox Biblical scholars explain the composition of the Genesis myth by later Hebrew prophets as a process of self-reflection projected back in history: "Because the human author was contemplating an object designed to reflect creation, and because he had a supernatural gift of insight into this object, he was able to offer an account of creation based on his reflections about Israel's history—he gazed *into* Israel's institutions and history and there saw mankind's beginnings" (Jeremy Holmes, unpublished paper "Genesis 1–11 and Science"). We imagine Rousseau did the same for modernity.

tranquil, dispassionate state by what Rousseau calls pity. This pity prevented him from harming other creatures or his fellow man. Only later, by a series of witless concessions of freedom, did mankind form families, cities, and states. Each step towards civilization further enslaved mankind.

But this myth makes of man a God, casting him in the form of an entirely self-sufficient and undetermined rational agent. As James Kalb observes:

> To refuse to talk about the transcendent, and view it as wholly out of our reach, seems very cautious and humble. In practice, however, it puts our own thoughts and desires at the center of things, and so puts man in the place of God. If you say we cannot know anything about God, but only our own experience, you will soon say that there is no God, at least for practical purposes, and that we are the ones who give order and meaning to the world. In short, you will say that we are God.[22]

In Pierre Manent's analysis, this is the dark myth lurking behind the progress of the democratic spirit: yearning for the pseudo-divine state of our ancestors.

> What would sum up in the same or a like way our society and its extraordinary or paradoxical character of dis-society? It would be the notion of the *state of nature*.... How can we be interested in the individual in the state of nature as Rousseau describes, eating acorns and quenching his thirst at the first stream? The animal nonetheless interests us since ultimately this individual is each one of us: he is what we want to be. To put it in a nutshell, the state of nature is defined as a state of independence, liberty, and equality. We want to live independent, free, and equal. In this sense, the state of nature forms our horizon.[23]

By seeking the ordering principle of society in the beginning, rather than in the end, the state of nature hypothesis inverts the tra-

---

22. James Kalb, quoted in Thaddeus Kozinski, *The Political Problem of Religious Pluralism: And Why Philosophers Can't Solve It* (Lanham, MD: Lexington Books, 2013), 229.

23. Pierre Manent, *A World Beyond Politics?: A Defense of the Nation State* (New Haven: Princeton University Press, 2006), 137.

ditional political order. For classical politics, it was not so much where man came from, or how he existed in an indeterminate past, but how he ought to be, and what he could be that mattered. Politics concerned itself about perfecting man's nature by bringing it to some end. Under the new mythology of autonomous mechanism, man springs forth fully formed from the womb of nature, in need of nothing but safety and fuel to keep his machine going. Since man is born perfect but unfortunately enslaved in society, modern politics strives to attain as much as possible for its citizens this original Edenic state of total autonomy. As a colleague put it, "Democracy is just the story of people trying to get as far away from each other as possible."

In light of this analysis, it is clear that modernity, for all its vaunted idealism and its supposed autonomy from history or tradition, is built on hidden theocratic foundations; it merely proposes a new mythology in place of an old one. In Thaddeus Kozinski's words: "It is not that modern liberal democracy has successfully desacralized politics, but rather it has changed the locus of sacralization from cosmic order, divine law, and the Church, to the human person, and the sacred freedom of individuals to choose their own sacred allegiances."[24]

Catholics believe a story: the story about man's original justice and original sin. The first moderns too believe a story: a new narrative of original justice, this time without original sin. In fact, the sin, in many cases, is precisely the entrance into society. Society itself becomes man's original sin, the act that separates man from a mythical primeval state of innocence and integrity. For Catholics, man can be saved from his enslavement to sin, but only in the next life, and only if he follows the rule of divine and natural law. Modern politics too has a salvation narrative, but it is this-worldly: man can find "salvation" in the free satisfaction of all his (non-predatory) desires in the democratic state. Modern politics tries to guarantee its citizens as large a share of Original Autonomy as circumstances allow, with the ultimate goal of freeing men as entirely as possible.

---

24. *Modernity as Apocalypse: Sacred Nihilism and the Counterfeits of Logos* (Brooklyn: Angelico Press, 2019), 121.

In this new mythological account, democracy becomes an indispensable tool for the modern religion. All other forms of government in some way deprive individuals of autonomy, by privileging one class over another, or cleaving to accidental historical arrangements. This is why the first moderns worked hard to eradicate all obstacles to the ascent of democratic forms of government. In the French Revolution, for example, the monarchy, aristocracy, guilds, monasteries, in short all the traditional threads of the fabric of society were rent to make way for the *novus ordo*.

But the paradox of modern liberty is that man is not deified: he feels himself subsumed into a Leviathan. Since his own autonomous choice is his only claim to self-worth, he is faced with a paradox: either consent to association and lose autonomy, or refuse to consent to anything. As Manent argues:

> The dilemma of modern liberty—the dilemma of modern liberty as experienced by the modern individual—could then be roughly formulated in the following way: Either I enter into a community, association, membership, and I transform myself into a part of a whole and lose my liberty, or I do not enter ... and I do not exercise my freedom. In brief, this is the dilemma of modern liberty: either I am not free, or I am not free.[25]

Man in modern democracy feels himself swallowed in the unrestrained motion of a majority devoid of a rational end. Government looms as the ambivalent referee of an orgy of blind desires, over a nation "swept with confused alarms of struggle and flight, where ignorant armies clash by night."[26]

III. Taming Leviathan: Logos-oriented democracy

If subsumed into such an anti-Logos modern religion, democracy cannot be reconciled in any way with the Catholic religion. Nevertheless, once these hidden religious foundations are exposed and repudiated, a Catholic is free to weigh democracy as one legitimate form among many others. The encyclicals of Pope Leo XIII

---

25. Manent, *World Beyond Politics?*, 119.
26. From Matthew Arnold's "Dover Beach."

Logos and Leviathan: Leonine Perspectives on Democracy

clearly teach the conditions in which democracy is a possible form of government for the modern world.

Leo expressly affirms that democracy is a legitimate form of government: "Again, it is not of itself wrong to prefer a democratic form of government, if only the Catholic doctrine be maintained as to the origin and exercise of power."[27] Under what conditions, then, would democracy be advantageous? I would argue that democracy is a form uniquely suited to the modern world, as long as it is not pure, and avoids the typical attitudes contrary to Catholic teaching. Leo suggests as much: "Neither is it blameworthy in itself, in any manner, for the people to have a share, greater or less, in the government: for at certain times, and under certain laws, such participation may not only be of benefit to the citizens, but may even be of obligation."[28]

To see how this might be so, we must turn to Tocqueville. In the introduction to his *Democracy in America*, Tocqueville argues convincingly that the tendency toward democracy is "the most continuous, the oldest, and the most permanent fact known in history."[29] As civilization increases prosperity, "all processes discovered, all needs that arise, all desires that demand satisfaction bring progress toward universal leveling.... When one runs through the pages of our history, one finds so to speak no great events in seven hundred years that have not turned to the profit of equality."[30] In light of this "providential fact,"[31] the duty of those who direct modern society is "to instruct democracy,"[32] not to oppose it. Unfortunately, because

---

27. *Libertas Praestantissimum* 44.
28. *Immortale Dei* 36.
29. Alexis de Tocqueville, *Democracy in America*, ed. Harvey C. Mansfield and Delba Winthrop (Chicago: University of Chicago Press, 2000), 3.
30. Ibid., 5.
31. Ibid., 6.
32. "To instruct democracy, if possible to reanimate its beliefs, to purify its mores, to regulate its movements, to substitute little by little the science of affairs for its inexperience, and knowledge of its true interests for its blind instincts; to adapt its government to time and place; to modify it according to circumstances and men: such is the first duty imposed on those who direct society in our day" (ibid., 7).

traditional society resisted democratic tendencies, democracy erupted by revolution,[33] rather than after careful circumspection.

I agree with this account, and believe that his trenchant comparison of aristocratic and democratic societies sheds light on several advantages of a democratic polity. First, democratic society "will be less brilliant, less glorious, less strong, perhaps; but the majority of its citizens will enjoy a more prosperous lot."[34] Democracy does not have the glorious potential of aristocracy, but it does improve the lot of the common man. Second, democracy can enliven the individual citizen by giving him political obligations. In his description of American townships, Tocqueville marvels at the energy of townsmen working for the common good together[35] while remarking that the citizen of an aristocratic country often feels like a colonist in his own land, "indifferent to the destiny of the place that he inhabits."[36]

Nevertheless, when bringing democracy into a Catholic state, several dangers must be avoided. Tocqueville envisions a future society that, "regarding the law as their work, would love and submit to it without trouble; in which the authority of government is respected as necessary, not divine and the love one would bear for a head of state would not be a passion, but a reasoned and tranquil sentiment."[37]

These observations point to the first difficulty in implementing democracy: the tendency it has to erode respect for authority. Frequent elections, for example, make people think authority does in fact reside in the general will, and does not make for stability and permanence in the legislative body. But this obstacle is not insurmountable, if it is balanced by a strong affirmation of the nature of

---

33. "Democracy has therefore been abandoned to its savage instincts; it has grown up like those children who, deprived of paternal care, rear themselves in the streets of our towns and know only society's vices and miseries" (ibid., 7).
34. Ibid., 9.
35. "The inhabitant applies himself to each of the interests of his country as to his very own. He is glorified in the glory of the nation; in the success that it obtains he believes he recognizes his own work, and he is uplifted by it; he rejoices in the general prosperity from which he profits" (ibid., 90).
36. Ibid., 91.
37. Ibid., 9.

authority: if the democratic state is ruled by a strong constitution that affirms authority's origin in God, if it submits itself to the laws of his Church, provides for God's public worship, and establishes the natural law as the foundation of all law.[38] Oaths of office must include similar elements. Under such a system of laws, there need be no difficulty in assigning a large share of self-government to the people. Instructed by their laws and the virtuous examples of their leaders, they will seek to build up the kingdom of God by the exercise of their rights. Also, reverence that in aristocracy is attributed to the aristocrat and his family can be transferred to the offices and assemblies themselves. A House or an Executive authority, through a solid history of illustrious leaders, can still command the sort of reverence proper for a God-given authority.

Another difficulty endemic to democracy, even if it succeds in establishing respect for its ruling political authority, is the maintenance of the authority of tradition. Care must be taken that the whims of the people do not destroy the religious and cultural foundations of society. There is a democracy of the dead, whose will must be taken into account in elections. Monuments of culture, traditional practices and lore, must not be allowed to be neglected. Of course, there are democratic ways to protect these things: guilds, cultural societies, churches, all can work to maintain tradition as democracy is implemented. In answer to Molnar's open question, we must affirm with Leo XIII that no society can remain robust without traditional religious foundations.

Conclusion

We have shown how democracy, as it exists within the ideological framework given to it by early modern thinkers, cannot be reconciled with Catholic principles. The classical and Catholic worldview holds that no social fabric can be woven without respecting the divine origin of authority and public profession of the true religion. Disengaged from a mechanistic mythology, democracy can be seen in its true light, as a form offering many benefits not found in more

---

38. As in the constitution of the Republic of Ireland, so rudely violated of late.

aristocratic regimes. Nevertheless, it is prone to self-will, improvidence, and contempt for authority, which must be combated with strong legal and cultural supports for tradition and religion. In the final analysis, the Leonine perspective on democracy can save modern man from the Leviathan, and help him return to the Logos.

23

The Politics of Nostalgia

Edmund Waldstein, O.Cist.

Introduction

I am very pleased to have been invited to speak here at the Pistori Palace[1] this evening. I have been told that this palace is closely associated with the disastrous political ideologies of the last century. During the Second World War it housed the representatives of National Socialist Germany, and later it became a Lenin Museum. This evening I am going to be criticizing an aspect of the dominant political ideology of our own time: liberalism. The history of liberalism in the last century is one of extraordinary triumph. After being widely questioned in the early part of the century, it triumphed over its totalitarian rivals, and today it surrounds us like the air we breathe, so that many of its ideas seem to people to be self-evident truisms. I am going to examine one example of this: the idea that democracy is the best form of government. Today it seems obvious to most people that democracy is the only reasonable form of government—indeed, even the only *legitimate* form of government. Democracy has become almost a synonym for legitimate government, for the rule of law. "Undemocratic" has become a synonym for "tyrannical," for a regime unconcerned with the good of the people.

Even those who are weary of the hypocrisy, vulgarity, and pettiness of democratic politics—the shortsightedness and divisiveness

---

1. I was invited to speak in Bratislava in 2014 by the Ladislav Hanus Fellowship; my thanks to the organizers, particularly Boris Bartho.

of politicians always looking toward the next election, the manipulation of the process through private interests, the dominance of prejudice over reason, and so on—even people who are sick of such politics cannot conceive of any un-democratic alternative.

Thus the "Occupy Wall Street" movement in the United States, weary of the mock representation of the people through magistrates who serve the interests of the "one percent," on whom they are financially dependent, can only propose a different model of democracy—a more direct, Athenian-style democracy—as a means to promote the common welfare. They do not dare to state the seeming implication of their criticism of the status quo: that democracy itself is part of the problem.

On a very different part of the ideological map one finds political strongmen such as Vladimir Putin. Fed up with the democratic chaos of the Yeltsin years, and the extraordinary loss of Russian power that they caused, Putin establishes an autocratic rule. And yet despite his evident contempt for democracy he thinks it necessary to go through democratic rituals of legitimation: elections, referenda, etc.

Why is it that even the enemies of democracy—American anarchists and Russian autocrats—have to pay lip-service to this form of governance?

It was not always so. The greatest philosophers of antiquity—Plato and Aristotle—both considered democracy a rather inferior form of political life. Plato has Socrates claim that democratic citizens are dominated by licentious passion rather than reason: "they call insolence good education; anarchy, freedom; wastefulness, magnificence; and shamelessness, courage."[2] He says that it is the sort of regime favored by children and women—i.e., those in whom reason is weak.[3] Aristotle distinguishes between good forms of government, in which the rulers have the common good of the whole city as their goal, and bad ones, in which they rule for their own private interests. He gives the name "democracy" to one of the bad regimes: that in which the poor rule for the private advantage of

---

2. *Republic* 560e.
3. Ibid., 557c.

The Politics of Nostalgia

their own class.[4] In the Christian Middle Ages monarchy rather than democracy was the most common form of government, and to many medieval thinkers this seemed perfectly reasonable.[5]

The great transformation that brought the modern world into being changed things, but this transformation took many centuries, and many resisted it—especially Catholics. When revolutionaries killed King Louis XVI of France, Pope Pius VI commented as follows:

> By a conspiracy of impious men, the most Christian king Louis XVI has been condemned to death, and the sentence has been carried out. But what sort of a sentence this was, and with what reason it was passed, We will briefly call to your attention: it was brought about without authority and without law by the National Convention—for that Convention, when the form of *the more excellent monarchical regime* had been abolished, placed all public power at the disposal of the People, who are governed by no reason or counsel; who perceive no distinction of things; who judge few things by truth, and many by opinion; who are inconstant, and easy to deceive and lead into every base deed; who are ungrateful, arrogant, and cruel; who rejoice in human blood, in slaughter and in funerals; and who are filled with pleasure by the pains of the dying, just as was seen in the amphitheaters of the ancients.[6]

At the time, his reaction was by no means extraordinary.

I want to examine why it is that today most people think about democracy and monarchy so differently from Pius VI. I will first consider the view of politics that one finds in the greatest thinkers of the Middle Ages: the ideal of Catholic monarchy that comes from a synthesis of classical philosophy and Christian theology. I then want to explain why modernity sees democracy as the best form of government, and how this is connected to the modern rejection of

---

4. *Politics* III.6–7, 1279a–b.
5. See, for example, Thomas Aquinas, *De Regno ad Regem Cypri*.
6. Pius VI, *Quare Lacrymae*, Allocution to the Secret Consistory of the Sacred College of Cardinals of June 17, 1793, translated by Coëmgenus, http://thejosias.com/2015/01/29/pius-vi-quare-lacrymae/.

classical philosophy and the Christian faith. I shall argue that the modern preference for democracy is unreasonable, that it flows from a false conception of the end or goal of political life, a false conception of the common good, and a false conception of the source of political authority. And then I shall ask whether any practical consequences can be drawn from my position; after all, it is hardly likely that there will be a restoration of the monarchy here in central Europe any time soon, and it is unclear how one could work for such a thing, if at all. I shall argue that nevertheless there *are* practical consequences: although it is not feasible to work directly for a restoration, one *can* work toward a more authentic realization of the common good. Moreover, seeing through the false self-evidence of liberal politics allows one to gain a necessary critical distance from the ideology of our time, thus allowing one to resist certain evils more effectively.

I. The Discarded Image

A. *The purpose of government*

Classical Greek political philosophy was deeply marked by the experience of the war with Persia. In Herodotus's *Histories,* the Greek Demaratus tells Xerxes, the Persian tyrant, that the Greeks will win, despite having many fewer men than the Persians:

> They are free, yet not wholly free: law is their master, whom they fear much more than your men fear you. They do whatever it bids; and its bidding is always the same, that they must never flee from the battle before any multitude of men, but must abide at their post and there conquer or die.[7]

The reason why the Greeks win is that unlike the Persians they are not the slaves of passion, they are the "slaves" of law. To be ruled by law is to be ruled by *reason,* since law is a decision based on reason. And this will become the Greek notion of freedom: the rule of reason. To be ruled by reason means to be free, because it means

---

7. *Histories*, ed. and trans. A. D. Godley (Medford, MA: Harvard University Press, 1920), Bk. VII, 104, 4–5.

understanding what is really good, what is really desirable, not being moved by a passing feeling toward an action which one knows does not really lead to anything good. The achievement of the true good is happiness, and since everyone wants to be happy, a law which "forces" one to do good and to avoid evil does not limit freedom, but rather makes the one who follows it free; able to achieve what he really, deep down, wants.

This conception of law presupposes that there is really an objective good that is knowable by human reason. Socrates argues this point with the sophists of his day. They hold that in fact there is no true good. "Justice is the advantage of the stronger." That is to say, what people happen to desire they call good, and if they are strong enough they force everyone to submit to their desire and they call this justice. But Socrates argues against this that there is indeed an objective good. The good is indeed what we desire, but it is not good because we desire it, but on the contrary we desire it because it is good; desire is awakened by the good when we recognize it.

So why doesn't everyone desire what is really good? The problem is that there are different powers in the human soul; there are the senses (touch, taste and so on) and then there is reason. The senses know a limited kind of goodness, and from this kind of knowledge come certain passions such as hunger and thirst and lust. Only reason knows the complete good, wherein happiness really lies, and *understands* it as good. Thus reason has to *order* and moderate the passions. Unfortunately most persons are like the Persian soldiers; there is a disorder in the soul, with the passions dominating reason. So man has to be educated, and habituated to act in an orderly way so that reason will rule over the passions. On this account, law has an educative task; it is meant to train the human soul, to order it, to help produce a harmony among its different parts, in which reason has the first place. This harmony is called virtue.

This harmony in the soul is more than a merely useful thing. It is not as though virtue is merely a means to getting the good, something that makes you more effective at getting the truly desirable good. Virtue is itself good, and it is a participation in a higher good. As Socrates says:

> For he, Adeimantus, whose mind is fixed upon true being... his eye is ever directed towards things fixed and immutable, which he sees neither injuring nor injured by one another, but all in *order* moving according to reason; these he imitates, and to these he will, as far as he can, conform himself.... And the philosopher holding converse with the divine *order*, becomes *order*ly and divine, as far as the nature of man allows.... And if a necessity be laid upon him of fashioning, not only himself, but human nature generally, whether in States or individuals, into that which he beholds elsewhere, will he, think you, be an unskillful artificer of justice, temperance, and every civil virtue?... And if the world perceives that what we are saying about him is the truth, will they be angry with philosophy? Will they disbelieve us, when we tell them that no State can be happy which is not designed by artists who imitate the heavenly pattern?[8]

I consider this to be one of the profoundest insights of Platonic philosophy: the human good is a *participation* in a higher, divine good. Thus our good exists not principally in our selves, but principally in the divine realm, and secondarily in ourselves. The divine good *is more our own good* than the good which exists in our own souls. This Platonic insight was developed by St. Augustine and then further developed by St. Thomas who synthesized it with Aristotle's account of the common good.

Note the importance of *order* in Plato's text. The divine order (harmony, beauty) is reflected in the order of the eternal forms; this is reflected in the visible cosmos, in the order of the virtuous soul, and in the order of the just political community. St. Thomas Aquinas teaches that order is what God principally intends in creation: every individual creature reflects some aspect of God's glory, but it is the order, the harmony, the beauty of their unity, that most perfectly reflects the Creator:

> The multitude and distinction of things has been planned by the divine mind and has been instituted in the real world so that created things would represent the divine goodness in various ways and diverse beings would participate in it in different degrees, so

---

8. *Republic* 500; emphasis added.

The Politics of Nostalgia

that out of the order of diverse beings a certain beauty would arise in things.⁹

At the beginning of Dante's *Paradiso* Beatrice makes the same point:

> e cominciò: Le cose tutte quante
> hanno ordine tra loro, e questo è forma
> che l'universo a Dio fa simigliante.

> And she began: All things whate'er they be
> Have order among themselves, and this is form,
> That makes the universe resemble God. (Canto 1)

The order of the whole of creation is what Charles De Koninck calls "the good of the universe" and "God's manifestation outside Himself." Man as the micro-cosmos can reflect this order in his own person through virtue. This is why virtue can be identified with happiness—because virtue is a participation in that order which is the greatest image of the divine beauty and goodness. And the order in a community is an *even greater* participation in the universal order. This is what Augustine shows with his analysis of the praises of "peace" in the Psalms: "If I forget you, O City of Peace, let my right hand wither! Let my tongue cleave to the roof of my mouth, if I do not remember you, if I do not set Jerusalem above my highest joy!"[10]

This is also how St. Thomas understands Aristotle's teaching on the primacy of the common good. Aristotle writes the following:

> Even if the end is the same for a single man and for a state, that of the state seems at all events something greater and more complete whether to attain or to preserve; though it is worthwhile to attain the end merely for one man, it is finer and *more godlike* to attain it for a nation or for city-states.[11]

It is good for man to realize the order of the universe in his own soul but it is *more godlike* for him to realize it in the state. St. Thomas takes this *more godlike* very literally; the community of men reflects God more than an individual man, just as the universe reflects Him

---

9. St. Thomas, *Compendium theologiae*, Lib. 1, cap. 102, end.
10. Ps. 136[137]:5–6. See my paper "On Peace as the Final Cause of the Universe."
11. *Ethics* I.2, 1094b7.

Integralism and the Common Good

more perfectly than any one creature. Recall what I said about participation a moment ago: my *own good* exists more in the divine than in my individual existence. A corollary can now be seen: the common good, the order of the community, is more *my good* than any private good of mine. The common good of order or peace is common in the fullest sense of the word: all the members of the community share it without it being divided or lessened by this sharing. Thus the common good is not merely a useful good; it is not merely the conditions that enable individuals to get what they want. It is the best good that individuals can have, it is that in which they find their happiness.[12]

Let me sum up the argument so far. The conception of politics that began with Socrates, Plato, and Aristotle, and that was developed by the great Christian thinkers, sees man as having an objective good. This good is a participation in the divine good, and consists primarily in the unity of order or harmony. This unity of order exists in the individual soul through virtue and in the community through peace. Law is ordered to producing this unity of order, both in the individual soul, and more especially in the community. Thus St. Thomas defines law as follows: "an ordinance of reason for the common good, made by him who has care of the community, and promulgated."[13]

Law derives its legitimacy from the good to which it is ordered; if it is ordered to the true common good then it is binding on all its subjects—not in a way that enslaves them, but in a way that makes them free. Similarly the ruler, who makes and administers the law, has his authority from the common good; to the extent that he serves the authentic common good he has legitimate authority and is not imposing on anyone. Legitimacy on this view does not depend on the "consent of the governed" given through democratic rituals, but rather it depends on the objective good.

B. *The form of government*

Since the purpose of government is to produce an order in the

---

12. See De Koninck, *Primacy of the Common Good*.
13. *ST* I-II, q. 90, a. 4.

The Politics of Nostalgia

community which is an imitation of a higher order, it is necessary to determine where exactly that higher order is to be found, how it is to be known, and in what way the political order is to imitate it. For many of the ancients that order was visible in the stars—which they thought of as eternal, immutable, living beings—but they were wrong about the stars. In Plato the divine order is found principally in the ideal forms, which are not visible to the senses, but can be apprehended by the intellect. But Plato's application of this order to the city is never presented in a straightforward way. In the *Republic* he spends the greatest amount of time "constructing" a city that is dominated by *thymos*, by passion, rather than by reason, since his interlocutors are not yet ready to comprehend the city of *logos*.[14]

In Christian thought the model for the "divine" order is the "city of God," the spiritual community composed principally of the hierarchies of the angels, in all their myriad myriads, to whom the saints are then joined. The "order of the universe" is principally an order of persons, related in a hierarchy of governance and subordination.[15] St. Thomas Aquinas is called the "Angelic" Doctor because of the clarity with which he investigated that order.

But how is the model of the heavenly city to be applied to the earthly city? Dante's *Commedia* is one of the finest examples of how this is done. The "dark woods" at the beginning of the *Inferno* are the loss of order both in Dante's soul (the loss of virtue) and in Italy as a whole (the loss of political peace).[16] Dante's journey through the divine order manifested in the punishment of the damned, the purification of the Church suffering, and the glory of the angels and saints, is the means not only to recovering virtue in his own soul, but also to showing Italy the solution to its woes.

One thing that Dante learns is that it is necessary, for good politi-

---

14. See Eva Brann, *The Music of the Republic* (Philadelphia: Paul Dry, 2011), esp. ch. 6.

15. See my blog-essay "Angelic Governance and Human Dignity," *Sancrucensis*, October 2, 2013, https://sancrucensis.wordpress.com/2013/10/02/angelic-governance-and-human-dignity/.

16. See Romano Guardini, *Dantes Göttliche Komödie: Ihre philosophischen und religiösen Grundgedanken*, ed. Hans Mercker (Mainz-Paderborn: Grünewald, 1998), 70–75.

cal order, to have a monarch. This is shown in poetic mode in the *Commedia*, but Dante also argued for it more pedantically in the *De Monarchia*. The *De Monarchia* is principally about the necessity of a universal monarchy, but the argument can also be used to show why a monarchy is preferable to a polyarchy in a particular state. Dante gives a number of arguments, but the most illuminating (from my perspective) are those that proceed from the idea of imitating the divine order. In I,VIII he argues that God makes everything to "represent the divine likeness in so far as their peculiar nature is able to receive it," but the human race is most like him when it is *one*, and it is most one when it has one ruler. Similarly, in I,IX he argues that humanity imitates the heavens (meaning presumably the stars, but the angelic hierarchies could have been taken as the middle term instead). Now, the heavens are moved by a single mover, therefore men should be ruled by a single monarch. These arguments are applied to the order that ought to obtain in humanity as a whole, but they are even more applicable to a particular state, where a more closely-knit community is possible.

Dante's arguments are very similar to those presented by St. Thomas Aquinas in the *De Regno*. St. Thomas there argues that monarchy is the best form of government since that which is itself one is better able to cause unity. But unity is the primary purpose of government, because government is for the sake of the common good, and the common good consists in a kind of *unity* (namely a unity of order that reflects the divine beauty).[17]

But of course there are different forms of monarchy. The kind favored by St. Thomas is not a pure monarchy, but one that is moderated by aristocratic and democratic elements to preserve the monarch from falling into tyranny, and to keep him in contact with the different parts of society. St. Thomas proposes that the aristocratic element be elected by and from the people, thus providing for a democratic element.[18] But here I disagree with St. Thomas. Most people are ruled by passion, and it requires education to acquire virtue and responsibility. Experience teaches that an hereditary aris-

---

17. See *De Regno ad Regem Cypri*, I.2.
18. See *ST* I-II, q. 105, a. 1.

tocracy, in which the members are raised with a sense of responsibility and *noblesse oblige*, is better able to bring to the fore a virtuous elite than popular election, which tends to bring ambitious liars to the top. Reginald Garrigou-Lagrange, the great Thomist theologian, writes: "Any regime which favors the ambition of demagogues who flatter the people in order to arrive at power, leads to political pharisaism and to ruin, for there is no durable union except in truth and justice."[19]

Thus Garrigou-Lagrange proposes another way of including the aristocratic and democratic elements in a monarchy. He proposes the model of medieval France:

> Under the *ancien régime* in France, the interests of the different classes of society and of the different regions were represented by the corporations and their delegates, by the provincial Estates, and by the Estates General: assembly of clergy, of the nobility, and of the third estate.[20]

The prevention of the rise of ambitious demagogues is also one of the reasons why I think that hereditary monarchy is superior to elected monarchy. Another reason is that election of the monarch tends to cause faction among the people, weakening their unity by causing enmity between the supporters of rival candidates. This is a grave disadvantage, because the monarch ought to instantiate the unity of the whole community. As St. Thomas writes:

> Since love looks to the good, there is a diversity of love according as there is a diversity of the good. There is, however, a certain good proper to each man considered as one person, and as far as loving this good is concerned, each one is the principal object of his own love. But there is a certain common good which pertains to this man or that man insofar as he is considered as part of a whole; thus there is a certain common good pertaining to a soldier con-

---

19. Réginald Garrigou-Lagrange, "On Royal Government," translation Andrew Strain, www.academia.edu/8384944/Translation_of_Garrigou-Lagranges_On_Royal_Government.

20. "On Royal Government." Garrigou-Lagrange does not clearly state that he is disagreeing with St. Thomas. See Alan Fimister, *Robert Schuman: Neo-Scholastic Humanism and the Reunification of Europe* (Brussels: Peter Lang, 2008), 111–12.

sidered as part of the army, or to a citizen as part of the state. As far as loving this common good is concerned, the principal object of love is that in which the good primarily exists; just as the good of the army is in the general, or the good of the state is in the king. Whence, it is the duty of a good soldier that he neglects even his own safety in order to save the good of his general.[21]

A great republican statesman, Robert Schuman, the father of the European Union, describes his own experience of this:

> It is in Luxembourg that I acquired the first notions of patriotism. It was in 1890 under the Grand Ducal balcony. The people acclaimed Grand Duke Adolf who came to make his solemn entry into the capital. I was a little boy of four years old lost in the crowd. I was enflamed by its enthusiasm and taken up in its pride. [...] Henceforth I knew what it is to love one's country, and the attachment to the sovereign who personifies and guarantees the unity, continuity and independence of the nation.[22]

This function of the monarch is fulfilled much better if he is the descendent of the kings for whom my ancestors shed their blood, than if he's just some bloke elected by a party to which I don't even belong.

An obvious objection to the hereditary system is that it often results in fools or evil men becoming kings. This is a great disadvantage, but as the libertarian philosopher and economist Hans Hermann Hoppe points out,[23] if one compares the record of hereditary monarchs to that of elected rulers, the system of hereditary monarchy actually harbors fewer fools and villains.

II. The Wasteland

Now I turn to the question of how the classical conception of politics that I have just tried to explain was replaced by the modern one

---

21. *De virtutibus*, q. 2, a. 4, ad 2.
22. Fimister, *Schuman*, 145.
23. Hans-Hermann Hoppe, *Democracy, the God that Failed: The Economics and Politics of Monarchy, Democracy and Natural Order* (New Brunswick, NJ: Transaction Publishers, 2001). See also Peter A. Kwasniewski, "Between Christ the King and 'We Have No King But Caesar,'" *OnePeterFive*, October 25, 2020, https://onepeterfive.com/christ-king-no-king-caesar/.

The Politics of Nostalgia

with which we are all familiar. I will only be able to give a few brief hints about this, because this was an extremely complex process: the genesis of the modern world.

One way of stating what happened is that freedom was disengaged from the good. Modern thought beginning already in the late Middle Ages with nominalism, but more in Renaissance humanism, and then fully in the Enlightenment, begins to see freedom not as "slavery to the law" as Herodotus did, but rather as *deciding for oneself what to do, without any determination from without, not even determination by the objective good*. Freedom is seen as an arbitrary choice in nominalism. In humanism the very indeterminacy of this free choice begins to be seen as the root of man's dignity. Man has dignity not because he can understand what is truly good and attain it; rather man has dignity because he can decide for himself wherein he wants to find his good, his end. We see this view in Giovanni Pico della Mirandola's *Oration on the Dignity of Man*—although Pico sometimes makes use of the older notion of freedom as well. Freedom thus comes to be seen as primarily *freedom from any interference with free choice, freedom from any kind of coercion*.

After the wars of religion that followed the Reformation this position was supported and aided by a similar but less radical view, namely, the view that the objective good for man is *too hard to know, too difficult to agree about*; that in order to avoid the bloodshed of religious wars, it is necessary to limit politics to the care of a bare minimum of peace necessary to allow for the non-violent coexistence of persons with different views of what the true good is.

For both of these views the *end* of politics came to be seen as the securing of *rights*—the *prevention* of interference with people's freedom.

In early modern thinkers such as Hobbes this view of politics was used to support a new kind of monarchy: absolutism. This was a corrupt form of monarchy that, instead of seeing the monarch as the principle of a beautiful harmony and order, saw him as the manager of a huge bureaucratic machine that was set up to give people security and allow them to get what they wanted. Later thinkers such as Locke came to see that the machine didn't need the sovereign at the top; it could run on its own.

Integralism and the Common Good

This view corresponded to a new cosmology, a new view of nature. It was this new cosmology, in my opinion, that did most to make modern political philosophy plausible to people. The spectacular success of modern natural science, and the technological developments that it enabled, have had a profound effect on our mentality; they have become inscribed in the very "material relations" of daily life through the industrial-capitalist economy. It is the mechanistic mentality fostered by capitalism and reductive natural science that makes modern political views seem so obvious.

Modern natural science begins with the *decision* of thinkers such as Francis Bacon and René Descartes to find a way of looking at nature that will enable man to have power over nature, to dominate it. The older, Aristotelian view had seen the purpose of science as *understanding the world as it is.* Thus for Aristotelian science the most important thing to study had been the *good*—what is the good that nature tries to achieve, what is the goal that a particular natural thing strives for and so on. But in the new science such questions became irrelevant. If the purpose of science is *power* over nature, then the whole point is not to find the goals that nature herself pursues, but to replace them with my own goals. Modern natural science thus began to ignore any aspect of reality that did not fit with this project. This would not in itself be problematic as a limited method for particular purposes, but of course it became a total way of looking at nature. Nature came to be seen as a giant machine—moved not by the attraction of the good, but by blind, mathematically defined "forces."[24]

---

24. Consider the following analysis by Sean Collins: "Where did the Hobbesian-Machiavellian politics come from? No doubt it originated, in significant part, from properly political experience, and interpretations to which that experience gave rise. But that experience could not have been interpreted in the way it was if it were not for a more universal postulate: the postulate that there is such a thing as 'force' understood not only as a political reality, but as a principle of politics and ethics. But it became a physical principle (articulated to various degrees at various times) before it became a political or ethical principle. If the former had not happened, the latter very likely would not have happened either" ("Imagine a World without Force," blogpost, October 5, 2009, http://sdcojai.wordpress.com/).

The Politics of Nostalgia

This view of nature inevitably affected the view of human nature. So we see, for example, that in psychology since Freud, human desire tends to be seen as kind of a blind force that randomly attaches itself to various objects—not as a something that is aroused by the objective goodness of things.

All this supports the idea of politics as ordered to allowing people the freedom to pursue whatever they happen to desire, without interference from anyone else. The older idea of law as educative, as that which orders persons and peoples toward their true good, then appears as tyrannical, as against freedom.

Thus, what I have called the more radical idea of the separation of freedom and the good is becoming ever more dominant in our society. The Supreme Court of the United States explicitly stated this idea of freedom in 1992:

> At the heart of liberty is the right to define one's own concept of existence, of meaning, of the universe, and of the mystery of human life. Beliefs about these matters could not define the attributes of personhood were they formed under compulsion of the State.[25]

On this account of freedom, if the state were to attempt to order its subjects to an authentic good it would be disrespecting their dignity as persons.

And so we can see a first reason why democracy seems so plausible to our contemporaries. Democracy gives people the illusion of being involved in making the laws. Thus to obey the law is really to obey oneself. The philosopher George Santayana once made this remark about the apparent futility of parliamentary institutions:

> Those who spoke spoke badly, with imperfect knowledge of the matter in hand, and simply to air their prejudices. The rest hardly listened. If there was a vote, it revealed not the results of the debate, but the previous and settled sentiments of the voters. The uselessness and the poor quality of the whole performance were so evident that it surprised me to see that so many intelligent men—

---

25. *Planned Parenthood v. Casey*, United States Supreme Court, 505 U.S. 833; 112 S.Ct. 2791; 120 L.Ed. 2d. 674 (1992).

for they were intelligent when doing their special work—should tamely waste so much time in keeping up the farce. But parliamentary institutions have a secret function in the Anglosaxon world, like those important glands that seem useless to a superficial anatomy. There is an illusion of self-government, especially for members of the majority; there is a gregarious sense of safety and reassurance in being backed, or led, or even opposed by crowds of your equals under conventional safeguards and guarantees; and there is solace to the vague mind in letting an anonymous and irresponsible majority be responsible for everything. You grumble but you consent to put up with the course that things happen to take.[26]

Moreover, the democratic process itself fits with the mechanical view of the world as a system of blind forces. As Sean Collins writes:

We have now built an entire civilization on the separation of final causes from efficient causes. Many noble souls still hope that the good will still prevail, and they act accordingly. But if one assumes that the good is brought about as an epiphenomenon from agencies which are at bottom blind, tyranny and not freedom will inevitably be the result.[27]

The counting and quantifying of mass opinion on which democracy depends is the fitting political expression of the view of the world as an arena of "force." Erik von Kuehnelt-Leddihn points out the contrast between this sort of politics and those of a hereditary monarchy:

Monarchy is not a thought-out, artificial, arithmetical form of government, rather it is in the strictest sense of the word "natural," proportioned to the nature of man. Begetting and birth are contrasted to poster-covered walls and nights at the computer after election battles.[28]

---

26. George Santayana, *Persons and Places*, vol. 2: *The Middle Span* (New York: Scribner, 1945), 160–61.
27. Collins, "Imagine a World without Force."
28. *Die rechtgestellten Weichen* (Wien: Karolinger Verlag, 1989), 94.

III. Consequences

When Boris Bartho and others interviewed me for the YouTube trailer of the *Bratislavské Hanusove Dni*,[29] they were particularly interested in the practical conclusions that might be drawn from my position. And rightly so: political philosophy is a practical science. But modern political ideas are so entrenched that it is hard to see what can be done at the level of practical politics.

At the level of constitutional law there is a limited amount that can be done to encourage the monarchical element within a republican form. One can see the constitution of the French Fifth Republic as an improvement over that of the Fourth in this regard. But such reforms are to my mind largely beside the point. The primary focus of our political action should be to encourage respect for the primacy of the objective good, and the natural law that follows on it, over "consensus values." I admire people who try to do this in current politics—such as the great Slovak M.E.P. Anna Záborská—but again, the amount of good that can be done in this way is limited by the nature of the system.

Perhaps more important than direct political action is the kind of work that the Ladislav Hanus Fellowship is doing here: education. To educate ourselves in the way of which Plato speaks: to look at the eternal and divine, and to form our souls according to the order there—*that* is the most practical thing that we can do. And then we can form communities at the local level where that order can find some (imperfect) embodiment, where we can seek authentic common goods together. A classic example of such a local form of community is the monastery, a way of embodying an alternative to the dominant model of authority, of community, and of economic life. Hence Alasdair MacIntyre at the end of *After Virtue*, his famous polemic against modernity, famously wrote that we are waiting for a new St. Benedict:

> What matters at this stage is the construction of local forms of community within which civility and the intellectual and moral life can be sustained through the new dark ages which are already

---

29. See http://youtu.be/fgfkLf.

upon us. And if the tradition of the virtues was able to survive the horrors of the last dark ages, we are not entirely without grounds for hope. This time however the barbarians are not waiting beyond the frontiers; they have already been governing us for quite some time. And it is our lack of consciousness of this that constitutes part of our predicament. We are waiting not for a Godot, but for another—doubtless very different—St. Benedict.[30]

Conclusion: In Praise of Nostalgia

People like to dismiss my position as nostalgic; as a kind of weak sentimental attachment to an idealized past that enables me to justify my shirking of responsibility in the present. This is the accusation that is invariably brought against critics of modernity, and usually they think it necessary to protest that they are not in fact nostalgic. Thus Alasdair MacIntyre in the Preface to the 3rd edition of *After Virtue* writes that there is "not a trace" of nostalgia in his book,[31] and another critic of modernity, Brad Gregory, concludes his latest polemic with a section entitled "Against Nostalgia."[32] But I am not going to let myself be bullied out of my nostalgia; I reject the whole notion that nostalgia is something bad. I have entitled this concluding section of my manuscript not "*Against* Nostalgia," but "In *Praise* of Nostalgia." Contempt for nostalgia is a sign of the vulgar philistinism of the age of "progress." Nostalgia is a deeply human sentiment. The greatest and most *political* works of Western poetry are all nostalgic: Homer is nostalgic, Virgil is nostalgic, Dante is nostalgic.

Pope Francis is hardly a shirker of the burden of the present, but in a reflection (written before he became pope) on the work of Luigi Giussani he offered some reflections on nostalgia that are very relevant here, and with which I conclude:

> I am convinced that [Father Giussani's] thought is profoundly human and reaches man's innermost longings. I dare say that this

---

30. MacIntyre, *After Virtue*, 263.
31. Ibid., xi.
32. Brad S. Gregory, *The Unintended Reformation* (Cambridge, MA: Belknap, 2012).

is the most profound, and at the same time understandable, phenomenology of nostalgia as a transcendental fact. There is a phenomenology of nostalgia, *nóstos algos*, feeling called home, the experience of feeling attracted to what is most proper for us, most consonant with our being.[33]

---

33. Quoted in Silvina Premat, "The Attraction of the Cardinal," *Traces*, June 2001, reproduced online at http://communio.stblogs.org/index.php/2013/03/the-attraction-of-the-cardinal/. For similar positive remarks on nostalgia by John Paul II and Joseph Ratzinger, see Peter A. Kwasniewski, "'What Is Most Deeply Human': Two Contrasting Approaches to Nostalgia," *New Liturgical Movement*, December 30, 2013, www.newliturgicalmovement.org/2013/12/what-is-most-deeply-human-two.html.

24

Hard Liberalism, Soft Liberalism, and the American Founding

Edmund Waldstein, O.Cist.

1. Hard liberalism: Patrick Deneen on Thomas Hobbes

In *Why Liberalism Failed,* Patrick Deneen identifies a double principle underlying the liberal conception of liberty: 1) an anthropological individualism and a voluntarist understanding of choice, and 2) a view of human beings as separate from and opposed to nature.[1] The two principles are intimately connected. Both are bound up with the Enlightenment's rejection of the objectivity of the good, expressed with unrivalled clarity by the protoliberal Hobbes: "*Good, and Evill, are names that signifie our Appetites, and Aversions.*"[2] Choice is therefore "voluntarist" in the sense that it is not elicited by the objective goodness of things, but is rather the arbitrary fixing of the will on some object. Such an anthropology is individualistic, since there is no common end uniting different human beings. Human life, under this conception, is indeed radically irrational—there is no final goal, and therefore no reason to do one thing rather than another:

> For there is no such Finis Ultimus, (utmost ayme,) nor Summum Bonum, (greatest good,) as is spoken of in the Books of the old Morall Philosophers. Nor can a man any more live, whose Desires are at an end, than he, whose Senses and Imaginations are at a

---

1. Patrick Deneen, *Why Liberalism Failed* (New Haven: Yale University Press, 2018), 31.
2. *Leviathan,* Part I, ch. 15.

stand. Felicity is a continuall progresse of the desire, from one object to another; the attaining of the former, being still but the way to the later.[3]

This is a profoundly lonely and pessimistic view of human life, and an aimless hurrying from one object of desire to another, a being swept this way and that by irrational passion, unable to find rest or lasting happiness.

In a Hobbesian world, the older notion of nature as an intrinsic principle of motion toward the good and rest in the good as an end is mere nonsense. Human beings cannot find their fulfillment in perfecting their nature through virtue and finding their place in the ordered hierarchy of natures that is the cosmos. Natures become merely the raw materials to be dominated by the human will through the process of technological progress sketched out by Hobbes's employer Francis Bacon.

2. Soft liberalism: Vincent P. Muñoz's objections to Deneen

A panel discussion[4] between Vincent P. Muñoz and Adrian Vermeule raised the question as to what extent Deneen's critique of liberalism applies to the understanding of political liberty articulated by the founders of the United States of America. Muñoz argued that Deneen's critique is accurate enough as applied to the heirs of Hobbes, but that it misses the mark when it is thought of as applying to the American *Declaration of Independence*. Certainly, as Adrian Vermeule pointed out in his response, the American Founders do not belong to any of the recognizable current schools of liberalism—Millian, Rawlsian, Hayekian, etc. Nevertheless, I claim that in certain key respects the American Founders were indeed liberal. It is necessary to distinguish between a *radical* or (as I have called it in the past) *hard* liberalism, based on a Hobbesian denial of the supreme good, and a *moderate* or *soft* form of liberalism that does not necessarily deny the supreme good, but does deny that politics should directly order human life toward that good. Soft liberalism

---

3. *Leviathan*, ch. 11.
4. Retrievable at https://soundcloud.com/thomisticinstitute/adrian-vermeule-vincent-p-munoz-the-crisis-of-liberalism-a-discussion.

converges with hard liberalism in conceiving of rights primarily in terms of subjective power and in seeing political life as being primarily for the sake of protecting rights thus understood. It is a form of liberalism because it sees the end of politics as being *liberty*, rather than the common good of human life.

The bridge between the hard proto-liberalism of Hobbes and the soft liberalism of the founders is of course John Locke, who gives a hard-liberal account of the good in *An Essay Concerning Human Understanding*,[5] but who in *The Second Treatise of Civil Government* often writes as though he were merely a soft liberal.[6]

The American Founders were not all consistent soft liberals in my sense. There is a current of classical Republican thought in the American Founding that sees the purpose of government as being the *res publica*, the common good. But there is a significant admixture of soft liberalism in the American Republic, seen most clearly in the *Declaration of Independence*'s account of the reason for the establishment of government. And in fact, Muñoz himself seems to give primary importance to that current and to be himself a soft liberal.

Muñoz argues that the *Declaration of Independence* presupposes a non-Hobbesian understanding of the good. Good and evil are not merely names for the arbitrary objects of appetite, but rather there is a *true good* based on the order that God has placed in His creation. Thus, the *Declaration* begins with an assertion of truth: "We hold these truths." The *Declaration*'s championship of a view of government as founded on the consent of the governed for the sake of the defense of their rights, as Muñoz argues, is based on an

---

5. In Book II, ch. 20, Locke defines good and evil with reference to pleasure and pain: "Things then are good or evil, only in reference to pleasure or pain. That we call GOOD, which is apt to cause or increase pleasure, or diminish pain in us." And, since pleasure and pain are said relative to the subject ("For when a man declares in autumn when he is eating them, or in spring when there are none, that he loves grapes, it is no more but that the taste of grapes delights him: let an alteration of health or constitution destroy the delight of their taste, and he then can be said to love grapes no longer"), the definition is practically the same as Hobbes's definition in terms of appetite.

6. My thanks to Felix de St. Vincent for this point.

Hard Liberalism, Soft Liberalism, & American Founding

understanding of human equality and human rights as part of the natural order created by God. Because human beings are endowed with a rational and free nature, Muñoz understands the *Declaration* to be arguing that it is in accord with their nature that they be self-governed and that rulers rule only by the consent of their subjects. And such rule should be, on his view, ordered to defending the rights that flow from the possession of reason and free will. The infamous moral relativism propounded by the United States Supreme Court in *Casey v. Planned Parenthood*, Muñoz argues, is not the logical conclusion of the natural-rights liberalism of the American Founding, but rather the betrayal thereof.

Although Muñoz succeeds in showing that the *Declaration* is not hard, Hobbesian liberalism, the soft liberalism that he finds there instead is itself still a seriously erroneous and dangerous understanding of politics. Instead of seeing the legitimacy of political rule as flowing from the common good, as Thomas Aquinas had, this soft liberalism sees it as flowing from the consent of subjects. The end of political life is then seen as the liberty of those subjects to pursue their own ends with a minimum of interference. Thus, while the soft liberal might still see a sovereign good to which human life is ordered, that sovereign good is separated from politics and thereby privatized. Moreover, this privatization of the sovereign good, and the structures that soft liberalism unites with hard liberalism in promoting, tend to dissolve the residual moral objectivity on which its softness rests, and thus the subjects of soft liberal regimes harden over time. Soft liberalism, in other words, is not only bad in itself, it also leads to hard liberalism, which is much worse.

The first questioner in the Vermeule-Muñoz panel raises the objection that such a rights-based idea of government will forbid the misuse of human nature only when such misuse is seen as injuring the rights of others. However, this apparently soft-liberal line of reasoning has led to hard liberal decisions of the United States Supreme Court, such as *Griswold v. Connecticut* (striking down laws against contraception) and *Lawrence v. Texas* (striking down laws against acts of unnatural vice). In his response, Muñoz simply points out that the same line of reasoning leads to the right of religious liberty: "A man may use his freedom not to properly worship

God, therefore do you take away his freedom to worship?" The question leads us to a crucial ambiguity in the notion of rights that shows why soft liberalism is indeed liberalism.

3. The ambiguity of rights

According to an influential view, liberalism simply is the doctrine that politics is ordered to the protection of rights. Thus Leo Strauss writes:

> If we may call liberalism that political doctrine which regards as the fundamental political fact the rights, as distinguished from the duties, of man and which identifies the function of the state with the protection or the safeguarding of those rights, we must say that the founder of liberalism was Hobbes.[7]

But this view of the matter is complicated by the role that the idea of rights plays in undoubtedly non-liberal or pre-liberal thinkers, such as Thomas Aquinas. Strauss of course recognized that there was a notion of "right" in pre-liberal thought, but he sees the moderns as having come up with a new notion of "right" based in a new primacy of self-preservation. Strauss's account of how this came about is deeply suggestive, but not (to my mind) completely precise. Recent work by the likes of Dominic Legge, O.P. (at the same conference as the Vermeule-Muñoz panel[8]) and Pedro Izquierdo (on *The Josias*)[9] gives a slightly more precise account that

---

7. Leo Strauss, *Natural Right and History* (Chicago: The University of Chicago Press, 1953), 181.
8. The talk "When Rights Go Wrong: Thomistic Reflections on Rights, Justice & the Common Good" may be found here: https://soundcloud.com/thomisticinstitute/dominic-legge-op-when-rights-go-wrong-thomistic-reflections-on-rights-justice-the-common-good.
9. "Notes on Right and Law," *The Josias*, May 16, 2017 (https://thejosias.com/2017/05/16/notes-on-right-and-law/); cf. the conversation with Izquierdo in *The Josias Podcast*, Episode III: Basic Concepts—Right, Rights, and the Law (https://thejosias.com/2017/11/22/the-josias-podcast-episode-iii-basic-concepts-right-rights-and-the-law/), and my reflections thereon in "New Episode of The Josias Podcast on Rights," *Sancrucensis*, November 22, 2017 (https://sancrucensis.wordpress.com/2017/11/22/new-episode-of-the-josias-podcast-on-rights/). The following paragraphs are in part re-worked from that blogpost.

shows the difference between the function that rights play in non-liberal and liberal thinkers. This fuller account does, however, support Strauss's thesis—against critics such as Brian Tierney[10]—that a political philosophy that identifies the end of the state with the protection of those rights is essentially different from pre-modern political philosophy.

The English word "right" is derived from the Indo-European root "reg," meaning straight (and hence, to move in a straight line, to lead straight, to put right, to rule, etc.). "Right" is the etymological equivalent of the Latin *rectitudo*. But in legal usage "right" is used to translate another Latin word, namely *ius*. St. Thomas, following the Roman jurists, uses *ius* in the sense of the *object of the virtue of justice*. That is, most basically, the *thing* due to another. The just *thing*. For example, the bread that a baker owes someone who has paid him for bread. St. Thomas's understanding of *ius* is thus bound up with his understanding of the whole order of justice. What is due to another will depend on the distribution of things that has been made with a view to the common good. This distribution of things is made in the first place by God's eternal law with a view to the universal common good of all things—both the intrinsic common good of the harmonious order of the whole of creation, and the extrinsic common good of God Himself as the object of happiness. In the second place, the distribution of things is made by human custom and law for the sake of the common good of temporal happiness and peace. Law is the *ratio iuris*, it gives the reason why a particular thing is due to a particular person. And what law is *is* an ordinance of reason *for the common good*.

Thus, in St. Thomas's conception, everything goes back to deliberations of reason about the common good, and what serves it. So,

---

10. Tierney criticizes Strauss for exaggerating the discontinuity between ancient and modern conceptions of rights. See Brian Tierney, *The Idea of Natural Rights: Studies on Natural Rights, Natural Law, and Church Law, 1150–1625* (Grand Rapids: Eerdmans, 1997), especially pp. 52 and 208. For a lucid critique of Tierney's theory of the continuity of premodern and modern natural rights theories, see Gladden Pappin, "Rights, Moral Theology and Politics in Jean Gerson," in *History of Political Thought* 36.2 (2015): 234–61.

Integralism and the Common Good

for example, the distribution of private property will be regulated with a view to what serves the common good. Therefore, the law can put limits on the acquisition of wealth, if it judges that too great an acquisition damages social peace. Or it can forbid certain kinds of contracts or loans that are judged to be prejudicial to civic friendship.

Now, the modern sense of "right" as a *moral power*, that is *what someone ought to be allowed to do without interference* was originally an analogical extension (anticipated already by late medieval Schoolmen such as Ockham, but most clearly expounded by Baroque Schoolmen such as Suárez), and originally meant that if a thing is one's right, then the power or license that one has to do certain things to or with the thing is also due to one, i.e., one's right. For example, if a piece of bread is someone's *ius*, then eating the bread is also his *ius*. That is, he ought *to be allowed* to eat the bread.

This analogical extension would be unobjectionable in itself. Such moral powers do indeed have some foundation in reality, and it makes sense to extend the name *ius* to them. But in the course of the extension, a fatal reversal takes place. The analogical extension of *ius*, right as a power, comes to be seen as the *prime analogate*, and objective right, the object owed to the other, as an analogical extension. On the basis of this reversal, Suárez and his Enlightenment imitators hold that something is due to another, because of the inviolable moral power that he has of demanding it, *rather than* the power being an effect of his being owed something. Henri Grenier explains the consequences with his customary concision:

> If objective right is understood as right in the strict sense, it follows that subjective right, i.e., right as a power, is measured by the just thing, according to conformity to law. Moreover, since law is an ordinance for the common good, it follows that the whole juridical order is directed to the common good. But, if subjective right is understood as right in the primary, strict, and formal meaning of the term, it follows that the juridical order consists in a certain autonomy, independence, and liberty. For subjective right is not measured by the just thing, but the just thing is measured by the inviolable faculty, which is a certain liberty. Therefore, according to moderns, the juridical order is directed to liberty rather

than to the common good. This gives rise to errors among moderns, who speak of liberty of speech, liberty of worship, economic liberty,—economic liberalism,—without any consideration of their relation to the common good.[11]

Here we see why even a soft-liberal acceptance of the primacy of rights (understood as subjective powers) in political life will lead to hard liberalism. If the political order is seen as being primarily ordered to the defense of subjective rights, then the ordination of the juridical order to the common good will quickly be lost. The relation of law and right will be reversed. Law will more and more be seen as a limit on rights for the sake of preserving them. That is, it will come to be seen as a limit on the moral power to do things for the sake of preserving the maximum moral power of doing things in the greatest number of persons. Thus, for example, it limits the power of taking stuff away from others, in order to increase the power of amassing possessions. The end ultimately is for each person to be able to exercise their will (whatever its object) to the maximum extent compatible with others doing the same. This is liberal*ism*, because *liberty* is seen as the primary aim of political life. It is only a small step from such a conception of law to the infamous dictum of the United States Supreme Court in *Casey v. Planned Parenthood*: "At the heart of liberty is the right to define one's own concept of existence, of meaning, of the universe, and of the mystery of human life."

When the *Declaration of Independence* laid down as a fundamental principle that governments are established among men to secure their natural rights, it was not laying down a hard-liberal, Hobbesian principle. But it was laying down a soft-liberal principle—a principle that tends to sever the juridical order from the common good, and that therefore has an inherent tendency toward hard liberalism.

But the American founders were not consistent in seeing the aim of government in soft-liberal terms. There has long been a debate between interpreters of the American Founding, with one side fol-

---

11. Grenier, *Thomistic Philosophy*, vol. 4, §950.

Integralism and the Common Good

lowing the mid-twentieth-century consensus of scholars such as Louis Hartz and Martin Diamond in reading the Founders as Lockean liberals, while the other side follows scholars such as Bernard Bailyn and J.G.A. Pocock, who in the later part of the twentieth century argued that in fact the Founders were classical republicans, seeing the end of government as being the common good. In his excellent dissertation, Matthew J. Peterson retraces the debate, and concludes that both sides are partly right.[12] The Founders saw the aim of government as being *both* the defense of individual rights (liberalism), and the public good (republicanism). Peterson warns, however, against concluding that the political thought of the founding was merely an incoherent *mélange*. He suggests that with a deeper understanding of the common good, one will see that the defense of individual rights makes an integral contribution to the common good of political life itself, but that the common good of political life finally goes beyond individual rights. On my reading, Peterson essentially comes down on the republican side, albeit with an important qualification. If one asks which the Founders saw as being ordered to which: the public good to individual rights, or individual rights to the public good? Peterson reads them as subordinating individual rights to the common good. He denies, however, that rights are seen as *merely instrumental*; rather they are integral to the common good.

Peterson's reading seems to me a possible interpretation of the Founders. But I think that to some extent he underplays the tension between the two ways of seeing the relation of rights and the common good. On the whole, I think that Charles Taylor is right to see a transformation going on during the American Revolution in which classical common good and natural law thinking is transformed by a liberal understanding of rights, so that the relation between the two is slowly reversed.[13]

---

12. Peterson, "The Meaning of the Public Good in the Rhetoric of Ratification," Dissertation, Claremont Graduate University, 2013.
13. See Edmund Waldstein, O.Cist, "Against the American Revolution," *Sancrucensis*, January 16, 2012, https://sancrucensis.wordpress.com/2012/01/16/against-the-american-revolution/.

4. Blackstone's account of law and rights

To a certain extent one can see the shift between a non-liberal and a liberal understanding of the relation of rights and the common good taking place already in an author whom the American Founders cited more often than any other, except Montesquieu: the English Tory jurist Sir William Blackstone (1723–1780).[14] Blackstone is rightly considered to be one of the main conduits of classical natural law and common good thinking to the American Founders. And certainly, Blackstone has a strong doctrine of natural law, holding that any positive laws that go against the laws that God has inscribed into nature are invalid. And his *Commentaries on the Laws of England* are largely an admirable exposition of how the natural law is embodied in the common law of England. Yet, in his general remarks on the nature of law in the Introduction to the *Commentaries*, and on the nature of right in Book I, the Tory Jurist introduces some surprisingly Whiggish conceptions that would justify us in calling him a soft liberal.

Blackstone's general definition of law is Suárezian in the sense that it omits any reference to the good: "Law, in it's [sic] most general and comprehensive sense, signifies […] that rule of action, which is prescribed by some superior, and which the inferior is bound to obey."[15] In discussing natural law, Blackstone does indeed bring in order to happiness, the human good, but to a Thomistic reader two features of his discussion appear strange. The first is that the relation of happiness and the natural law seems to be conceived of in a strangely extrinsic manner. The second is that happiness seems to be conceived of as a purely *individual* good, rather than as the attainment of the common good. It is worth quoting Blackstone at length:

---

14. The top-three most cited authors are, in order, Montesquieu, Blackstone, and Locke; see Donald S. Lutz, "The Relative Influence of European Writers on Late Eighteenth-Century American Political Thought," in *The American Political Science Review* 78.1 (1984): 189–97.

15. William Blackstone, *Commentaries on the Laws of England*, Book I, *The Rights of Persons*, ed. David Lemmings (Oxford: Oxford University Press, 2016), 33. For Suárez's similar definition, see Legge, "When Rights Go Wrong."

Integralism and the Common Good

For as God, when he created matter, and endued it with a principle of mobility, established certain rules for the perpetual direction of that motion; so, when he created man, and endued him with freewill to conduct himself in all parts of life, he laid down certain immutable laws of human nature, whereby that freewill is in some degree regulated and restrained, and gave him also the faculty of reason to discover the purport of those laws. [...] These are the eternal, immutable laws of good and evil, to which the creator himself in all his dispensations conforms; and which he has enabled human reason to discover, so far as they are necessary for the conduct of human actions. [...] But if the discovery of these first principles of the law of nature depended only upon the due exertion of right reason, and could not otherwise be attained than by a chain of metaphysical disquisitions, mankind would have wanted some inducement to have quickened their inquiries, and the greater part of the world would have rested content in mental indolence, and ignorance it's [sic] inseparable companion. As therefore the creator is a being, not only of infinite *power*, and *wisdom*, but also of infinite *goodness*, he has been pleased so to contrive the constitution and frame of humanity, that we should want no other prompter to enquire after and pursue the rule of right, but only our own self-love, that universal principle of action. For he has so intimately connected, so inseparably interwoven the laws of eternal justice with the happiness of each individual, that the latter cannot be attained but by observing the former; and, if the former be punctually obeyed, it cannot but induce the latter. In consequence of which mutual connection of justice and human felicity, he has not perplexed the law of nature with a multitude of abstracted rules and precepts, referring merely to the fitness or unfitness of things, as some have vainly surmised; but has graciously reduced the rule of obedience to this one paternal precept, "that man should pursue his own happiness."[16]

Blackstone's notion of the connection between natural law and happiness as a sort of ingenious contrivance of the Creator seems to obscure the fact that law of its very essence is directed to the common good of creatures, in which their happiness consists. Indeed, Blackstone's words would seem to imply an individualistic under-

---

16. Blackstone, *Commentaries*, Bk. I, 34.

standing of happiness, and therefore the "self-love" of which he speaks would not be the properly ordered love of the common good, in which the highest good of the individual is found, but rather the love of a private good.[17] Such a conception will tend to destroy any notion of the subordination of the juridical order to the common good.

In his definition of civil (or municipal) law, Blackstone again manages to avoid any mention of the common good. Civil law is "a rule of civil conduct prescribed by the supreme power in a state, commanding what is right and prohibiting what is wrong."[18] Right here should be taken as meaning *rectitudo* rather than *ius*. But in his general discussion of right, Blackstone shows how the two meanings are related. Again, I quote at length:

> Now the rights of persons that are commanded to be observed by the municipal law are of two sorts; first, such as are due *from* every citizen, which are usually called civil *duties*; and, secondly, such as belong *to* him, which is the more popular acceptation of *rights* or *jura*. Both may indeed be comprized in this latter division; for, as all social duties are of a relative nature, at the same time that they are due *from* one man, or set of men, they must also be due *to* another. But I apprehend it will be more clear and easy, to consider many of them as duties required from, rather than as rights belonging to, particular persons. Thus, for instance, allegiance is usually, and therefore most easily, considered as the duty of the people, and protection as the duty of the magistrate; and yet they are, reciprocally, the rights as well as duties of each other. Allegiance is the right of the magistrate, and protection the right of the people.[19]

Here Blackstone has seemingly derived the classical notion of *ius* from the notion of *rectitudo*. Right is *what is due to another*, the

---

17. For the relation of happiness and the common good, see Edmund Waldstein, O.Cist., "Whether it is Sinful to Desire Happiness: Martin Luther's Critique of Aristotelianism," lecture given at Thomas Aquinas College, March 29, 2019, www.academia.edu35314634Eudaemonism_and_the_Common_Good_Martin_Luther_vs._Thomas_Aquinas.
18. Blackstone, *Commentaries*, Bk. I, 36.
19. Ibid., 83–84.

object of justice. The right of the magistrate is the allegiance due to him from the people. But when Blackstone begins to explain what he calls the "absolute rights of persons" (that is, rights that belong to them apart from any particular human community), he explains them in terms of subjective power or liberty:

> The absolute rights of man, considered as a free agent, endowed with discernment to know good from evil, and with power of choosing those measures which appear to him to be most desirable, are usually summed up in one general appellation, and denominated the natural liberty of mankind. This natural liberty consists properly in a power of acting as one thinks fit, without any restraint or control, unless by the law of nature: being a right inherent in us by birth, and one of the gifts of God to man at his creation, when he endued him with the faculty of freewill.[20]

The laws of human society are seen as limiting these natural liberties or subjective powers, and here Blackstone does introduce something like the idea of the common good:

> Political therefore, or civil, liberty, which is that of a member of society, is no other than natural liberty so far restrained by human laws (and no farther) as is necessary and expedient for the general advantage of the publick.[21]

But what is meant by the "advantage of the publick"? A little earlier in the discussion, Blackstone makes it clear that this public advantage is nothing other than the widest amplitude of subjective rights compatible with security:

> For the principal aim of society is to protect individuals in the enjoyment of those absolute rights, which were vested in them by the immutable laws of nature; but which could not be preserved in peace without that mutual assistance and intercourse, which is gained by the institution of friendly and social communities. Hence it follows, that the first and primary end of human laws is to maintain and regulate these *absolute* rights of individuals.[22]

---

20. Ibid., 85.
21. Ibid.
22. Ibid., 84.

Hard Liberalism, Soft Liberalism, & American Founding

This is soft liberalism in a nutshell. There is much in the rest of Blackstone's account of the common law that accords ill with this understanding of the end of law and politics. But this understanding does indeed color some of his interpretations. Take, for example, the interpretation of compulsory purchase (i.e., eminent domain) in his discussion of the right of property:

> So great moreover is the regard of the law for private property, that it will not authorize the least violation of it; no, not even for the general good of the whole community. If a new road, for instance, were to be made through the grounds of a private person, it might perhaps be extensively beneficial to the public; but the law permits no man, or set of men, to do this without consent of the owner of the land. In vain may it be urged, that the good of the individual ought to yield to that of the community; for it would be dangerous to allow any private man, or even any public tribunal, to be the judge of this common good, and to decide whether it be expedient or no. Besides, the public good is in nothing more essentially interested, than in the protection of every individual's private rights, as modelled by the municipal law. In this, and similar cases the legislature alone can, and indeed frequently does, interpose, and compel the individual to acquiesce. But how does it interpose and compel? Not by absolutely stripping the subject of his property in an arbitrary manner; but by giving him a full indemnification and equivalent for the injury thereby sustained.[23]

There is something almost comical about this passage, since Blackstone in one breath denies and affirms the same thing. First, he denies that the law allows land to be taken from someone for the sake of the public good. But then he affirms that this is in fact what happens (although the person must be paid for his losses). But the problem is that the relation of the person's *ius* and the common good is explicitly viewed upside-down and backwards: "the public good is in nothing more essentially interested, than in the protection of every individual's private rights." Similarly, with taxation:

---

23. Ibid., 94.

Nor is this the only instance in which the law of the land has postponed even public necessity to the sacred and inviolable rights of private property. For no subject of England can be constrained to pay any aids or taxes, even for the defence of the realm or the support of government, but such as are imposed by his own consent, or that of his representatives in parliament.[24]

Here we have of course the principle of *no taxation without representation*, so central to the American Founding. And the way in which Blackstone expresses it shows how an originally pre-liberal understanding of rights as the object of the virtue of justice, arising from the division of things made with a view to the common good, was in the process of being colonized, corrupted, and reversed by a liberal view of rights as subjective claims, liberties as ends in themselves, to which the whole legal and political order was to be subjected.

5. The problem of religious liberty

If Blackstone was in some respects a soft liberal, one respect in which he was still free of liberalism was in his High Church Anglican view of the necessity of established religion. "Doubtless," he writes, "the preservation of christianity, as a national religion, is, abstracted from its own intrinsic truth, of the utmost consequence to the civil state."[25] Blackstone's way of considering the question is somewhat backwards from a Catholic point of view—he considers the benefits that supernatural religion brings to the common good, rather than the order of the temporal to the spiritual. Moreover, as a good Anglican, he denies the superiority of spiritual to temporal authority.[26] But the juridical standing of religion that he defends is much closer to the traditional ideal than to liberalism. It was of men

---

24. Ibid.
25. William Blackstone, *Commentaries on the Laws of England*, Book IV, *Of Public Wrongs*, ed. Ruth Paley (Oxford: Oxford University Press, 2016), 28.
26. In justifying the laws against "papists," Blackstone writes: "while they acknowlege a foreign power, superior to the sovereignty of the kingdom, they cannot complain if the laws of that kingdom will not treat them upon the footing of good subjects" (Blackstone, *Commentaries,* Bk. IV, 36).

of Blackstone's type that St. John Henry Newman was thinking in the "Biglietto Speech" when he looked back at the place of religion in English life during his youth: "Even in countries separated from the Church, as in my own, the *dictum* was in force, when I was young, that: 'Christianity was the law of the land.'"[27]

Newman begins the Biglietto Speech with a discussion of "the spirit of liberalism in religion," against which he had striven all his life. This spirit denies the objective truth of religion: "Revealed religion is not a truth, but a sentiment and a taste; not an objective fact, not miraculous; and it is the right of each individual to make it say just what strikes his fancy."[28] This can be seen as a form of hard liberalism: there is no supreme good, but only subjective will which decides to consider the supreme good to be found in some religion. Hence, persons of different religious opinions may "fraternise together in spiritual thoughts and feelings" without sharing a common doctrine. The immediate result of this religious liberty is that religion becomes a private matter, and is separated from political life:

> Since, then, religion is so personal a peculiarity and so private a possession, we must of necessity ignore it in the intercourse of man with man. If a man puts on a new religion every morning, what is that to you? It is as impertinent to think about a man's religion as about his sources of income or his management of his family. Religion is in no sense the bond of society.[29]

Therefore, the dictum of his youth about Christianity being the law of the land is gone and "by the end of the century, unless the Almighty interferes, it will be forgotten."[30] Newman recognizes that the same political conclusion can be derived from softer doctrines than that of liberal religion. In England, he explains, the doctrine that religion should be banished from public life has been pro-

---

27. John Henry Newman, "Biglietto Speech," in W. P. Neville, ed., *Addresses to Cardinal Newman with His Replies etc. 1879–1881* (London: Longmans, Green, and Co., 1905), 61–70, at 65; online at https://www.newmanreader.org/works/addresses/file2.html.
28. Ibid., 64.
29. Ibid., 65.
30. Ibid., 65–66.

moted by the various non-conformist Protestant sects that arose after the Reformation. It is worth quoting him at length:

> At first sight it might be thought that Englishmen are too religious for a movement which, on the Continent, seems to be founded on infidelity; but the misfortune with us is, that, *though it ends in infidelity as in other places, it does not necessarily arise out of infidelity.* It must be recollected that the religious sects, which sprang up in England three centuries ago, and which are so powerful now, have ever been fiercely opposed to the Union of Church and State, and would advocate the un-Christianising of the monarchy and all that belongs to it, under the notion that such a catastrophe would make Christianity much more pure and much more powerful. Next the liberal principle is forced on us from the necessity of the case. Consider what follows from the very fact of these many sects. They constitute the religion, it is supposed, of half the population; and, recollect, our mode of government is popular. Every dozen men taken at random whom you meet in the streets has a share in political power,—when you inquire into their forms of belief, perhaps they represent one or other of as many as seven religions; how can they possibly act together in municipal or in national matters, if each insists on the recognition of his own religious denomination? All action would be at a deadlock unless the subject of religion was ignored.[31]

Newman's point here is extremely important. The disestablishment of religion need not necessarily proceed from the unbelief of hard liberalism, but it will tend toward such unbelief. When religion is bracketed out of deliberations about the common life of political animals, it will come to be seen as a matter of sentiment and opinion rather than of truth.

The situation of a multitude of Protestant sects that Newman describes in England was even more firmly established in her American colonies. And so it is not surprising that the American Constitution forbids the establishment of religion, at least at the federal level. As Matthew Peterson explains:

---

31. Ibid., 67–68, emphasis added.

Hard Liberalism, Soft Liberalism, & American Founding

What both sides [i.e., Federalists and Anti-Federalists] explicitly eschew in the debate is the idea that the government should take a stance as to which denomination of Christianity, or even which religion more generally, at least at the federal level, best leads to man's highest end. They indicate that this is consonant with Christianity itself. James Wilson and John Dickinson see the aims of the federal government as at least pointing towards and harmonious with religion. Dickinson asks whether any government could be "more conformed to the nature and understanding, to the best and the last end of man?" and Wilson sees "liberty, virtue, and religion go hand in hand, harmoniously, protecting, enlivening, and exalting all!"[32]

William Lee Miller has even argued that this view of religion is the most essential element of the liberalism of the American Constitution.[33] But what are we to make of the claim that this is "consonant with Christianity itself"? It is true that Christianity, in contrast to pagan religion, distinguishes between spiritual and temporal. Moreover, Christianity has always taught that Baptism must be accepted freely. Both points were reiterated with great force by the Second Vatican Council in *Dignitatis Humanæ*. But, as we have attempted to show on *The Josias*, this does not mean that religion ought to be banished to a private realm.[34] Rather, it means that it is under the authority of a higher power than temporal rulers: the spiritual authority of the Church. And it is the duty of temporal rulers to recognize the spiritual authority of the Church and

---

32. Peterson, "The Meaning of the Public Good," 347.
33. William Lee Miller, *The First Liberty: America's Foundation in Religious Freedom*, 2nd ed. (Washington, DC: Georgetown University Press, 2003).
34. See Edmund Waldstein, O.Cist., "*The City of God*: An Introduction," *The Josias*, August 28, 2017 (https://thejosias.com/2017/08/28/the-city-of-god-an-introduction/), "Religious Liberty and Tradition," *The Josias*, December 31, 2014, and subsequent dates (for the complete text: https://thejosiasdotcom.files.wordpress.com/2014/12/pater-edmund-dignitatis-humanae2.pdf), and "Integralism and Gelasian Dyarchy," *The Josias*, March 3, 2016 (https://thejosias.com/2016/03/03/integralism-and-gelasian-dyarchy/); Joel Augustine, "Dyarchy is Dyarchical: A Reply to Meador," *The Josias*, May 8, 2017 (https://thejosias.com/2017/05/08/dyarchy-is-dyarchical-a-reply-to-meador/); and Peter A. Kwasniewski, "The Catholic State: Anachronism, Arch-enemy, or Archetype?," *Latin Mass Magazine* 23.3 (Fall 2014): 18–22 (https://thejosiasdotcom.files.wordpress.com/2014/11/tlm-2014-fall-kwasniewski2.pdf).

Integralism and the Common Good

order the temporal common good of this life to the eternal common good of the Heavenly City. *Dignitatis Humanæ* "leaves untouched traditional Catholic doctrine on the moral duty of men and societies toward the true religion and toward the one Church of Christ" (§1). Including the duties laid out by Pope Leo XIII in *Immortale Dei* §6:

> Since, then, no one is allowed to be remiss in the service due to God, and since the chief duty of all men is to cling to religion in both its teaching and practice—not such religion as they may have a preference for, but the religion which God enjoins, and which certain and most clear marks show to be the only one true religion—it is a public crime to act as though there were no God. So, too, is it a sin for the State not to have care for religion as a something beyond its scope, or as of no practical benefit; or out of many forms of religion to adopt that one which chimes in with the fancy; for we are bound absolutely to worship God in that way which He has shown to be His will. All who rule, therefore, should hold in honour the holy name of God, and one of their chief duties must be to favour religion, to protect it, to shield it under the credit and sanction of the laws, and neither to organize nor enact any measure that may compromise its safety.

It would be unfair to blame the American Founders too much for not following the teaching that was to be enunciated in *Immortale Dei*. Inheriting, as they did, the religious disunity that followed in the wake of the Reformation and the tradition of aversion to established religion that had formed among non-conformists who left England to escape Anglicanism, and formed as they were in an English legal and political tradition that was already in the process of being transformed and corrupted by liberalism, it is small wonder that the Founders made non-establishment of religion one of the pillars of the order that they founded. One can even be grateful that the order they founded is not as hostile to religion as the totalitarian republic of the French Reign of Terror or the totalitarian atheism of the Soviet Union, was later to be.[35] But one should not

---

35. Pope Leo XIII himself says as much in his encyclical letter *Longinqua Oceani*: "For the Church amongst you, unopposed by the Constitution and govern-

lose sight of the fact that America's arrangement lacks something essential to the true common good, and that it has an inevitable tendency to bring forth other evils. Muñoz himself admits that the same liberal logic of rights that grounds the American understanding of religious liberty also grounds the moral insanity of *Griswold v. Connecticut* and *Lawrence* v. *Texas*.

ment of your nation, fettered by no hostile legislation, protected against violence by the common laws and the impartiality of the tribunals, is free to live and act without hindrance. Yet, though all this is true, it would be very erroneous to draw the conclusion that in America is to be sought the type of the most desirable status of the Church, or that it would be universally lawful or expedient for State and Church to be, as in America, dissevered and divorced."

25

Liberalism's Fear[1]

Adrian Vermeule

I want to thank the Consul-General for arranging this event. It's always a pleasure to have a chance to honor Prof. Legutko, whose book helped to awaken so many of us from our modernist slumbers, into the light of a new dogmatism.

The title of the panel is "Democratic Reformers or Illiberal Backsliders?" And my answer is "Both." Let me start with a puzzle. I know, or know of, a number of U.S. and U.K. academics, journalists, and other intelligentsia who spend their careers in a state that can only be described as professional hysteria, particularly directed at Poland, Hungary, and Brexit. In this state of hysteria, the meanings of words are redefined. The Polish election, although free and fair, represents a threat to "democracy"; the passage of legislation according to constitutional procedures, such as the Polish parliamentary law on the judiciary, becomes a threat to the "rule of law"; and so forth. What is the root cause of this extraordinary reaction?

Many have observed that Poland and Hungary have been experimenting with nonliberal versions of democracy. Assuming this to be true for the sake of discussion, it still does not explain the hysteria; it actually sharpens the puzzle. Why should a country like

---

1. In honor of Prof. Ryszard Legutko and his book, *The Demon in Democracy*, the Consul-General of Poland, Maciej Golubiewski, convened an event on May 9, 2018, to address "Democratic Reformers or Illiberal Backsliders? Poland and the Challenges of Sovereign Politics in the West." This chapter presents the illuminating remarks of Adrian Vermeule at this event. One need not think democracy is the best form of government to realize that it is not, in and of itself, liberal. Liberalism, however, needs democracy, or more precisely it needs the "periodic ceremony" of democracy.—*Eds.*

Liberalism's Fear

Poland be more an object of hysteria on these particular grounds than, say, Saudi Arabia or China? After all, those regimes are *neither* democratic *nor* liberal in any conventional sense. Why would a regime that is democratic but not liberal be *more* objectionable than a regime that is neither democratic nor liberal?

I think the key to the puzzle is liberalism's longstanding anxiety about its uneasy relationship to democracy, indeed its somewhat parasitic relationship. Here I will draw upon Carl Schmitt's Introduction to the second edition of his *Crisis of Parliamentary Democracy*, in which Schmitt explains the polemical and political problem that liberalism has faced since its triumph in the long century between 1789 and 1918. As the doctrine of the nineteenth-century politics of parliamentary monarchomachy—the political opposition to monarchy—liberalism made an alliance of convenience with democracy and for immediate advantage helped to cement the pervasive and seemingly irresistible notion that the fundamental criterion of political legitimacy is democratic—something to which all regimes of any kind at least pay lip service today. When this liberal-democratic alliance somewhat unexpectedly came to power everywhere starting in the second half of the nineteenth century, however, the alliance—now lacking its common enemy, the monarchy—immediately started to fracture. John Stuart Mill, as of 1861, was already frightened by the possibility that democratic majorities would constrain experimental individualist projects of self-actualization by educated elites, who should therefore be given multiple votes in a representative system, among other privileges and other institutional checks on majoritarianism.

It has since become undeniable that liberalism both needs and fears democracy. It needs democracy because it needs the legitimation that democracy provides. It fears, however, that its dependence on, yet fundamental difference from, democracy will be finally and irrevocably exposed by a sustained course of nonliberal popular opinion.

In this environment, the solution of the intellectuals is always to try to idealize and redescribe democracy so that "mere majoritarianism" never turns out to count as *truly* democratic. Of course the majority's views are to count on certain issues, but only within constraints so tightly drawn and under procedures so idealized that any outcomes threatening to liberalism can be dismissed as inauthentic, often by a constitutional court purporting to speak in the name of a higher form of democracy. Democracy is then reduced to a periodic ceremony of privatized voting by secret ballot for one or another essentially liberal party, safely within a *cordon sanitaire*. In the limit, as Schmitt put it, liberalism attempts to appeal to a "democracy of mankind" that erases nations, substantive cultures, and the particularistic solidarities that are constitutive of so many of the goods of human life. In this way, liberalism attempts to hollow out democracy from within, yet retain its outward form as a sort of legitimating costume, like the donkey who wore the lion's skin in the fable.

We are now in position to answer our puzzle, to explain why democracies that flout liberal pieties are so much more threatening to liberalism than polities that are neither liberal nor democratic to begin with. The democratic polity that rejects liberalism offends on two counts. For one thing, the apostate is always more detested than the pagan. If the democratic but nonliberal polity seemed for a time to be a community in good standing under the liberal imperium, then its turn against liberalism represents a threatening retrogression. On its own premises, given its historicized and immanentized eschatology, liberalism may expand, but must never contract. To adapt something that the defining mind of our era, Nigel Farage, said about the European Union, liberalism has its analogue to the Brezhnev Doctrine that no nation might ever leave the Warsaw Pact.

But this is a contingent issue, depending on the nature of the *status quo ante*. The second and more systematically offensive thing about a democratic-but-nonliberal regime is that it threatens to expose the elite character of the liberal project. Liberalism is in many respects an enterprise created by and in the service of elites who capture most of the upside gains of ever-greater release from customary, moral, and economic constraints, and who are buffered—economically and personally—from the downside risks and losses. Liberalism's agents know and fear that the broader demos may reject their aspirations for ever-more-satisfying forms of creativity and self-fulfillment. Liberalism's agents know and fear that the demos may rebel when the customary norms and liturgies of the people are cleared away to make room for the restless and ever-changing liturgy of liberalism. In this sense, Judith Shklar was right to emphasize the "liberalism of fear," but in a different way and for different reasons than she offered. The fear at the base of liberalism is that it will be left alone and visibly alone, expelled from the host within which it has fed and sheltered for so long.

26

"According to Truth"

Adrian Vermeule

One of the most curious features of life under political liberalism[1]—for present purposes, the doctrine that the central task of politics is to promote individual autonomy and to secure its preconditions—is that all politics and political conversation happens at one step removed, one meta-level up. Instead of pursuing substantive excellence and justice, we have circuitous conversations about statistical properties like "diversity"; instead of deciding what ought to be permitted, what condemned, we debate "civility"; instead of discerning truth, we quarrel over "religious liberty"; instead of protecting the most vulnerable, we conceal our vices and crimes under the rubric of "choice," in both market and non-market spheres (although to be fair there are almost no non-market spheres left any more). When we ask about Truth, liberalism answers "What is 'Truth'? Your truth is not someone else's truth, and it is no more legitimate to make your truth into public policy than it would be to force your taste in ice cream upon everyone else. All this is solely of private concern."

Many have observed this, and traced its causes and consequences, including a number of important recent diagnoses of the fragility or even failure of liberalism.[2] It seems to me that some of these diagnoses, acute though they may be, have left out or at least underplayed something simple but important: a deep human revulsion

---

1. See *The Josias Podcast*, Episode V: Liberalism (Part 1), February 2, 2018, https://thejosias.com/2018/02/02/the-josias-podcast-episode-v-liberalism-part-1/.
2. See chapter 24; Deneen, *Why Liberalism Failed*.

at this muffled, perpetually repressed, and indirect anti-political politics. One cannot perpetually stand at a remove from the substance of our common life, pursuing a shadowy half-life of consumerism in the commercial Market while seeing the civic Forum through a glass darkly. Human nature wearies, sickens, and eventually rebels. The Second Vatican Council speaks of man's restless desire to "live fully according to truth."[3] It seems to increasing numbers of people that living fully means living according to the truth not only in the family and local community and marketplace, but in the polity as a whole.[4] Liberalism, in its myopia, has left this out of its calculations, and as a result the liberal order is not ultimately compatible with the deepest desires and beliefs of its subjects. The Achilles' heel of liberalism is this hunger for the real as expressed in politics, the hunger to come to grips with the substance of the common good.

The most interesting conversation I've had lately in an academic setting was with a colleague—a man of the left who thinks of himself as "secular," but who is in fact animated by a vibrant faith in the progress of history—who asked me to lunch and pressed the question "in a fully Catholic polity, the sort you would like to bring about, what would happen to me, a Jew"? (Nothing bad, I assured him.) This was no second-order discussion of "political liberty" or "rights" or "overlapping consensus." This was a passionate concrete question about the fate of an individual, a people, and the shape that a polity might take, all inseparably linked. It was, at last, after all the academic workshops on "procedural justice" and "tolerance," a genuinely political conversation.

We are witnessing, with increasing tempo on many fronts, the outbreak of rebellions against anti-political politics. This is a phenomenon of both the "left" and the "right." That very fact suggests that the left-right dimension is no longer, if it ever was,[5] a particu-

---

3. *Gaudium et Spes* 19.
4. See Henri Grenier, "The Dignity of Politics and the End of the Polity," *The Josias*, June 17, 2015, https://thejosias.com/2015/06/17/the-dignity-of-politics-and-the-end-of-the-polity/.
5. See chapter 28.

larly useful guide to our politics, and that we need categories more relevant than the seating-chart of the French National Assembly. Trump, Brexit, the recent electoral results in Austria, Germany, Hungary, Italy, Poland and elsewhere—none of these are easy to fit into a standard left-right frame.

One way of understanding the fault-lines emerging in many liberal polities is to cast them as a conflict between liberal elites of the "center" on the one hand, and "populists" who contest the center's fanaticism[6] on the other, as witness the coalition of left and right populists in Italy. It is sometimes suggested that the main issue is economic—that populism is a reaction by the have-nots against the self-dealing of the haves. In a somewhat more sophisticated variant, the idea is that populism reacts against not only the economic superiority of the haves, but their insufferable cultural smugness, born of conviction of their own merit.

Although all this unquestionably captures something, I don't think it is the whole story, in part because it leaves out the essentially spiritual dimension of the hunger for the real, of the desire to live fully in the Forum as well as the Market. Consider the offspring of liberalism that goes by the name of "progressivism." (Let me bracket here inevitable and interminable controversies about taxonomy— whether progressivism counts as a species of the liberal genus, as a corrupted version of true liberalism, or what have you. In my view progressivism is a descendant of classical liberalism, especially in its Lockean and Millian variants, and may justly be termed "liberalism" in the same way that the child traditionally takes on the family name of the father—even if, as in this case, the child and the father are often at odds. Yet these taxonomic and genetic questions are not critical for the questions I pursue here.) In some versions, at least, progressivism gets one big thing exactly right: It attempts to grapple with the real, to make politics and our common life fully and vibrantly political again. And it does so because of the animating

---

6. See Pierre Manent, "Populist Demagogy and the Fanaticism of the Center," *American Affairs Journal*, vol. I, n. 2 (Summer 2017), https://americanaffairsjournal.org/2017/05/populist-demagogy-and-the-fanaticism-of-the-center/.

faith of its adherents,[7] complete with liturgies[8] and sacraments and hope for salvation and an account of final things, of the end times. To be clear, I believe it to be a corrupted and heretical faith, an odd and distinctive mix of Pelagianism and Gnosticism,[9] but it has this one excellent quality, that it hopes to escape the spectral underworld of liberal politics.

From this point, there are two ways to go wrong. The politics of reality might be, from anyone's own standpoint, the wrong politics, substantively speaking. A stock liberal claim is that this possibility is so fearsome that everyone prefers or at least ought to prefer public "neutrality"—as among religious views, visions of justice, or any of the other things that people care about most deeply. On this claim, all are risk-minimizers, and liberalism will emerge in equilibrium as the cautious second choice of all. Yet it quickly becomes apparent that this "neutrality" is just another substantive view about who should be allowed into the Forum for what purposes, and what may be said there. The hunger for the real might then make people so desperate, so sick of the essential falsity of liberalism, that they become willing to gamble that the Truth (what liberals would call "their version of truth") will prevail—or at least willing to gamble on entering into coalition with other sorts of anti-liberals, as in the Italian coalition of "populists" of left and right. In an even better version, the willingness to take one's chances with post-liberalism is not the spirit of the desperate gambler, but is rather the spirit of faith—never certain, but inspiring and inspired by theologically-inflected hope. This last answer is hardly confined to, say, Catholic traditionalists. The faith in the triumph of a secularized-but-providential history that animates so many strands of progressivism manifestly also fills its adherents with a (warped) version of theological hope. Of course it is true—it's obvious—that there are ver-

---

7. See my review-essay "Integration from Within," *American Affairs Journal*, vol. II, n. 1 (Spring 2018), https://americanaffairsjournal.org/2018/02/integration-from-within/.
8. See my article "Liturgy of Liberalism," *First Things*, January 2017, https://www.firstthings.com/article/2017/01/liturgy-of-liberalism.
9. See the Congregation for the Doctrine of the Faith, Letter on Certain Aspects of Christian Salvation *Placuit Deo*, January 24, 2018.

sions of non-liberalism that are worse than liberalism. At a certain point, however, people can no longer abide perpetually living in fear of the worst-case scenario. A "liberalism of fear"[10] is ultimately intolerable for creatures fashioned to live in hope.

There is another and somewhat more subtle way that things can go wrong. Liberalism muffles the political in second-order concepts like "civility" and "tolerance" and "choice," and the hunger for real politics rightly rebels against this. But it does not follow that these concepts have no value at all, when rightly placed within a larger ordering to good substantive ends. If civility, tolerance, and their ilk are bad masters, and tyrannous when made into idols, they may still be good servants. The shibboleths of liberalism all have chastened, nonliberal counterparts, justified in nonliberal terms. J.F. Stephen, the withering Victorian critic of John Stuart Mill, was clear-minded about this, pointing out the many reasons why a prudent sovereign ordering affairs to the common good might choose for that very reason to leave particular matters to individual choice, or might be reluctant to employ the "rough engine" of the law even where serious wrongs occur.[11] "Free trade" and "the free market" are idols, but merchants benefit the community and must be given a duly regulated scope within which to ply their trade. "Civility" and "tolerance" may be cryptic terms in which to measure and regulate the substantive bounds of the views and conduct that will be permitted in a rightly ordered society, but such a society will also value charity, forbearance, and prudence. Hence rejecting liberalism doesn't entail that men should be allowed to assault teenagers wearing offensive hats.[12] Most generally, as Aquinas observed, a well-ordered society will not use law to suppress all vices and to prescribe all virtues,

---

10. See "Judith Shklar: The Liberalism of Fear," *Political Not Metaphysical*, February 25, 2016, https://politicalnotmetaphysical.wordpress.com/2016/02/25/judith-shklar-the-liberalism-of-fear/.

11. *Liberty, Equality, Fraternity*, ed. Stuart D. Warner (Indianapolis: Liberty Fund, 1993).

12. Ben Tobin, "San Antonio police probe alleged assault of teen wearing a Make America Great Again hat," *USA Today*, July 5, 2018, https://www.usatoday.com/story/money/2018/07/05/san-antonio-police-investigate-alleged-assault-teen-wearing-maga-hat/761370002/.

except to the extent conducive to the common good.[13] Such a society, after throwing down the idol of Liberty, will allow liberties. But even where the nonliberal order happens to reach the same conclusions as a liberal order, it justifies them in different ways and on different grounds.[14]

My main suggestion is not so much about what should be done, but about the constraints that man's political nature places on what can be done. Ought implies can. The prerequisite for successful political arrangements is that they must in the long run be compatible with the ineradicable human impulse to live fully in a political community ordered towards the truth. As Joseph de Maistre observed, following Aquinas and Aristotle, "before the formation of political societies, man was not a complete man."[15] Now this impulse to live fully in the civic community of the Forum, not merely in the half-way life of liberalism, is alarming in many ways, but it cannot be denied altogether. It follows that in one way or another it must be controlled and channeled into substantively admirable directions; there is no alternative. The hunger for a real politics must, in some way or another, be sated. Better that it be sated through a sacramental feast.

---

13. *ST* I-II, q. 96, a. 2.
14. See chapter 3.
15. See *Study on Sovereignty*, Book I, ch. 2: http://maistre.uni.cx/sovereignty.html.

27

Integralism Versus the Marxist and Post-Marxist Left

Vincent Clarke

In this essay, we will be asking whether there is anything of worth on the intellectual left. We will not be considering more pragmatic disciplines such as economics. Rather we will be focusing on philosophical and expressly political ideas. Some thinkers in the post-fusionist Catholic sphere have pointed to these ideas—typically formulated as some sort of Catholic Marxism—as being a way forward. Others—including the integralist movement—have rejected the worldview lying behind these ideas but have claimed that there are interesting components that can be refashioned.

So far, the discussion of these ideas has not considered that they emerged as a response to and ultimately as a replacement for the liberal ideas that arose during the Enlightenment. The original proponents attempted to incorporate the Romantic critiques that arose against liberal Enlightenment ideas in the eighteenth and early nineteenth century into the liberal Enlightenment project. By taking this perspective we hope to show that these left-wing ideas are ultimately the flipside of the liberal Enlightenment project that was formulated against classical and Catholic systems of thought. For that reason, they should, at best, be viewed coolly, at worst, with extreme suspicion.

For reasons of space we will stick closely to what appear to be the core ideas. This will allow us to give a full contextual and historical overview of the idea and how it relates to classical and pre-Enlightenment thought.

Alienation, or Marxian metaphysics

Whether we argue that liberalism began to emerge with Hobbes or Locke or even Bacon, we can say that it was originally formulated as a mechanistic and dispassionate intervention in politics and culture. These ideas were, from the beginning, a response to the passions of religion as manifest in the Wars of Religion. The first generation of liberals were not antinomian revolutionaries so much as they were nervous administrators—social and political managers preaching tolerance in the hope of avoiding civil war.

But it soon became clear that Man was not made for management. The Romantic thinkers brought the question of passion and affirmative personal freedom back on the stage. Whether this was in the immature fantasies of Goethe's young Werther or in the sophisticated political mythology of Rousseau's Man-in-the-state-of-nature, the message was clear: notional freedom coupled with drab political management was not enough; Man was built for love, transgression, self-actualization, and the Enlightenment project must recognize that.

Accusations soon followed: It was thought that the liberal Enlightenment project, with its dull bourgeois rationalism, crushed Man in his project to be free. In throwing off the shackles of religion, the Romantics argued, post-Enlightenment Man had signed himself up to the slave ship of dreary rationality. Man, they claimed, was alienated by liberal bourgeois society.

"Alienation," or "Entfremdung" in the original German, is an unusual term. At the time when the Romantics, especially Hegel, were discussing it, there were three general meanings. One was a legal meaning which denoted the selling of a man's rights over his own property. Another was a social term meaning the estrangement of a man from his peers. The final medico-psychiatric meaning—connected to the previous usage—was the loss of a man's capacity for reason and his falling into insanity.[1] Indeed, until the mid-twentieth century it was not uncommon for psychiatrists to be referred to, especially in France, as "alienists."

---

1. R. Felix Geyer and David R. Schweitzer, *Theories of Alienation: Critical Perspectives in Philosophy and the Social Sciences* (Dordrecht: Springer Books, 1976), 5.

The original Hegelian use of the term was most closely associated with the medico-psychiatric meaning. In his *Phenomenology of Spirit*, Hegel discusses "the Alienated Soul" or, in his terminology, "the Unhappy Consciousness" as "the consciousness of self as a divided nature, a doubled and merely contradictory being."² Hegel describes a consciousness that looks upon itself as an object—that judges itself and deems itself unworthy. In modern pop psychological language, Hegel seems to be discussing something like self-hatred. Hegel takes the alienated consciousness to task saying that this self-judgment rests on a contradiction: if the consciousness is judging itself, this is equivalent to a judge judging his own judgment. Infinite regress follows. This is overcome for Hegel when the alienated consciousness recognizes itself as its own judge and in doing so overcomes the contradiction and becomes unified.

Note that Hegel does not project the alienation onto the external world. This, for him, would merely be a cop-out—a manifestation of blaming the world for problems that the Spirit or psyche has not sufficiently overcome. Later on, Hegel will warn against this projection of the alienated consciousness outward:

> The heartthrob for the welfare of mankind passes therefore into the rage of frantic self-conceit, into the fury of consciousness to preserve itself from destruction; and to do so by casting out of its life the perversion which it really is, and by straining to regard and to express that perversion as something else. The universal ordinance and law it, therefore, now speaks of as an utter distortion of the law of its heart and of its happiness, a perversion invented by fanatical priests, by riotous, revelling despots and their minions, who seek to indemnify themselves for their own degradation by degrading and oppressing in their turn—a distortion practised to the nameless misery of deluded mankind.³

---

2. G. W. F. Hegel, *Phenomenology of Mind* (1807), B. IV, (b), n. 207, https://www.marxists.org/reference/archive/hegel/works/ph/phbb.htm. Interestingly, this important sentence, taken from J.B. Baillie's 1910 edition of the *Phenomenology*, is left out of the popular 1977 A.V. Miller translation. Yet in his introduction Miller discusses Hegel's concept of alienation nine times. A strange discrepancy, as he obviously finds the category very important to Hegel's thought.

3. Ibid., AA., B, (b), n. 377; my emphasis.

Integralism Versus the Marxist and Post-Marxist Left

Of course, some of Hegel's followers decided to do just that. The most prominent was Ludwig Feuerbach who used Hegel's dialectical apparatus—built to accommodate a fusion of post-Enlightenment rational deism and a defense of Christian morality—against religion. In his *The Essence of Christianity*, published in 1844, Feuerbach argued that religion was a product of alienation. Man thought that he was worshipping God, Feuerbach argued, but really this was just a projection of his own consciousness. Feuerbach could not be clearer:

> The consciousness of God is the self-consciousness of man; the knowledge of God is the self-knowledge of man. Man's notion of himself is his notion of God, just as his notion of God is his notion of himself—the two are identical. What is God to man, that is man's own spirit, man's own soul; what is man's spirit, soul, and heart—that is his God. God is the manifestation of man's inner nature, his expressed self; religion is the solemn unveiling of man's hidden treasures, the avowal of his innermost thoughts, the open confession of the secrets of his love.[4]

From here it was not long before Feuerbach and his followers were denouncing—just as Hegel warned they would—the "perversions invented by fanatical priests." But that was not enough. The French Revolution, in its attempt to fuse liberal Enlightenment Reason and Romanticism, was content with directing its ire against the priests and the kings, but in nineteenth-century Europe it was becoming clear that a new ruling class was ascendant: the bourgeoisie. So, it was inevitable—especially after the revolutions of 1848—that the notion of alienation would be pushed further than Feuerbach had attempted.

Feuerbach's account was purely negative. It counseled that Man should throw off the shackles of religion and worship at the altar of himself. Perhaps that would require murdering a few priests, but it did not require upending the social order: it could not be used to justify the 1848 revolutionaries. Marx would soon make the point that Feuerbach's thesis was ahistorical and it "does not see that the

---

4. Ludwig Feuerbach, *The Essence of Christianity* (1844), I, §2, https://www.marxists.org/reference/archive/feuerbach/works/essence/eco1_2.htm.

'religious sentiment' is itself a social product, and that the abstract individual whom he analyses belongs to a particular form of society."[5] Here the critique moves up the ladder, from the relation between the individual and the Church, to the relation between the individual and society as mediated by the Church.

Now a new avenue for social criticism is opened. We have swung all the way back from the medico-psychiatric meaning of "alienation" to the social. Social alienation was, until now, largely seen as the product of a defective individual consciousness. But Marx would turn that around: it was not the alienated man who felt his alienation like a weight on his shoulders that was the problem; it was the society itself.

Marx conceived of alienation in bourgeois society as being tied up with the production process under capitalism. The key passage is as follows:

> The worker becomes all the poorer the more wealth he produces, the more his production increases in power and size. The worker becomes an ever-cheaper commodity the more commodities he creates. The devaluation of the world of men is in direct proportion to the increasing value of the world of things. Labor produces not only commodities; it produces itself and the worker as a commodity—and this at the same rate at which it produces commodities in general. This fact expresses merely that the object which labor produces—labor's product—confronts it as something alien, as a power independent of the producer. The product of labor is labor which has been embodied in an object, which has become material: it is the objectification of labor. Labor's realization is its objectification. Under these economic conditions this realization of labor appears as loss of realization for the workers; objectification as loss of the object and bondage to it; appropriation as estrangement, as alienation.[6]

---

5. Karl Marx, *Theses on Feuerbach* (1845), n. VII, https://www.marxists.org/archive/marx/works/1845/theses/theses.htm.

6. Karl Marx, *Economic and Philosophical Manuscripts* (1844), I, IV, https://www.marxists.org/archive/marx/works/download/pdf/Economic-Philosophic-Manuscripts-1844.pdf.

Integralism Versus the Marxist and Post-Marxist Left

The solution to this is obvious: to change the relations of production in such a way as to ensure that Man sees the objects of his production *as objects of his production*. We have come a long way from Hegel. Whatever one thinks of Hegel's Panglossian post-Enlightenment liberal Protestantism, at least he was dealing with an issue that was straightforward: the psychological problem of self-alienation. Hegel was playing philosopher as psychologist and encouraging his readers to reflect on themselves until they occupied a place of coherence and mental comfort. It is not hard to see how Hegel expects the Alienated Soul to get from A to B.

With Feuerbach this becomes rather dubious. He seems to be suggesting that the problem is the priest. His solution would then be to throw off the shackles of religion. If the notion that *less* religion would lead to *less* personal alienation appeared dubious in the first half of the nineteenth century, today it appears absurd—the very opposite of the truth. One need not even cite statistical studies[7] showing much less alienation amongst the religious, but just reflect on the fact that modern sociology as it emerged in the work of Durkheim was premised on the idea that secularization led to alienation or "anomie."[8] Still, on his own terms we can at least take Feuerbach's argument seriously: if it really is the priest that is the cause of personal alienation—presumably through the spreading of some nefarious morality—then it is clear how the removal of the priest will remove the source of alienation.

Few have commented on it, but from a common sense point-of-view Marx's thesis seems very strange indeed. It seems to imply that self-alienation—effectively a psychological problem—will disappear if Man gets greater consciousness of the fact that the goods he is producing in a factory and then buys at the market are actually the goods he produced. How does this work exactly? Would the same effect be achieved if Man is sat down and made to watch hours

---

7. See, for example, Y. Chen and T. VanderWeele, "Associations of Religious Upbringing with Subsequent Health and Well-Being from Adolescence to Young Adulthood: An Outcome-Wide Analysis," *American Journal of Epidemiology* 187.11 (November 2018): 2355–64.

8. See Emile Durkheim, *Suicide: A Study in Sociology* (1897) (n.p.: Snowball Publishing, 2013).

of film about the production and distribution systems of a modern, decentralized economy? It is hard to see why the latter should not work in the Marxian frame of reference. Marx's theory sounds impressive when pitched at a high theoretical level, but when closely examined it seems a little silly.

How does it relate to Catholic thought? Well, first it should now be clear that it arises out of a system that is totally at odds with Catholic thought. It starts with the well-meaning liberal Protestantism of a Hegel that encourages Man to overcome his alienation through rational self-reflection—not unlike contemporary psychotherapy—and then counsels a combination of post-Enlightenment deism and stripped down Christian morality as a principle on which to organize an effectively liberal society.[9] It then mutates into belligerent atheism with Feuerbach who is quick to blame the Church for psychological distress—a very common underbelly of post-Enlightenment rationalism. Finally, it turns into a critique of the production process in capitalism and religion is tossed aside as the "opium of the masses." At best, this final development is a form of naïve Pelagianism; at worst, it is the sort of ideology that led to everything from the Spanish Red Terror to the violent suppression of the Church in the Soviet Union. Lying within every Marxist is an angry Feuerbachian—and this especially so when the seizing of private property fails to ameliorate psychological distress.

In Catholic thought, alienation is simply a product of a disordered Will that is not sufficiently aligned with God and the natural law. "Our heart is restless," St. Augustine writes of his former alienation, "until it finds its rest in Thee." Alienation is the product of Sin. Even abstracting from the deep theological components of this account, it lines up remarkably well with common sense. A person likely feels alienation because he is living poorly. He is devoting himself to various false gods and not recognizing the truth of the

---

9. The Hegelian prescription bubbles up constantly in our society. Recently it has found expression in the popular figure of Jordan Peterson. See Vincent Clarke, "Jordan Peterson: Shepherd of the Easily Freudened," *American Affairs Journal*, May 17, 2018. https://americanaffairsjournal.org/2018/05/jordan-peterson-shepherd-of-the-easily-freudened/.

Integralism Versus the Marxist and Post-Marxist Left

real God. His desires are clamorous and disordered because he will not submit his Will to the natural law. Thus, for integralists and promoters of Catholic thought it is obvious how mass alienation should be overcome: by ordering our societies to the natural law. The better aligned societies are with the natural law, the less people will experience alienation, because by being ordered by the natural law, man is being ordered in accordance with his own nature. It is a simple, straightforward account and one that lines up remarkably well with the statistical studies that post-Durkheimian sociology would have us believe. It is also—last time this author checked—the official position of the Catholic Church.

Even if some Catholic Marxists accept this broad account, they might argue that a more streamlined version of Marx can be helpful in achieving precisely that. It is to this that we now turn.

Commodity fetishism, or Marxian anthropology

One line of defense of Marxist thought is to say that the concept of alienation was a product of the "young Marx's" thinking which was superseded in his later mature works—most notably *Capital*. The idea here is that Marx in his "Hegelian phase"—as a young man concerned with personal feelings of alienation—got caught up in questions that would later become irrelevant. On this account, Marx's later work represents an "epistemic break" from his earlier work; Marx moves from the vague realm of metaphysics into the precise world of science.

The most notable proponent of this argument was Louis Althusser. In his seminal 1965 collection of essays *For Marx* he writes:

> [I]f we are prepared to stand back a little from Marx's discovery so that we can see that he founded a new scientific discipline and that this emergence itself was analogous to all the great scientific discoveries of history, we must also agree that no great discovery has ever been made without bringing to light a new object or a new domain, without a new horizon of meaning appearing, a new land in which the old images and myths have been abolished—but at the same time the inventor of this new world must of absolute necessity have prepared his intelligence in the old forms themselves, he must have learnt and practised them, and by criticizing

them formed a taste for and learnt the art of manipulating abstract forms in general, without which familiarity he could never have conceived new ones with which to think the new object.[10]

Althusser dismisses the young Marx as a naïve man caught in the trappings of outmoded philosophical idealism and contrasts him with the mature Marx, the scientist, and his objective theory of History and Communism. If we accept this interpretation, the theory of alienation slips into the background—an embarrassing product of an immature and underdeveloped mind.

Despite the fact that Althusser dismisses the idea of "commodity fetishism" as a product of the pre-scientific Marx and replaces it with his own theory of ideological apparatuses,[11] some claim that the notion of commodity fetishism is a viable anthropological theory that can be deployed by Catholics in defense of the natural law. This is supported by the fact that, although the notion of alienation is dropped in his mature work, Marx nevertheless discusses commodity fetishism. In his *Capital* he explains it as such:

> As against this, the commodity-form, and the value-relation of the products of labour within which it appears, have absolutely no connection with the physical nature of the commodity and the material relations arising out of this. It is nothing but the definite social relation between men themselves which assumes here, for them, the fantastic form of a relation between things. In order, therefore, to find an analogy we must take flight into the misty realm of religion. There the products of the human brain appear as autonomous figures endowed with a life of their own, which enter into relations both with each other and with the human race. So it is in the world of commodities with the products of men's hands. I call this the fetishism which attaches itself to the products of labour as soon as they are produced as commodities, and is therefore inseparable from the production of commodities.[12]

---

10. Louis Althusser, *For Marx* (London: Allen Lane, 1969), 85.

11. See Louis Althusser, "Ideology and Ideological State Apparatuses" in *Lenin and Philosophy and Other Essays* (New York: Monthly Review Press, 2001).

12. Karl Marx, *Capital* (1870), vol. 1 (London: Penguin, 1992), 165.

Integralism Versus the Marxist and Post-Marxist Left

Here we see more echoes of Feuerbach. But only by analogy. Marx is no longer discussing the psychological or metaphysical phenomenon of alienation. Instead he is highlighting the fact that the highly abstract social relations that capitalism gives rise to lead to a mystification of the production process and hence of the nature of society. In turn, this gives rise to an ideology, a false consciousness, that tricks Man in capitalist society to think that his lot is a natural one and not the product of political forces that can be altered. This is not metaphysics, but anthropology.

But is it good anthropology? Again, Marx's theory sounds good from a high theoretical level but when we start to think it through it becomes a little muddy. And again, the questions that we raised about alienation rise to the surface, albeit in different form. If Man is told clearly the actual relations of production, will he instantly recognize them as unjust and rebel against the system? Certainly, if *Marxists* are told what Marx thinks to be the relations of production they will come to this conclusion—there is plenty of historical evidence in favor of that proposition—but it does not follow that *everyone* comes to this same conclusion. Many have studied Marx's work and concluded that the capitalist relations of production are, if not ideal, at least a best approximation of how to organize a functional society. Others have concluded that these relations *are* deeply flawed, but that this does not mean the whole system need be overthrown—rather they should be ameliorated by the State. The point is that, even with Marx's critique laid out, it is not obvious that one accepts it as true as one might a mathematical demonstration. It has, embedded within it, more than a few value judgments—not just on the utility of capitalism but also on the prudence of revolutionary social change.

From this perspective, Marx's notion of commodity fetishism is not neutral anthropology. Rather it is a statement that we are only likely to accept if we accept Marx's broader vision—that is, if we ourselves are socialists or communists. It is also slightly dubious. Take the former Soviet Union as an example—whether the Soviet system was a true socialist economy or not, it was certainly not capitalist. Relations of production in the Soviet Union were extremely opaque—"plans" were handed down by the Gosplan without much explanation. Most people, it would be fair to say, experienced the arbitrariness of Actually Existing Socialism as utterly mystifying—especially when a triple order of toilet paper arrived but no soup. Does it therefore follow that the centrally planned economic system, in the manner it produced and distributed commodities, provided ideological cover for the system? This seems unlikely. In fact, it was the opaqueness and dysfunction of the system that led citizens to look across the West enviously at the societies of abundance. If anything, the opaqueness and dysfunction generated cynicism and opposition to the system.

Yet, if Marx's account is right, why does commodity fetishism "work" in the relatively functional capitalist economies, but not in the dysfunctional centrally planned economies? After all, the same mechanism of opaqueness of production relations exists in both. Yet they generate different responses. Under capitalism, most of the time, most people accept the system as relatively natural. Yet under Really Existing Socialism people had a lingering sense that the system was dysfunctional and performed poorly in comparison with the Western capitalist systems. The more we think about it the stranger and less convincing Marx's account is, even on its own terms. Again, it sounds good when stated *theoretically*—but when *applied* it becomes vague and strange.

What about its relation to Catholic thought? Certainly, Catholic thought is sympathetic to the idea that people should have more immediate control over their lives, including in their economic relations. It states this in its principal of subsidiarity. But it certainly does not call for the overthrow of markets or capitalism. Rather its response to this problem has been one of corporatism; of the organization of society into empowered corporate entities that gain some modicum of control over blind market forces.

As with Catholic thought's description of alienation as arising from Sin, this comes across as much more in line with common sense. It is not hard to see how the Catholic policymaker gets from A to B. Without the "corporations," the capitalist system is bewildering and punitive. But after they are introduced it is tamed to the needs of the community. This is much more specific than Marx's vague notion that an imprecisely defined "communism" will overcome the opaqueness of the system—and it makes no grandiose claims that the opaqueness of the system is fooling people into not joining the Church and becoming virtuous. Indeed, the idea that people are not joining the Church because of the opacity of economic relations comes across as so ridiculous as to be funny—but it is functionally equivalent to what Marxists are claiming when they claim that the only reason that the masses do not join the Marxist revolution is due to the opacity of economic relations.

Finally, we will turn to the post-Marxist left. Although no Catholic thinkers are counseling that we embrace the postmodern theories of desire and identity, there may be something interesting there that some have missed.

Desire and pleasure, or post-Marxist politics

Defining the post-Marxist left is not altogether easy. It encompasses everything from identity politics to the sexual revolution. It encompasses thinkers as broad as Jacques Derrida, Roland Barthes, and Jacques Lacan. In what follows we will stick with two key thinkers, Michel Foucault and Giles Deleuze, as these best articulated the goals and methods of their politics. This is not to dismiss other thinkers. Lacanian neo-Marxists, for example, have drawn on Lacan's theory of alienation as being superior to Hegel's and integrated it into a post-Althusserian Marxism that reintegrates something resembling metaphysical critiques.[13] These are interesting, albeit flawed, from a Catholic perspective, for the same reason that Marx's original alienation theory is flawed. But Foucault and Deleuze articulate the politics that we see on the left today in the most concise manner.

Foucault and Deleuze, in their respective ways, shift the focus away from the production process as such and onto what they think

---

13. In brief, this neo-Marxism posits that alienation is overcome simply by taking part in the revolution. See Badiou, *Theory of the Subject* (1982) (London: Bloomsbury Academic, 2013). A cruel critic would say that the neo-Marxists have moved from Hegelian psychotherapeutic intervention to post-Lacanian group therapeutic intervention—and such a cruel critic would see those criticisms confirmed if they ever went to the embarrassing self-help spectacle that is a post-1968 radical leftist meeting.

to be a repressive society that suppresses the best tendencies—the true desires—of the individual. We are back, therefore, to the pre-Hegelian Romantics. It does not take long for them to find behind the curtain the oppressive figure of the priest. We are back, once more, to Feuerbach.

Foucault and Deleuze view society as a collection of institutions that repress individuals and force them to conform. Foucault is more inclined to examine institutions that are overtly punitive—the school, the hospital, the prison; while Deleuze is more inclined to examine institutions that shape the culture—most notably, psychotherapeutic intervention. But both recognize that the real repressive tool is morality. They argue that morality did not disappear after the Enlightenment destroyed religion but, rather, snuck in through the backdoor into social science and psychology and deployed via social and political institutions.

Foucault is quite explicit about this return to morality and ethics in his review of Deleuze's book *Anti-Oedipus*, co-authored with Felix Guattari:

> I would say that *Anti-Oedipus* (may its authors forgive me) is a book of ethics, the first book of ethics to be written in France in quite a long time (perhaps that explains why its success was not limited to a particular "readership": being anti-oedipal has become a life style, a way of thinking and living).[14]

Here we get the gist of the whole project. The revolution is not so much about changing society as about changing oneself. True, the institutions that are not allowing oneself to self-actualize must be destroyed—and in that sense society must be changed—but the focus is on oneself, on lifestyle. Post-Marxist leftism is a *lifestyle leftism*. In this it is much closer to religion than the old Marxist framework. This is because it is much more about cultivating a sort of anti-morality; a rejection of all moralities and the following of the raw, unstructured instinct.

---

14. Gilles Deleuze and Felix Guattari, *Anti-Oedipus: Capitalism and Schizophrenia* (1972) (Minneapolis: University of Minnesota Press, 1972), xiii.

Integralism Versus the Marxist and Post-Marxist Left

It is not surprising then that these thinkers eventually find at the root of the contemporary pseudo-scientific morality the Christian—and indeed, Catholic—morality of old. They set their work up as an opposition to this. Foucault jokes about this in his introduction: "Paying a modest tribute to Saint Francis de Sales, one might say that *Anti-Oedipus* is an *Introduction to the Non-Fascist Life* (ibid.)." In his later work Foucault became obsessed with the old Jesuitical ethical manuals, especially those that dealt with the confessional—which he saw as a prototype of psychiatric and psychotherapeutic repression. He also found this type of subjectivity—which he defines as the problem that creates alienated social beings—to have been invented by St. Augustine.[15]

Foucault and Deleuze are, in more ways than one, completely correct. They are not so much a repudiation of the Catholic tradition as an attempt to turn it on its head. For that reason, they are much closer to the Catholic thought tradition than is Marx. They understand that the key question is a moral one—to what extent society is organized in line with the natural law. But for them, the natural law is oppressive and the source of misery, whereas for Catholics it is liberating and the source of contentment. Where St. Augustine tells of his decadent lifestyle, the misery it brought him, and his finding of peace in God, Foucault and Deleuze tell us that peace in God is an illusion and that St. Augustine would be much better off pursuing his carnal desires.

How they come to this conclusion is mystifying. Neither seemed like a happy man. Foucault died from AIDS and Deleuze from suicide. For all the talk of self-actualization in their work, it seems that the lady doth protest too much and the writing is really flowing from a deep unhappiness and personal alienation. One suspects that their politics does not really have the goal of flourishing but instead of self-destruction. They are the theorists of decadence and death because *they* are decadent and death-oriented. Since no one

---

15. B.E. Harcourt, "Foucault's Keystone: Confessions of the Flesh. How the Fourth and Final Volume of *The History of Sexuality* Completes Foucault's Critique of Modern Western Societies," *Columbia Public Law Research Papers*, n. 14–647 (2019).

succeeded in talking them out of this, they tried to convince others to follow them—and called on the destruction of Western Christian society. The story of the post-Marxist left is the story of the snake in the garden.

Yet for all that, integralists have much to learn from these thinkers. Since they are dealing with the same problem as integralists—namely, the moral regulation of the Good Society—their tactics and critiques only need to be flipped over to be useful. Where they implore transgression, integralists simply implore moral restraint and regulation. Where they implore the pursuit of instinctual satisfaction, integralists warn of the dangers of such libertinism and catalogue its effects. Where they call for post-1968 libertarian "liberation," integralists point out that the only true freedom is freedom from one's whims and desires. The key project for integralists when it comes to leftist thought should not be trying to repurpose Marx's dubious concepts, but rather turning the post-Marxist left on its head.

28

Right, Left, Forward, or Back? Or Why I Am Neither Left nor Right

John Francis Nieto

The following remarks propose to explain why I have no expectation of political gains from either right or left and why rather I distrust both movements, at least in so far as they are political movements arising within modern political theory. Nonetheless, several things I am not claiming should be made clear in the beginning.

1. First, I am not claiming that either the left or the right is, simply speaking, one movement. Each has many elements and I have no intention of speaking to what is proper to these elements. Rather my comments concern groups or individuals only insofar as they assent to the political principles that have formed right and left as distinct "sides" or "factions" in the modern political system.

2. Second, I am not claiming there is no difference between right and left. I shall argue that both sides work to advance things they hold in common more than those things proper to them. These common principles (in my opinion) are or should be reprehensible to the most earnest partisans of either side. And I do think each side has some who work with the intention of bringing about a greater good, however much I may disagree with them.

3. Third, I therefore am not denying the need to work with one side rather than another in particular political battles. I note however that in doing so the political battle becomes distorted insofar as the

principles at hand must be conformed to those commonly accepted. Hence, the fight against abortion becomes for the right a question of a personal right to life, since "rights" are the commonly received political principle. More fundamental in abortion is the destruction of the common good attained in sexual union. But our political culture is too corrupt to recognize the horror of such destruction. Again, concern for the land we live on and encouragement of small-scale farming have their champions on the left. But this must be pursued within the exploitative, industrial conception of man's relation to the earth that defines our political debates. We have lost any sense that the earth provides for our needs. Rather, we seek from it satisfaction of desires.

4. Fourth, I do not propose these remarks with any suggestion of demonstrative certainty insofar as they contain judgments of particular political movements. I am not surprised that I, when young, or that other young people maintain political positions with great certainty and vehemence. I was so determined that I was willing to incite revolution, if given a chance. But it does surprise me that many who have the air of political wisdom pronounce in the same fashion as the young.

5. Political matters involve all the complexity of any moral judgment. Hence, questions of motives and circumstance, concerns about consequences, dangers of misstatement and misapprehension crowd about political acts. Further, political judgments involve the assumption of wisdom not demanded by the moral life. Everyone must live the moral life and attempt to attain to some measure of happiness. To go beyond the most general political truths and begin to judge in this realm is to suggest that one possesses the good attained in morality and politics in a manner sufficient to help others do so. Even the wise must fear such a step. (Of course, in saying this I have already opposed some principles common to both right and left.)

6. Hence, although, in the following remarks, I will propose some things which I believe to be of complete certainty, though difficult

Why I Am Neither Left nor Right

to articulate, such things are of a general and fundamental character. What I say against particular factions assumes that they reject, most often implicitly, these foundations of political order. They may well assume the same things at one time or another, insofar as they lack the consistency of well-conceived political opinions. But nowhere do I claim more than a probable, reasonable certitude in judging particular political opinions or actions. Only God can grasp these things with perfect clarity and determination. Any partisan who claims to understand these matters without any admixture of error fools himself; as likely, he is a liar, most likely a *petit*-demagogue.

7. What I propose therefore in the following remarks about particulars is incomplete, overstated somewhere, poorly substantiated elsewhere. I would have no one agree with me by the fact that I have said it. Rather, I urge each to reflect upon his moral and political experience, to confirm his understanding of true political principles, to judge political opinions and actions to the extent that true principles make them intelligible, and to refrain from opinions and judgments beyond these. To the young I particularly recommend moderation. To form political judgments is as much a burden as it is a privilege.

8. Now to take up this burden myself. I will first make clear in a schematic way my own associations with right and left (9–11). Next I will state my distrust of these movements in a general manner (12). Then, I will propose the political principles most necessary to true political order (13–25). Finally, I will state in a specific manner how right and left reject these principles in common (26–51).

9. For several years, from sixteen to twenty-two, I consciously considered myself a member of the political left. I first identified myself as a communist and a Marxist, then distinctly a Maoist—to my shame, a deceived admirer of the Chinese cultural revolution—, and finally, for nearly four years, an anarchist. As an anarchist I would have allowed myself to be called socialist or communist, so long as these terms were not taken in a particular, narrow sense.

10. Near my twenty-second birthday I began to question various of my political principles and after several months I recognized that several were wrong, though I did not claim to know the correct principles. Several things I never questioned: my distrust of the political influence of wealth, my sympathy with workers, my contempt for the ugliness and inhumanity of technology, my sense that man has been estranged from nature, and thus from his own nature, and so on. This re-haul of my political thought led to a moral reevaluation and thus to my return to the Catholic faith. But the political reevaluation came first.

11. Returning to Catholicism, I was determined to hold to the faith in its purity. I believed, for a short while, that this demanded I align myself with the right. Yet I could never champion capitalism, at least insofar as the word refers to industrial or high-finance capitalism. While I rejected the near-pacifist position central to my anarchism, I could not find enthusiasm for any of the military engagements so readily supported by the right. And thus, for many years, since my early thirties, I failed to feel any deep sympathy with left or right. Further, I have come to reject the distinction of right and left as an appropriate approach to political order.

12. My sense that the distinction and opposition of left and right do not arise from the principles proper to political order coincided with the sense that left and right agree on much that each side takes for granted. More and more it became clear to me that they take for granted an opposition to the principles that make real political order possible. Some of these principles are found explicitly in traditional teachings about politics, especially in traditional Catholic social teaching, although others are found there only implicitly. In effect, left and right, to my mind, are in general agreement with modern political and economic thought and disagree with how that thought should play out.

13. To make the principles where left and right agree more clear, I shall first discuss some of the principles I understand to be central to traditional political thought. None is more fundamental than the

notion that according to the very nature of man the common good gives rise to the political order.

14. The common good insofar as it is good is a final cause. Thus, victory is the purpose and cause of an army, and polyphonic music is the purpose and cause of a choir. Insofar as it is common, the common good brings many into a community and orders the members of the community to it and to one another. The nature of polyphonic music, for example, brings those capable of singing it together and makes a soprano of one, an alto of another, and so on.

15. By means of this order to the good and to one another a society becomes one agent pursuing the good common to them. This is to say that the common good makes the many members of the community a single agent in pursuing that good. The common good as final cause brings into being a city as an agent cause that pursues that good.

16. This common good must be some one thing belonging to all the members of the community. Nonetheless it belongs to the various members in distinct ways and some share more in this good and others share less. In the political order, the common good is nothing other than the common life lived by citizens. This life has many elements and is conceived in many ways. It is called "peace," "prosperity," "justice," insofar as we pay attention to one or another of its various aspects or elements.

17. To be a citizen, not in name alone but in reality, is nothing other than to pursue and possess this good by loving it and by sharing the power to bring it about and maintain it. Some make laws, some enforce them, some judge those who are subject to laws, some elect those who make laws, and so on. Each pursues and maintains the common good according to his share in political power. But every citizen as such must love the good not merely as it belongs to himself but also as it is a whole belonging to the entire community. Thus, he loves the common good as his own good, yet as a good greater than any private good belonging to him as an individual. So

the soldier offers his own share in the common good from love for this good as it belongs to the whole. Likewise, Saint Paul says,

> I am speaking the truth, in Christ, I am not lying, and my conscience in the Holy Spirit bears me witness: there is great sorrow and incessant pain in my heart. I could have wished to be outcast from the Christ myself for the sake of my brothers, who are my blood kindred.

18. While the common good belongs to the entire community of citizens, some part of the community must be dedicated to pursuing and maintaining this good for the whole. This is the government, which in its very nature is ordered to the good of the whole community. Though the government rules the community and thus some men are subject to any government, many, if not most, of those subject to government are themselves citizens. Thus government must rule citizens not for the good of the government, but for the good of the whole citizen body insofar as they form a community possessed of a common life.

19. Now there are many aspects of political life that must be found in all political communities: murder and stealing, for example, are wrong everywhere. Nevertheless, since the common good is nothing other than the community's common life, it must be determined in time and place. Where a people lives determines many aspects of its common life: the balance of agriculture and commerce in its economy, the kinds of food cultivated, and so on. Again, the particular history of a people influences that life. For example, the experience of a regime particularly good or evil affects the future attitude toward that kind of regime.

20. Two attributes of the common good demand particular attention. The common good must be attained in a manner that is stable and self-sufficient. These are rooted in the relation of the common good to the community that pursues it. If it is not stable, retaining more or less the same character over time, it will not really be common to the members of the community over time. Grandparents

will not share political life with their grandchildren, or even parents with their children, but mere biological life. If the common life is not self-sufficient, the members will depend upon other communities with which they will form a larger community. This larger political community will possess its own life, less distinct and less in the control of the original community.

21. Above I claimed that by his nature man is inclined to the common good. This can be seen in many ways, but most obviously insofar as man is inclined to happiness, which cannot in fact be attained by oneself. Man cannot be born or grow up without others. Nor can he attain to language, knowledge, or virtue in a sufficient way without the help of others.

22. But man cannot attain happiness, taken as perfecting himself alone or as perfecting the community, merely by means of his natural powers. The principal cause of this lies in his passions. Man's sensitive desires, arising from the concupiscible and irascible appetites, respond immediately to the sensible objects that appear by the exterior senses and the imagination. Nor are they wholly subject to reason.

23. Hence, man needs habits in these appetites and in his will, by which he will follow the good perceived by reason, even when the sensible appetites incline toward another good. Again, by these habits the sensible appetites will themselves incline in a manner appropriate to them toward the good perceived by reason. Traditional political thought therefore proposes the necessity of virtue for sound political order: temperance in the concupiscible appetite, bravery in the irascible appetite, justice in the will, and prudence (which knows the good for man) in the intellect.

24. For this reason, because the cardinal virtues are necessary in pursuing and maintaining the common good, traditional political thought suggests that good government is something rare, not to be expected everywhere, not likely to last a long time. This is not to say that men should not aim at good government. But they should not

be surprised that good government is so difficult to bring about and they should cherish the institutions that do so, if such institutions should be hit upon.

25. Let me underscore one point here. No loss in political thought is greater than the loss of the understanding that happiness, whether for one man or for a community, depends upon possession of the cardinal virtues. However bad society became in ancient and medieval times, anyone influenced by the great civilizations, such as the Greek or the Chinese, would have heard that these virtues are necessary for happiness. A bad man might scoff at such a position, but at least he was aware of it. And if this position is true, it is in some way a principle of action to anyone who becomes happy. In our day few come to know of this truth and, of course, even fewer have any share in happiness.

26. In describing the opposition to these principles common to the political right and left (at least insofar as they are movements), I shall first discuss the notion of social contract, which is at the heart of modern political theory (27–40). Next, I shall propose that the political thought of right and left is founded on the social contract (41–44). Then, I shall propose the manner in which right and left are themselves opposed while agreeing in the notion of a social contract (45–47). Finally, I shall make some remarks about the United States in particular: where it stands regarding this theory (48–51).

27. As stated above, modern political theory in common establishes political order on what is called the social contract. These thinkers do recognize that any society works toward some kind of good. They display various defects in their understanding of the common good. But all these thinkers reject the natural inclination to the common good. The common good, in their view, is not a final cause by nature. Rather, it must be established as the good of the community by some community or some part of a community, as by an agent cause. But, as stated, these thinkers hold that that agent cause cannot come into existence through the natural inclination to the common good.

28. Instead, the modern political theorists propose that the community comes into existence through the inclination of its members to their own private good. Each man about to enter into community recognizes that he will attain to some private good through association with others. This agreement constitutes a contract, generally implicit, by which the city or state is constituted.[1] So constituted, the community determines some part to serve as a government and this government pursues the good of the city or state.

29. The relation between the good of the community and the individual citizen is not described in the same way by the various philosophers. Nonetheless, the manner of establishing the community implies that this good belongs to the government more or less as the private good of the member, the good that prompted him to enter into society, belongs to that member. The government becomes more or less another individual pursuing its own private good, as is said most clearly by Hobbes.

30. There results an opposition between the good of the state and the good of the citizen. For the citizen enters into society for the sake of his own private good. But his participation in the state and consequent enjoyment of this private good demand subordination to the good of the state. The state will work to bring about his private good only insofar as citizens work toward the good of the state. But the good of the state is not properly the citizen's good. Rather it is a good proper to the government.

---

1. The author is somewhat simplifying matters. There are certainly modern political theorists who do not conceive of the state as being constituted by a contract. Hegel, for example, rejects the idea of a social contract (see *Philosophy of Right*, §75). But all modern political theorists propose something other than a natural inclination to the common good as the foundation of politics. Thus, Hegel replaces the natural inclination to the common good with history. The dialectic of history brings about the political community, and this dialectic is certainly driven by "desire" for private goods, but the coming into being of the community is not based on an implicit agreement between already existing individuals (contract)—rather it is only in the community that desire becomes self-conscious and individual subjectivity comes into being. Nevertheless, the result is similar to that of social contract theory; natural inclination to the common good is excluded.—*Eds.*

Integralism and the Common Good

31. Insofar as modern governments are totalitarian, they assume the supremacy of the good of the state, mistakenly understood to be a common good. Insofar as these governments partake in "Western liberalism" (which has nothing to do with "liberal vs. conservative") they recognize a citizen's "rights." Such rights are here understood to constitute a reservation of some private good against the claims of other citizens, but more profoundly, against the claims of the state.

32. Citizens do not live in such a social order for a common life, but each lives for his own sake a life he conceives as properly his own. He orders his action to his own success and prosperity, to his own pleasure, perhaps a bit beyond this to his family. He sees the political order as useful to these purposes of his own. He does not find in it an opportunity to participate in government, whether by legislating, ruling, counseling, judging, or even electing. If he shares in any of these, he looks to his own ends.

33. The government likewise looks to its existence and flourishing as an institution. Those who belong to it work to maintain themselves in power and see individual citizens either as an instrument or as a threat to that power. The citizen is promised his private good in exchange for maintaining the government.

34. There is nonetheless a kind of balance that can be found, at least for a time. The exchange of private goods allows the government to pursue its power as a private good and the citizen to pursue whatever life pleases him as his private good. They may recognize the other's intentions; they may flatter and deceive each other. In either way such a system can last for some time.

35. But this is not government or politics in the ancient sense, which demands that a people organize themselves so as to pursue a common life. Rather, the social contract introduces a system of management by which the government offers the various elements of a satisfactory private life to citizens in exchange for its own power.

36. Those who developed the theory of social contract were certainly proponents of virtue. Nonetheless such a system has no need of virtue. The citizens support the government through their inclination to their own private good. No one needs virtue to desire this in a stable and vehement manner. The passions incline us sufficiently to what is in one way or another our own. In a system of "human management" the passions can be counted on by a government to keep citizens satisfied with various pleasures and excitements, while it strengthens its own place in the world.

37. Virtue may, however, be necessary to distinguish and desire what is truly good from what appears to be good. For this reason, virtue may be an impediment to such a system. If virtue allows someone to recognize that a truly common life, a stable and self-sufficient life shared with others in one place and through time, is more desirable than the satisfaction of passions, he becomes an impediment to such government-as-management.

38. Let me briefly point out some reasons such a conception of government is incompatible with the stability and self-sufficiency that are attributes of the common good. Since what is provided to citizens is not a common life but the satisfaction of passions, which each works out in his own way, a system of human management must provide new and various satisfactions to its citizens. Food, sex, violence, wealth become central to any system like this. But they must have the increase and variety that keeps the senses and the passions alert and excited. Hence the life of citizens demands constant changes and this can be supplied at least in part by import. This alone is reason against stability and self-sufficiency.

39. But the government also seeks to augment its own power and security. This will always suggest further control and regulation of the citizen's life, which will demand change of one sort or another. But it also tempts a government to interest itself in the doings of other governments. Greater interdependence among such governments means greater power and security, at least for the government that does the most successful meddling.

40. Now, when government is viewed as mere management of individual satisfactions—a system that does not demand the attainment of any virtue—good government will not seem to be something rare and difficult to maintain. Rather, it will be thought to flow according to some kind of formula from mere power and will. Good government will bring about "happiness" by managing men and goods as they already are, by ingeniously shifting them about, while traditional political theory assumed that men must become good to become happy, especially insofar as they are in community.

41. Now I do not think it difficult to see that the political right and left, at least in our times, both accept the conception of government as a social contract. We see both pandering to the citizen's desires for his private good. More and more each conceives of the political order as arising from and serving individuals and not families, neighborhoods, and towns.

42. Generally speaking, both right and left conceive or propose themselves as the true defenders of the citizen's rights. Both conceive the opposite side as more or less totalitarian. And each side has some justice, since totalitarian governments have at times been on the right and at times been on the left. In fact the opposition of totalitarianism and Western liberalism is woven into the principles of government accepted by both sides.

43. Hence, whatever their long-term dreams and utopias, each side proposes that good government is synonymous with its own establishment in power. Right and left each proposes to solve society's problems on the condition that it becomes the government, while the other side is destroyed or fades away into ignominy and then obscurity. For me this makes clear that neither side can ever be successful. Even granted that each of them changes, perhaps even to become more and more like each other, neither side can bring about what it aims at, because they cannot get rid of one another.

44. For this reason, I believe that right and left are both proceeding "forward" toward a more and more perfect system of human man-

Why I Am Neither Left nor Right

agement. This demands global government, a fluid worldwide economy, a thorough-going leveling of individuals through society, so that no one can remain outside the reaches of this management and thus present a danger to its integrity. Everyone can enjoy his private satisfaction so long as he submits to the system, so long as he is "with the program," as it is vulgarly put.

45. Where then do right and left differ, if they are in fundamental agreement about the social contract? I think there are many illusions lurking here and do not have time to consider them. Let me merely propose for the moment that the fundamental difference is this: the left holds that the original formation of society is a system of oppression and must be superseded by a true social contract, while the right accepts this original formation as a binding contract.

46. The position of the left, described in the *Second Discourse* of Rousseau, holds that the conditions of man when he first "found" himself in nature encouraged him to establish a system of property, racism, sexism, and so on, by which he used others for his private good. This system must be replaced by a true social contract that orders men and wealth to bring about the private good of all society's members. For example, the left holds that American slavery was part of the American system at its founding. The undoing of that slavery introduced a new element of a true social contract.

47. The right claims that the systems in place at the time the doctrine of social contract arose were more or less sufficient to bring about that good. They may hold that the contract has been insufficiently fulfilled at one time or another, as, for example, in American slavery, but that the principles in the American social contract are sound and capable.

48. This leads me to speak a moment about the United States. I speak as someone who has always looked at his own country from within and from without. From my childhood I recognized the good that I have received and share in through the American system

of government. But I have also seen this system as belonging, at least temperamentally, to the Anglo-American race, more than to my own. I say this merely to avoid any dissembling.

49. I believe that any true government must be founded on true political thought. I think that there is evidence in American history of such a foundation. In fact, one part of this is the claim in the Federalist papers, that the members of the proposed union have the same language, culture, and political institutions. At the same time the founders used the language of the times to explain their foundation. Some believed it fervently; others may not have. The people themselves, I expect, conceived the political order more or less as they had when they began to live in this country.

50. Over time, however, we have come to live more and more by the principles enunciated in our foundation. One of the most impressive facts about American political life, one paid only the slightest attention, is that it has in fact proceeded more or less according to the words and formulas used in its institution. I do not deny that these have been used with more and less precision and with changes in meaning. Nonetheless, our government has in fact gone forward more or less according to these "instructions." This is something very rare.

51. As we have stuck to these principles, we are therefore living more and more according to the contract theory embedded by the founders in their account of the foundation. Hence, we have lived more and more for the rights of individuals and we have established the government more and more as an entity that serves its own ends in opposition to our own. As we continue forward, however much we imagine that we go right or left, we will be furthering a system of government that consists in human management. The only true direction is back—not back in time, but back to the true principles of human political order.

About the Editors

EDMUND WALDSTEIN, O.Cist. is a monk of the Cistercian Abbey of Stift Heiligenkreuz in Austria, lecturer in moral theology at the Abbey's theological college, and parish priest of Gaaden and Sulz. Born in Italy and raised in the United States and Austria, he studied at Thomas Aquinas College in California, the Hochschule Benedikt XVI in Heiligenkreuz, and the University of Vienna, where he was promoted Doctor of Theology in 2019. His research has focused on eudemonism, the common good, Catholic integralism, and theological readings of literary fiction.

PETER A. KWASNIEWSKI is a former professor of theology, philosophy, music, and art history, a composer of sacred choral music, and author and speaker on topics concerning Catholic Tradition. He has written or edited over a dozen books, including, most recently, *The Ecstasy of Love in the Thought of Thomas Aquinas* (Emmaus Academic, 2021) and *From Benedict's Peace to Francis's War* (Angelico Press, 2021).

www.ingramcontent.com/pod-product-compliance
Lightning Source LLC
Chambersburg PA
CBHW022102150426

43195CB00008B/230